Numero 6

Reliving A Historic Year Following Liverpool Football Club

Numero 6

Reliving A Historic Year Following Liverpool Football Club

The Anfield Wrap

Edited by Josh Sexton

First published as a hardback by deCoubertin Books Ltd in 2019.

First Edition

deCoubertin Books, 46B Jamaica Street, Liverpool, L1 OAF
www.decoubertin.co.uk
ISBN: 978-1-909245-99-0

A CIP catalogue record for this book is available from the British Library.

Cover design by Matthew Shipley.

Printed and bound by Jellyfish.

This book is dedicated to Emma Johnson.
'Rave safe, Duckies.'

CONTENTS

INTRODUCTION

THE Anfield Wrap have aspired to be your companion home and away since 2011.

Some of those seasons have been slogs. Times where you may have wondered why you commit so much time and money to this mad leisure activity. But there are other times which give us purpose and perspective. But above all joy.

This season was a joy and a great one for Liverpool Football Club, but also for The Anfield Wrap. We've loved evolving our content across several platforms and testing out new things, all while committing ourselves wholly to being your companion at home, away and even abroad.

That's why we've produced this book. It's a collection of our work over the last 12 months but also a reflection of the hard work everybody concerned puts into producing the content you consume. It's a labour of love because we love what we do – and we hope you do to.

We want to share the journey of supporting Liverpool Football Club and rarely have they taken us on such a journey as they did in the last year. This book is about retelling that tale. Before, during and after the event.

It features contributions from our weekly columnists who give up their time from Monday to Friday and on matchdays. We're rightly proud and eternally thankful for what they do.

It starts from the morning after defeat in Kyiv and runs until the end of the week that followed The Reds being crowned Champions of Europe for the sixth time.

So, sit tight. Share the journey again with us. Relive your own journey. Remember what a joy it was to be alive. Fall in love again.

Josh Sexton

FOREWORD

By Clive Tyldesley

NOTHING compares. Nothing.

When you support a football team and that team wins the ultimate honour, the moment lives with you forever.

It paints a silly faraway smile across your face on a crowded train, it bonds you infectiously with random strangers that just happen to share the same heart flutters at the very mention of Madrid.

It is not your wedding day or the birth of your child, but it is true love just the same.

Love thrills and spills. Love flirts and hurts. You have no say about the route it takes, no control over the hold it has on you. It is an affair of the heart, it is not supposed to make any sense.

Looking back now, we can all chart the incredible journey that this Liverpool team completed aboard that open-topped bus on June 2, but not until Divock Origi steered his unlikely shot into the corner of the Tottenham goal long into the previous night did we know for sure that they would.

In the pursuit of love, you can sense that something different is happening but you are never quite certain what it is until…

And therein lies the excitement, the wonder, the hope that can as easily kill as thrill you. It is the search that makes the discovery worthwhile. If it were easy to find, it would have no magic.

Liverpool deserved it, they earned it over the course of the whole season. They probably played better against Real in Kyiv but in the 12 months between the two finals, they learnt how to win. And we learnt with them.

It would have been nice if the crowning triumph had been adorned by a display of memorable verve, dash and artistry but, in its way, Liverpool's showing in the Wanda Metropolitano was a defining performance. It was a job done. The biggest job of all.

I was commentating at the finals of 1978, 1981 and 1984. Great teams, poor games. Glory is not always glorious.

(Name-drop alert) I was discussing the final with Gareth Southgate the following week and I suggested to him that the three-week break had stripped the game of energy and drive. He disagreed.

Gareth felt that the timing of the opening goal set the tone for the night, that it was a match that Liverpool needed to win more than Spurs and that consolidating the early lead became an overriding priority for them.

Overriding and achievable. Game management has been the team's biggest single area of improvement during the last year. Liverpool fans can raucously dismiss taunts that the sixth European Cup was won in 'a League 2 of a match' because it was actually won with the worldly maturity and hardened edge that Jürgen Klopp has added to the mix.

There were times during the season when the manager needed to turn up the amps and blow away opponents with a burst of heavy metal football. The Anfield semi final will always be the year's signature night – their Bat out of Hell performance – but this was the season when the wildlings found a controlled confidence that plotted and planned paths to victory. Liverpool are all grown up now.

And that is the greatest source of optimism for the future. The age and culture of the team suggest that foundations have been laid for a period of sustained success, their ongoing development is indisputable.

The fifth European Cup was lifted by a team that finished fifth in the Premier League, 37 adrift of the champions. The sixth was won by a team that finished just 11.7 millimetres adrift.

The hard yards gained on the trail of the Premier League title provided the training and conditioning for the critical moments of the European campaign. All of those crafted, grafted victories over Fulham, Southampton and Cardiff in the spring did not quite strike gold in the national championships but they proved to be good dress rehearsals for the Olympian final ahead.

And Liverpool fans came to know their team and came to trust them more and more. The patience grew restless at times. Those of you that crawled home through the roadworks from West Ham on that endless Monday night in early February will recall the bristling unease about an opportunity escaping, but Liverpool never went away.

The glow in the reception for the runners up after the Wolves game sent the players an unmistakable message. Fans pay good money to watch their team and there is no onus on them to show gratitude and respect unless it is earned, unless they can see a mirror reflection of their loyal support in the players' pride and sustained effort.

This team are a credit to the badge. The bond between these players and you fans was only strengthened by the disappointment of finishing second.

It is a tight bond now. You can see yourselves and your commitment to the cause in Robbo and Trent and Hendo. Even the Nivea For Men adverts are kind of engaging. The silly season will always spawn gossip stories of Real Madrid targeting anyone and everyone but there is no sign at all of Mo or Sadio or Virgil wanting out now or in the future. Why would they?

Gareth was right. The trophy is important. The season would still have been a good one if Spurs had won the final but the return of the crown jewel to Anfield is a solid and tangible affirmation of all of the progress made, all of the promise taking shape.

It has quietened some of the noise in neighbouring shires, it has silenced some of the questions that would have been asked. And it has consummated the love affair. Liverpool and success are an item again.

For some of you, it will be the first time. You'll have heard about it but now you know what it's like, how it feels. Now you've got memories. Your special moments, your special places. You're already missing the players, the match days, the buzz, right?

That's love…

Clive Tyldesley, June 2019

PROLOGUE

Real Madrid 3 Liverpool 1

Saturday May 26, 2018

PAUL COPE

I FEEL duty bound to write this.

I hoped my last piece would be the end. The article I could retire on after a European Cup win.

The movie didn't go the way I hoped, or expected.

I've not long woken up and wandered into Twitter. It's an incredible scene and completely predictable. I saw Evertonians liking my tweets yesterday, keeping them to one side in case we got beaten. In case my confidence and hubris were misplaced.

They're happy today. The supporters of all the other teams are happy today. They can have it.

But imagine that. Imagine if your happiness depended on someone else's misery.

I know you're sad. I'm sad as well. I said before the game that we'd destroy them if we turned up, but we didn't. Not really. Not any of us. There's a question mark over so many things – not least my own record at finals and whether I should just stop going to them.

But what are we in this for? Success? Victory? Trophies?

I'm in this for the last three days.

I'm in this for dancing in airports and singing in train stations.

I'm in this for fun, laughter and pure, unadulterated joy. I'm in this for meeting you, saying hello and having a drink in some far foreign land together, disbelieving that this can all be real.

They can never take that away from me, from us.

We still had an absolute ball. We still went to a European Cup final.

It won't be remembered, though. Not like Istanbul. Like it or not, but we all only remember the winners. First is first and second is nowhere. We finished nowhere, make no mistake. We were destroyed by the masters. By the ultimate warriors. There was a moment around the 60th minute when I knew it was all over, but I didn't want to let on to anyone near me.

Sergio Ramos just sat on the floor.

In the middle of a European Cup final he just sat on the floor and looked at the referee. It was like peak Steven Gerrard on speed.

That's why they've won three European Cups on the run.

They won because their first substitute is a lad who can score an overhead kick in a European Cup final, and our two subs are lads who haven't run for months.

We can't afford to lose one of the best players in the world after 20 minutes. They've got about 20 of them.

We said going into the game that we needed to score four to win. We said that if we turned up as the best version of ourselves we'd beat them.

4

We didn't do either.

So, what now? What are your choices?

Be very clear, what you do next is a choice.

Whether you laugh or cry is up to you, nobody else. Whether people taking the piss out of you for being confident of a win and enjoying yourself upsets you or makes you laugh is up to you.

Today they get to laugh. But what they don't realise is that I'm still laughing. I'm still away on a holiday with my best mates getting drunk and singing while they're sitting at home reading this. Their lives are spent watching us have fun and being bitter about it. I feel bad for them all. I feel sorry for everyone whose lives are built around the failure of others.

That's not us. We're in it for us to win and to enjoy every second along the way.

We'll come back bigger and better than ever having had this experience.

They'll revel in it for a few days, but deep down they know. Deep down they realise this team got to a European Cup final with 11 players. Imagine what it would be like if our first sub was Gareth Bale.

They know that Naby Keita joins us in the summer and makes us better. They know that, regardless of losing this game, this is just the start.

It amazes me how many people are revelling in this as though it's the end of the story. It's not.

This is the *Empire Strikes Back*. This is the middle of the trilogy. This is the part where the world crushes your soul to make sure that when you come back you savour every second.

Winning is always better when you've tasted defeat. Unbeaten boxers are great, but they're not my favourites. My favourites are all of the people who've had to pick themselves up from the floor when they didn't think they had it in them. The fighters who refuse to submit.

You have a choice now. Pick yourself up and face the world or don't. It's up to you. All I can tell you is that I'm picking myself up. I'm going for a drink with my best mates and talking about all the laughs we've had along the way.

I'm walking down the street with my shoulders back and my head held high, proud of Jürgen Klopp and the team he's created. Proud of the football we've played, the goals we've scored and the games we've won. Proud of you, proud of me and proud of the Mighty Reds.

We lost a game of football, I got that wrong. I said we'd win and we didn't. But I wouldn't change a second of it. It makes me laugh that people don't think I know what I'm doing when I post super-confident messages on the internet. As if they don't realise that I know I'm exposing myself for whenever we lose, when I know that we all lose sooner or later.

I'll never change. I would do it all again and I will do it all again. I will keep putting myself on the line. I will keep risking defeat in the knowledge that one day, one glorious day, it will all be worth it.

I talked in my pre-match piece about being winners. The bit I didn't say was that the best winners know how to lose. They know how to pick themselves up off the floor, congratulate the victors and keep moving forward.

We'll keep moving forward. Together. A team united in defeat. A family making sure everyone is OK. Safe in the knowledge that our day will come. Failure can't beat persistence. We will win. Sooner or later.

Smile today. Remember the goals, the celebrations and the songs. Remember how glorious this has been. Remind yourself that this is just another step on the journey. There isn't an end. There are only moments. Stepping stones on the road.

PROLOGUE

There isn't a destination, all we can do is make sure we enjoy the adventure. Wherever you are now, choose to enjoy what we've had. Choose to focus on the positives. I know it's hard, that's part of the game. If it wasn't hard it wouldn't be worth playing. But just remember that this isn't the end.

This is just the beginning.

CHAPTER ONE - THE FAST START

The Pre-Season Tour

July 2018

LIVERPOOL tour, we tour.

Three games, three Anfield Wrap live shows. Charlotte, New York, Detroit. These are three profoundly different places.

Charlotte is an ever-growing financial and legal hub for the south east of the United States. It's a city trying to work out what it actually is, springing up around itself, enjoying a sprawl. It's the south on spreadsheets.

New York is New York. So good they named it etc. It is both world city and city of the world. It overwhelms you and whatever you want to do you can do. If you haven't been you know you should go if you can afford it – a live question, by the way – and if you have been you will be thinking of when you can go again.

But Detroit. Oh, Detroit. Charlotte sprawls, Detroit contracts. People work in Charlotte but they live in Detroit. They die there too. It's a city which has so many problems but a city which just vibrates and shimmers and drinks and dances and asks you if you are going to get some tonight.

Go to Detroit because Detroit Hustles Harder. It's a museum, and a petri dish, and a party.

Detroit feels like home but very much isn't home. We have to be careful of these things because identity is complicated and we cannot decide to have other people off because it makes a neat line.

A quick Wikipedia tells you that Detroit's black or African American community makes up 82% of its residents. The collapse of industry is on an unprecedented scale. Detroit could be the most post-industrialised place there has ever been.

We can draw some parallels, though.

Liverpool was spoken of in the context of 'managed decline'. Well, Detroit's decline has been managed, mismanaged, just plain organic and quite possibly systemically malevolent. There has been a mass migration from Detroit due to this.

When we said to people elsewhere in the US we were going to Detroit there was that intake of breath between teeth, that little face, that bit of 'be careful' hinted at or stated openly. Say to someone in Godalming you are popping to Liverpool.

Our live shows, especially abroad, are massively about identity. People come because they identify with Liverpool, both place and city. People are much more than just one thing.

The desperation in populist political circles to define people for or against something by just one facet on their complex being should be resisted at all times. It's our responsibility to challenge and remember that at every opportunity.

CHAPTER ONE - THE FAST START

No one embodies this more than Mo Salah, Egyptian King.

When he came on against Manchester City in New York, when he stood on the sidelines, it was like Beyonce was about to get on stage. Prior to the Kyiv final everyone wanted to talk about Salah, talk about him being a Muslim hero. But there is so much more to him than that. He is African and North African. Arab and Egyptian. He is a Liverpudlian icon.

He stood on the sidelines in New York and it was as though the world's city was about to acclaim the world's player. And then he scored straight away, Beyonce opening with Crazy In Love.

America was a blur. Everyone gave us shots to drink and we drank them. The shows went brilliantly, a celebration of supporting Liverpool.

The line about overseas supporters from jealous rivals is that they are 'glory hunters'. If they are, they are bad ones. Liverpool have won one League Cup this decade. But if they are anything, they are journey hunters.

They came for the football, fell in love with the city, wanted this football club and the urban sprawl that defines it to define part – only part – of their personalities. We've got them sprung and they don't care who sees.

We have Liverpool in common, they all get together in supporters' clubs as we do in Anfield. In that common ground, the facets of our identities can mingle. We can enjoy our differences. Those who want to define us by one thing don't want that common ground. It is counter to their goals.

They are wrong. We are right and Liverpool leave the United States having again brought people together having seen the Egyptian King in action.

Neil Atkinson

Liverpool v West Ham United

Sunday August 12, 2018

DAN MORGAN

'I LOVE the first day, man, everybody all friendly and shit.'

Namond Brice in *The Wire* had it right. School is in as of this weekend and we all get to go back to an environment where fun and enjoyment is just as fundamental as the learning process we continue to go through with Jürgen Klopp's Liverpool.

When Liverpool open their Premier League campaign against West Ham United at Anfield this Sunday they do so on the back of a summer holiday filled with ambition and optimism.

The summer transfer business, pre-season form and general vibe in and around the club, particularly with the conscious efforts to integrate players and fans, has left many of the opinion that this is the year that Liverpool take the next step and achieve major honours.

The contrast of The Reds' pre-season versus a summer of World Cup and premature transfer window chaos that has engulfed those around them represents an opportunity, there is no doubt about it. Liverpool are well aware, however, that they are completely at the behest of a Manchester City side who achieved 100 points last term.

Nothing is guaranteed in the football world, especially in England where you would be foolish to dismiss the likes of Manchester United, despite them having a manager who represents that fella you used to work with who told you every day how shit his job was but stayed there for 30 years.

Nothing is guaranteed, this much we know. Everyone starts on nil, nobody has the right. Don't do it for you, do it for Lucas.

Opening day clichés apart, an opportunity does present itself in the first four fixtures of the campaign for Klopp's men to set a pace at the top of the table.

With chaotic pre seasons and the likelihood of opposition absentees following those who went deep into the summer in Russia, the Liverpool boss has no doubt earmarked the early fixtures as a chance for his team to open up a gap on the rest.

You feel Klopp has become more ruthless over the summer. His margin for error and willingness to rehabilitate, which could be to the detriment of the team, is now at its slightest.

The signing of Alisson Becker, on the heels of some concerning pre-season displays by Loris Karius – which in turn came after the manager had briefed his support for the German stopper to continue as number one despite what happened in Kyiv – is evidence of his desire to take the next step.

The thought of Karius as Liverpool's number one turning up to a rambunctious Selhurst Park on a Monday night in August was potentially a recipe for disaster.

The prospect of needlessly dropping points in the second game of the season could be the difference between winning a title in May and, more importantly, setting the wrong type of tone for a squad that need the utmost concentration and desire from the get go.

Klopp and his team have rectified a major weakness in Liverpool. His side look ready to step up and will need to do so from the first whistle.

CHAPTER ONE - THE FAST START

There is a historic body of evidence to suggest that themes to a season can be set as early as the first day. Emile Heskey smashing one in the roof of the Anfield Road net against Bradford in 2000-01 set a precedent for him to spearhead a treble-winning Liverpool attack and have the best season of his career.

In 2013-14, Liverpool earned a 1-0 victory against a horrible Stoke side after a Daniel Sturridge strike and, more importantly, a late penalty save by Simon Mignolet. That day I came out the ground thinking Liverpool could really do something on the back of that result and the impending return of Luis Suarez.

Conversely, there is a moment on the opening day of the 2011-12 season campaign where Stewart Downing smashes the crossbar of Sunderland's goal from 25 yards in a frustrating 1-1 draw, which not only set a frankly weird tone of repeatedly hitting the woodwork throughout that season, but also one that ensured Downing himself didn't get to kick on.

These things can be brushed off as coincidental. However, in the subconscious mind of a player and team, they matter in the same way positive reinforcement does. If opposition clubs and supporters have spent the summer stating Liverpool will challenge for honours, then a strong start will only add to their proclamations and fears.

Liverpool already have a lot of miles in their legs and look strong entering the new campaign. They have played on average three games more than everyone else. This, we know, is a trademark of Klopp's, to get his boys in the best possible physical shape to start strong, yet don't be surprised to see similar levels of rotation to last season once 2018-19 hits its full stride.

The amount of players at the manager's disposal, in line with the sheer weight of a league and cup campaign he now knows is so weathering, means there remains an element of hope surrounding the fitness and reliability of the likes of Sturridge and Adam Lallana, coupled with keeping key players fit throughout the campaign.

Regardless, you feel The Reds haven't been in such a healthy position going into the opening day in a long time. West Ham will provide a difficult test and are, in many ways, very hard to read due to their manager and player turnaround. Yet it will be solely down to what Liverpool and Anfield do on the day to ensure we get off to the start we all want.

The manager and club have gone to great lengths in pre-season to harness the feeling of togetherness that grew with the Champions League run of last season. There has been a responsibility placed on the supporters now to ensure that the team feels the full support of the crowd and the opposition feel the full wrath of Anfield as often as possible.

There is now, more than ever in my lifetime, a feeling of all of us being in this together. If we take our lead off anything it should be how much these players are going into work every day with a smile on their face, loving being a part of what is happening at this football club.

As we enter the new campaign, it is vital to remember everything good we're feeling about going the match right now, the concept of everyone enjoying themselves and being the envy of the football world in the process. This manager demands it. He won't stand for anything less. It is, in his eyes, as much a route to success as signing world-class players.

The first day awaits us all. Comb your hair and shine your shoes. Liverpool Football Club, class of 2018. The best days of your life.

Liverpool 4 West Ham United 0
BEN JOHNSON'S RATINGS

THAT was a summer, weren't it?

What have you been up to? I'll be honest, I've tried to swerve The Reds; I haven't seen a minute of pre season, didn't really get involved in all the transfer voyeurism, just sort of lived for a bit, which was sound. It meant going into the game today I was genuinely excited to see what all our new lads are like. That's nice, isn't it?

When I say I tried to swerve The Reds, I mean that's a bit like trying to swerve your own face. It's always there, gegging in, bouncing around in mirrors like there is no tomorrow. Here he is, the big bellend. I mean I can literally see my nose as I am typing this, just there in my peripheral vision; cooey, here I am. The Reds are the same, lad.

I mean this is me below trying not to think about The Reds:

Picture the scene... A man sits at a desk, gazing into the middle distance, he looks weary, worried, pain etched across his face. All around him is a scene of utter greyness. Everything is grey, or shades thereof, in spite of the scorching weather outside.

He is reliving something over and over in his mind. The opening, slow, somewhat haunting bars of Fiesta by the Pogues is on a loop in his head, forever looping with no end in sight. No payoff.

Something snaps him out of his slumber – the record jumps.

The Joycey alarm.

@_pauljoyce: 'Liverpool agree fee with AS Roma for Alisson in region of £66m. Nothing to stop other clubs doing likewise, but Liverpool the first. Permission granted to speak to player.'

Colour fills the screen. Every colour imaginable. Flowers are falling from the sky, filling the room, rainbows shoot across the vista. A whistle blows, the beat kicks in. All of a sudden the man is marching around the room, party poppers are going off all around him.

Dancing safari animals are marching in a procession behind him, three rhinos on their hind legs swinging their arms in unison to the beat. Monkeys wearing Bermuda shorts are hanging from the light fittings playing tiny guitars.

The man leading the march is transformed. Gone is the worry, the stress, his hair is growing back, he looks 15 years younger. His kecks have somehow disappeared and he is marching, cock and balls swinging in the breeze underneath a rainbow-coloured grass skirt, a coconut filled with rum in one hand, pyro in the other.

He leaves his house, door ajar and turns right towards town. The postman joins the back of the conga. Next door's cat is getting a piggyback off the dog from over the road, happiness fills the world, as far as the eye can see.

The procession carries on in an endless party, towards town, the townest of towns. At the end of time, if you look closely enough, on the horizon, as the sun sets for the final time you will still see that dancing party, forever lost in a world of happiness. Fiesta.

Anyway. Yer, jibbed The Reds there, didn't I?

Alisson: 9

Pretty sure if he made a video of his summer holidays I would project it onto the

Liver Buildings. Fucking transcribe it onto rock in hieroglyphics then grind the rocks up and shoot them into my toe. Extra two points for not being Big Si or Lagos Kagos. Was made up with him catching it and that. Haven't seen that for ages.

Trent: 7

Thought he looked a bit rusty but then in fairness he's just come back off holiday. I was away last week and was still falling asleep at me desk on Thursday and eating me dinner at 11am. Went the gym Friday had to get off after half an hour on the bike and have a breather in me car before I started driving. So you know, he will be sound next week.

The ball to Keita for the second was pretty special.

Joe Gomez: 7

Looks skinny, doesn't he? Just had to ask the lads what his name was there which seems a bit harsh. Soz Joe. Reckon he has been on the same diet over the summer that Shaqiri is currently been lashed on. Just beans and the occasional fish. Didn't have much to do but done it all pretty well.

Virgil: 9

Jesus Christ. He's like a giant playing with kids mate, got a Snozzcumber in his arse pocket. He makes it look so easy. Imagine playing next to him.

Andy Robertson: 9

Did he set up all the goals and all the chances? How long has it been since we had two boss full backs? Twenty years? Absolutely brilliant, there. What a fella.

Gini: 8

We played so well he didn't really even need to play, but he pinged it about and looked sound. Wanted to see him playing a bit further forward and so did he.

Milner: 9

Thought he was man of the match, there. The sinew. Joined us together like no-one's business. Grafted more than everyone and does unbelievably for the second to keep it in. I wonder if he has to wear that headband all the while. On the ale like fucking McEnroe.

Keita: 9

First time I've seen him play. Fucking hell, he is glorious. He might be one of the five greatest players to play for Liverpool, the other four are Gegsi and our front three.

Mo Salah: 9

He is class, isn't he? Scored, has grew his hair a bit and still loves Allah. Is right, lad.

Sadio Mane: 9

Bloody hell, this might the best Liverpool team I have ever seen. Seriously. Mane isn't our best player. That's crackers that, isn't it?

Firmino: 8

Thought he grew into it. He isn't our best player either and is better than almost all our players since 1990. These Reds, mate. It's hard to see how this front three could get any better. How many times were they all stood in row ready to tap it in?

SUBS...

Karius: 9

Looks boss on that bench, there. Wear your jeans next week, kid.

Sheridan Shaqiri: 7

Wasn't arsed in the slightest about him till Charlie Adam questioned his professionalism. Got his whole body tattooed on my body the next day. My chest hair is doing a pretty good impression of his jig, there. Had to stitch some paper to my sides there, as I wasn't wide enough. Built like a fucking big armchair, isn't he? Might be my favourite ever.

(Sheridan courtesy of Adam Melia Entertainment plc.)

DAN Sturridge: 8

Lovely wrigglies. I've missed them so much.

Non Sub – Big Si The Mig: 8

I hope we didn't even give him a ticket. Tux in town times when he leaves, la.

NEIL ATKINSON'S REVIEW

IT was a pleasure to be back.

Anfield was expectant of a win but it was also eager to play a part. It wanted to embrace its globetrotting heroes and remind them this is where the action is.

They didn't need reminding. Liverpool look like a side enjoying their work but also look like a side deadly serious about it. There was a steeliness about the enterprise. They spurned chances but then refused to stop creating them. And there, then, was the opener.

It was all about overwhelming opponents by using and driving into space. Naby Keita had the ball, Sadio Mane vacated, Andy Robertson arrived and then so too did Mo Salah, and so too did the moment everyone had been waiting for. Liverpool's opening goal of the campaign and the return of the Egyptian King.

Sadio Mane could well be the barometer of the season. If he hits what he can then Liverpool may just be unstoppable. He was magnificent today. His intelligence dictates so much of our attacking and his finishing was terrific.

There is so much threat in the way Liverpool attack, they come from all angles and are capable of so many different types of goals. Fifteen-stitch James Milner was incredible for the second. It was a lung-busting run, but full of nous. Liverpool scoring tap ins is great news. And Liverpool scoring offside goals was nice.

Alisson is going to drive some people mad, but the plan and the approach is absolutely correct. Let's say this now – it will occasionally go badly wrong, and when it does we must back it wholeheartedly. It is the way to go about our business, there. Bringing them on to us.

Gini Wijnaldum ran the show in the middle of the park. He showed something in all phases of the game. He won it, gave it quickly, gave it intelligently, gave it with purpose. His was a tour de force. There was just more of him than any other midfielder on the pitch.

But there was more Liverpool than West Ham on the pitch. There was a relaxed intensity about Liverpool. It will come. But we will find our way.

It has started now; 37 more hurdles, 37 more challenges to come for Liverpool. But most of them will be similar to this. Relaxed intensity is the way forward. Liverpool are certain. Liverpool have other ideas. Liverpool are on the march.

Liverpool are serious.

Let's be serious. Let's have the time of our lives.

The city motto: *Deus nobis haec otia fecit.* God has given us these days of leisure.

Let's enjoy every single one of them. It is the least we can do.

An Ode to James Milner

Tuesday August 14, 2018

DAVID SEGAR

'MILNER'S a phenomenon, a guy with big balls...'

That was Manuel Pellegrini back in March 2015, quite literally talking bollocks.

Three years and five months later, the Chilean was reminded of just how big James Milner's are. Significantly more so than Jack Wilshere's and Mark Noble's after their unfortunate blocking of Liverpool shots at Anfield on Sunday. There may have been temporary enlargement, but purely down to the swelling. Poor lads.

Pellegrini was Manchester City manager at the time of that quote, and in an interview with Sid Lowe from *The Guardian* he was being questioned about Milner due to the increasing rumours that the utility man was on his way to Merseyside to sign for The Reds on a free transfer the following summer.

He added: 'I'm Milner's number one fan. Find me a more complete English player. There are players who are better technically, yes. Quicker players, yes. Players who head better, yes. But show me one who does all the things Milner does well. There isn't one.

'It's hard to leave him out. Respect, commitment and performance level: 10/10, fantastic. He's polyfunctional: full back – the only position he doesn't like – attacking midfield, wide. I played him as a forward and the team averaged three goals a game.

'He gives everything. You leave him on the bench and he's absolutely furious but watch him during the game: encouraging, shouting, supporting. And in the next training session he kills himself.'

In his first game as West Ham manager, Pellegrini's new side were up against Milner, and the Yorkshireman put in the sort of performance that would have had his former boss pining for the days he could call on him for his team.

Not many Reds had picked the 32-year-old in their predicted 11s for the season opener against The Hammers, assuming Fabinho, Adam Lallana or Jordan Henderson would be preferred, and also because Milner still had 15 stitches holding his head together following a clash in the friendly win over Napoli a week prior.

However, Jürgen Klopp opted for 'Millie', and he was right to do so. Milner was sensational in the middle of the park. At one point you could see West Ham's bench checking their tablets to make sure Liverpool's midfield set up wasn't Milner-Wijnaldum-Milner-Keita-Milner.

The former City man was quite the sight as he took to the field in his black headband, though it did feel like a missed opportunity that he didn't get it sponsored by Yorkshire Tea or Ribena.

The official reports were that it was to protect his head injury, though rumours spread that it was to keep the lid on his bonce so it didn't fly off mid game and let everyone see the motherboard inside that powers RoboMillie.

The numbers behind Milner's performance only went to confirm what most felt at the time, that his performance was something quite incredible.

He had 122 touches, more than anyone else, completed 95 of his 102 passes, made 57 passes in the West Ham half, put in seven crosses, made three key passes, came away with two assists, regained possession four times and even found room for an interception. All that, and he covered over 12.5km, more than anyone else of course.

It should hardly have been a surprise. The second-oldest player in the Liverpool squad set the benchmark on his first day of pre-season, running laps of Melwood during the lactate test with such dismissive ease that next year the fitness team might want to consider putting obstacles in the way, like water hazards or firing paintballs at him.

It's not just the impressive engine though, but his attitude, his game intelligence, and his genuine quality.

To not only have the nous to go for the cross from Andy Robertson with seconds to go in the first half, but to reach it on the stretch and control the ball back for Sadio Mane to score showed the touch of a man who deserves more credit than just 'works hard, doesn't he?'

Particularly in the first half, he was all about quality decision making. He kept it when he needed to, he made runs out wide when he needed to, and he fired early crosses in when the time called for it. With a bit of luck and better finishing from his teammates he could have gone in at the break with three assists to his name.

His performance was up there among equally impressive showings from Gini Wijnaldum and debutant Naby Keita. You could argue that one performance raises the other, in a chicken and egg sort of way, but in particular when someone like Keita arrives and sees a 32-year-old Milner putting in the shift he does, it can only serve to inspire and set the bar.

Keita is a hard worker by nature, and will be thrilled to see that attitude turned up to 11 by his new teammates.

These levels of performance are nothing new from Milner though. He showed what he was capable of last season when he came top of the assists table in the UEFA Champions League, not just achieving the most for 2017-18, but the most ever in a single campaign.

When Milner's rumoured move to Liverpool in 2015 became a reality, there wasn't exactly universal fanfare.

He was well respected in the game, and fans remembered the time he came off the bench to nearly single handedly turn things around at Anfield in the 3-2 win over City in 2013-14, but there was plenty of scepticism that he would bring The Reds what they needed as they looked to get back to the football elite.

Since then, Milner has gone from strength to strength. First he conquered penalties, then he conquered the left-back position for a whole season, he even managed to conquer Twitter within minutes of joining the social media site. He probably would have finished the Tottenham stadium on time as well if he'd been appointed as project manager.

Liverpool's vice captain can sometimes be the forgotten man. Perhaps his unquestionable reliability counts against him on occasion, but see him on a teamsheet and you know you're getting dedication, creativity and at least one thundering tackle that leaves you shouting, 'Well in, Millie'.

Despite the summer additions, he will continue to get plenty of minutes this season, and oppositions will hate that. As a midfielder coming to Anfield, or inviting Liverpool into your home, looking up and seeing Milner on the other team must fill you with a certain sense of dread. 'I've got to follow him around all day? I've got dinner plans later.'

The man with the big balls is leading by example, and everyone sees it. Particularly Klopp, whose celebration at Milner's fantastic assist for the second goal was quite clearly in honour of that fact.

Impressed? You'd be nuts not to be.

Controlled Aggression:
The Final Piece Of The Puzzle

Wednesday August 15, 2018

PAUL COPE

I'M excited.

Excited and a little bit afraid, if I'm being completely honest.

Excited that this could well be the best Liverpool team and squad that I have ever had the pleasure of watching in my entire adult life (which I count as 1998 onwards, for those who aren't familiar with my age, but could easily extend before my adult years to 1990 onwards if I could remember that far back).

But a little bit afraid because there are no guarantees that being this good will be enough to win the league.

In fact, I've realised I have an acute fear that Jürgen Klopp could create the greatest ever Liverpool side in the history of the club, accumulating more points than any previous side has ever managed, and we still might not win the title.

I think if I was a bit younger I'd be petrified at the thought.

As it stands though, I'm not going to waste too many of my waking hours worrying about how good Manchester City might be. There might not be much I can do about jumping up in the middle of the night in cold sweats about it, but I can control what I think about during the day.

And I'm choosing to think about how good we are now.

We were all excited heading into the first game of the season, but I'm not sure many of us would have predicted such a stroll in the park for our opening-day victory.

The consensus seems to be that we didn't leave second or third gear in order to completely dominate a rejuvenated West Ham side packed with new signings and led by their highest paid manager of all time. A Premier League winner, no less.

But for all of our opponent's new-found optimism heading into the new season, we swatted them aside with ease. After half an hour I wondered how they could find a way into the game and a goal just before half time made me question whether they might just declare in the dressing room.

Let their fans get an earlier train back to London, having already been through their entire 1980s back catalogue of anti-Liverpool songs and spending half an hour telling us how quiet we were before sinking into their own silent protest for the second half. It's depressing to see that some things never change.

We all hoped that we might send out a message to the rest of the league, and I'm not sure we could have done it much more emphatically.

A 4-0 victory that could easily have been eight. A goalkeeper making his debut without being tested in any meaningful way. Goals for our returning hero, new number 10 and long-lost lover continuing his pre-season form, breaking out the wriggly arms to the glee of the crowd, to put the cherry on the cake.

But, more than that, a look of aggression across the pitch. World-class players strewn around the Anfield turf. Pace, power and trickery at every turn.

CHAPTER ONE - THE FAST START

We're right to be excited, and we're right to get carried away as quickly as possible, regardless of how good anyone else might be. Let's not waste any time being cautious about what happens next.

For so many years now, I have been with many of you in bemoaning how lightweight and timid we've looked. Even when we've had sides packed with ability, we've always just lacked that aggression that all great sides have. That bit of needle that the best take with them to every party.

When Trent Alexander-Arnold got booked for pushing Felipe Anderson in the chest I couldn't have been happier. Our young right back showing that it doesn't matter who you are or what your reputation is, you can't just waltz past us like we're not there anymore.

There's Virgil van Dijk gliding around the pitch from centre back barking orders at everyone around him, a man mountain in goal oozing a calm control.

There's a terrier at left back who looks ready to 'take this outside' at any given moment, and a centre midfielder playing with 15 stitches in his head and another who's no stranger to getting a red card, strutting around the place with the kind of arrogance I love in footballers.

These lads mean business. For the first time in a long time, it looks as though a team and squad has been built that combines the flair and skill we've seen in past Liverpool teams, with the aggression, desire and determination that's been missing in so many of those sides, and we're seeing it across the pitch and across the squad.

The iron fist in a velvet glove we've been dreaming of for so long. And what a velvet glove it is. Lads everywhere who look able to take a touch that makes us drool, beat opposition players with ease and play intricate one-twos in tight spaces that leave their adversaries chasing shadows.

I left Anfield on Sunday with the never previously experienced feeling of looking forward to when we play against a team which traditionally sets up shop in their own box and challenges us to break down their defence. A team that turns up each season laughing about how easy it is to stop Liverpool by frustrating us. Good luck with that this season, lads.

Leave this team with the ball for long enough and it looks as though it has the cool heads and tricky feet needed to slowly drive you insane. Calmly passing the ball from side to side, moving your tired legs around the pitch while prodding and probing for space then, out of nowhere, bursting past three of your players as though they don't exist.

Maybe they don't. Maybe you're playing with fewer players than us. Can that be right? We started with the same number, didn't we? But it feels like these red bastards have got more. Didn't I just clear that ball? Why is it coming back at me so soon? Why the fuck have I got three men to mark? SOMEONE COME AND HELP ME FOR FUCK'S SAKE, THERE'S LOADS OF THEM.

But no one can come to help, mate. They're all fucked as well. They've got three men to mark and no one can understand why. Van Dijk's meant to be a centre back but he's standing 40 yards from your goal as our deepest-lying defender, staring you straight in the eyes with a knowing grin on his face.

I know it doesn't seem fair but you're just going to have to live with it. Take a 4-0 defeat now and we might go easy on you. But, then again, we might score 10. We could need the goal difference in May. No hard feelings, it's just business.

I'm not sure there could be a more glowing compliment for a Liverpool team in the modern era than me actually looking forward to watching it trying to break down a packed defence. Even as I write that I think of Jose Mourinho's depressed face and whining voice and how wonderful it would be to tear his negative, defensive setup to bits while we dance in the aisles.

This team is capable of anything and everything. The games against Manchester City are going to continue to be epic battles, and there's nothing we can do about how they get on against everyone else, so we might as well just enjoy every second of watching this beautiful red machine in action for the next 37 games.

It's going to be incredible.

Crystal Palace v Liverpool
Monday August 20, 2018
ROB GUTMANN'S PREVIEW

IT'S funny being the buzz. Being the noise.

Outside of our bubble we've always been regarded as a big team, obviously, but ultimately always supporting cast actors rather than the lead. Now feels different. Now feels like it may just be our time. Let's tempt fate and go for this. All around the world, they're talking about The Reds. Liverpool are the insurgency. The new force.

And it's more about the personality of this team than its accomplishments, because let's face it, we've won nothing. Yet.

But opposition managers, players and supporters just can't stop themselves talking about Liverpool. Sergio *fucking* Ramos can't stop talking about Liverpool. Pep Guardiola can't. Jose Mourinho loves getting into it about The Reds. Kevin De Bruyne's got some thoughts too. And in every pub, club and on every social media platform, the word is Liverpool.

The bookies now have us at bit over 3-1 to win the league. Just one game into the new season. This level of anticipation about what this Liverpool team might do feels unprecedented, in my memory at least. And it's not just because this team are good, it's the way in which they're good.

There are many different types of winning forces in sport. Often, they are characterised not just by talent but by will, by character, by 'winning mentality'.

Jürgen Klopp's team feel like they are trying to transcend traditional formulas. Like marathon runners who train to run further than an actual marathon to give themselves spare capacity, this Liverpool seem geared to overbeating teams. Yeah, that sounds a bit mad, but you know what I mean. If you watched Liverpool last season, you will definitely know what I mean.

Liverpool scored at least four goals on 16 occasions last campaign.

By way of context, the last Liverpool title-winning side managed to score that many just eight times. The free-scoring, Luis Suarez-inspired side of 2013-14 that came within two points of the title put at least four past opposition on 12 occasions. Rafa Benitez's best team of 2008-09 – again near champions – only notched four or more on six occasions.

Last season's title winners Manchester City – the greatest team of the Premier League era, in terms of points – managed to score four and over on 14 occasions. Very good but not Liverpool very good.

Liverpool have played one, scored four so far this season. Liverpool don't just try to beat teams, they try to unravel them. To dismember them. To bomb them back to the Stone Age. And making those things the objective doesn't always work. It's why Man City were first and Liverpool weren't.

Against Roma at Anfield in May, Liverpool were five up inside an hour. Roma should've done the decent thing and walked off the pitch. It was shaping up to be the biggest battering any side had ever taken at that stage of the world's premier club competition.

But Liverpool, having gorged on goals, were full and allowed themselves to become distracted. Roma pulled two back and the entire tie was kept alive when it had most definitely been declared dead.

Klopp and the club have spent the last year preparing and making fixes to weaknesses. For all the excitement and fear generated by Liverpool's much vaunted attack, the consistent propensity to concede at crucial moments demonstrated that this promising side were not yet the real deal.

The additions of Virgil van Dijk, Alisson Becker, Naby Keita and Fabinho represent a determination by the manager and his support staff to build a more complete and complex team.

This is what has got the wider football world in a lather. All are sweating now because they sense that Liverpool can't now be dismissed as mere fancy dans, all style and fragile substance. Liverpool now have backbone. A spine to supplement all that artistry and brio in the forward positions.

Klopp will probably look to go with a very similar 11 to that which beat West Ham on the season's opening day. There is little need to consider change. There will have been eight days between games, and all of his big guns were available and looked in good fettle in the swatting aside of The Hammers.

The only selection dilemma will come in midfield where the manager must decide if either Gini Wijnaldum or James Milner deserve to lose places to accommodate now battle-ready captain Jordan Henderson. The truth though is that both Milner and Wijnaldum are playing so well at the moment that it would be hugely unjust if either had to make way just yet.

Palace won't be pushovers and this may need to be a match won from the bench. Handy then that Liverpool's should feature such options as Henderson, Xherdan Shaqiri, Daniel Sturridge and Adam Lallana. These are luxuries we would have only dreamed of in the near past. Now the power in reserve serves to exemplify just how full bodied this latest Liverpool vintage is.

Monday night is a scrappy night for football, but we are where we are. Number one and shooting towards the sun.

Crystal Palace 0 Liverpool 2
BEN JOHNSON'S RATINGS

HAD a boss ratings there, you know. Fucking boss one, on me phone, work in motion, type as you watch. Real-time shit.

Then some mad fella come into The Croc and started asking everyone mad questions about whether they supported Liverpool or not on about 41 minutes and then me notes on my phone ended up in me notes deleted bit. And I went in to restore it, and The Reds scored, and I deleted it – lost forever, like a big fucking dope.

Anyway, fancy some re-hashed jokes, not only re-hashed from last season, but also from about 20 minutes ago? Sound. Go 'ed.

Alisson: 8

Cool as fuck, isn't he? Like the fucking Fonz. If you don't know who the Fonz is ask your auld fella, or a random auld fella. He was very cool. I mean he was a 40-year-old mechanic with one T-shirt, who lived in his mate's ma's garage and didn't have a bird or that, but you know, you will have to take the auld fellas' word for it.

Fucking hell, made a good save, looked boss, they cut to Mignolet's big stupid head for one second and then he went berserk and ran away from the ball. Put Si the Mig blinkers on him so he doesn't ever have to see him, just in case.

Trent: 8

Defended well there, didn't he? Zaha, if we are all honest with ourselves, is boss, isn't he? Isn't he? Reckon he's had a harder game against Trent than the other way round, you know.

Big Virg: ?

I'm not rating him anymore because it's always a nine or a 10. You decide, lazy balls. Especially if you're making an article out of it…

Reads it better than anyone ever, you know. Do they have a Reading World Championship? What are the rules? Do they have to all read the same book? It would have to be a surprise book, maybe a new book? Why are you banging on about books, lad? Speaking of books, I could write one about his two headers in the last minute, in fairness. Best seller.

Joe Gomez: 9

Made a great tackle when they were in first half. Thought he was just as good as the fella playing next to him, in fairness, which is praise indeed. When Degsi comes back from his jarg stomach injury he will struggle to get back in.

Andy Robbo: 8

Should have done better with that one in the first half. Did alright, set up a few great chances, and defended better than any left back we have had in donkey's years. Lashed that one right over the bar there though, didn't he?

Naby: 8

Oh, lad. That might be the greatest thing I have ever seen. The turn, the ball – if Salah scores, mate, (and he nearly does) it's probably the greatest goal of our lives, you know. He never though, and then Naby had a mad 10 minutes, probably because he was fuming.

Milner: 7

Gave it away twice in a minute in the first half and then tried to kick Zaha over the moon, which was sound in fairness. Scored a pen. Is right.

He was good first half, if a little slow in possession, but then ghosted into the shadows second half, until he reappeared like he was on a Scooby Doo in our box to stop their lad scoring late on. Great tackle.

Mo Salah: 8

Lost a point for the Naby miss. Weren't at his best, but could have scored a hat trick, won the pen, and got their lad sent off, and then sent Mane through at the end. Absolute golden touch. Grafted as well.

Firmino: 7

Not at his best but still better than most. Ran himself ragged.

Sadio Mane: 8

Say what you want, but there is nothing better than the payoff of a last-minute 2-0 fella. Sadio there was amazing, the strength the pace, the power, the persistence, the this that and the other. Fucking is right, lad.

SUBS...

Henderson: 9

Come on when we were stretched for five and boxed us, made it look easy. A captain's cameo.

Lallana: ?

Hmm, head like a badger. Gave away a freekick.

Sturridge: ?

Came on after 94 minutes, lad. Come on. Only putting it here so you don't moan.

NEIL ATKINSON'S REVIEW

THE season starts.

God, you felt that, didn't you?

God, you lived that, didn't you?

God, you loved that, didn't you? Didn't you?

What it is to be alive. Liverpool gave us that tonight. Being fair, so too did Crystal Palace.

It was visceral football from both sides. It was meaty football. It was the real deal, the first proper great game of the season. It had heft and presence. It kept announcing itself over and over and Liverpool had to cope with it.

Before a ball had been kicked on this fixture list this was a game that stood out. Monday night, under the lights, Selhurst Park. Palace v Liverpool. And, therefore, fair play to Palace. They brought the best of themselves.

Andros Townsend nearly scores a Tony Yeboah, nearly produces the full business. Wilf Zaha is so potent, every time he picks the ball up he screams danger. Patrick van Aanholt is a footballer. And Aaron Wan-Bissaka is marvellous and, under duress, does the right thing, and my God what a player he is.

Let no one tell you otherwise. They are quick, strong, brilliant on the ball. They finish top half. They terrify our rivals. They have 12 games against the top six. That we have won one should not be diminished. What a game to win.

Liverpool play 38 games and at least 15 of them will be, in comparison to this one, utterly sterile. It should not be such. But we all know it will be. This game was alive. It was vivid and it was active. Until the 93rd moment this was a contest. It was a contest Liverpool won.

Liverpool defended brilliantly. What is important there is the idea that defending wasn't just about sitting deep and blocking. Liverpool played some brilliant front-foot football to aid their defending.

Both Joe Gomez and Virgil van Dijk were able to pick their moments to influence play. They got to be excellent centre halves as part of a unit rather than excellent emergency measures. James Tomkins was on the stretch. Mamadou Sakho was on the stretch. Liverpool's players rarely were.

Through the whole game Liverpool had a guiding intelligence that Palace struggled to deal with. All of their moves were improvised whereas Liverpool felt rehearsed, in the best possible sense. These Liverpool players love and adore each other and want to know each other's every move from the outset.

There were exceptions: Naby Keita turned away and found Mo Salah with the most glorious inspiration imaginable. Liverpool's finest footballer should have found the net but instead punted over. It would have been a remarkable goal, a goal to tell one hell of a story. Instead Salah ended the game goalless and perhaps slightly frustrated. Yet he assisted both Liverpool goals.

We won 2-0 and we deserved to win 2-0. We were the better side across the board. Yet there was a ton going on. Wan-Bissaka against Mane; where James McArthur was at any one time V what the momentum suggested; Christian Benteke V himself. An ongoing battle that last one. But everywhere else on the pitch football was happening. Players had to demonstrate their qualities.

It was a joy to behold. The easiest thing in the world when Liverpool come to town is for a side to hide. But that didn't happen this evening. Palace wanted to know. They faced down Liverpool and came off second best.

They won't be alone come May. Liverpool have the presence to face the nation down, to want to swagger wherever they go. It is marvellous and it is incredible. But it is a side maturing in front of your eyes.

The strange thing is this: They have done and lived and experienced the hard part. Most sides never properly get that, not the precocious ones, but Liverpool very much have. They know the hard part. But right now they want to make the hard be easy.

Liverpool win the game. They deserve it. But there are 36 more. Nothing stops now. But imagine being these Reds.

They march on, knowing the burden placed on them by their rivals, knowing that perfection is required by September. It is arduous and it is tough. But it is what Liverpool are built to deal with. Tonight was a sensation. Tonight was a ball. Tonight was a joy to be alive. It is exhausting how many more of them we need but this is our reality.

We have to keep winning. We have to be hard faced. We have to not apologise. We have to work, bitch.

Liverpool v Brighton & Hove Albion

Saturday August 25, 2018

ROB GUTMANN'S PREVIEW

IF you're not beside yourself with excitement at the prospect of watching The Reds at home to Brighton & Hove Albion then you're in the wrong business.

This Liverpool side are building dreams and momentum. All that stands in our way is the bearing of the psychological burden that accompanies great expectation.

Greater tests lie ahead than the already despatched West Ham and Crystal Palace, and indeed this weekend's opponents, but fulfilling minimum requirements has proved too much for countless Liverpool setups over the decades. Ruthlessness must be the new watchword.

It's been a long, long time since we've been able to go into a season sensing that something special was brewing. In my Liverpool-supporting life the most redolent example has always been the early phase of the 1987-88 campaign.

Truth be told, optimism wasn't particularly great on the eve of that season. Yes, Liverpool had been busy in the transfer market – bringing in John Barnes, Peter Beardsley and John Aldridge – but we'd finished the 1986-87 season well behind champions Everton and had lost top scorer and main man, Ian Rush, to Juventus in a record-breaking summer transfer.

It was the early results and the nature of the performances that quickly changed attitudes.

After a narrow opening day win over Arsenal, The Reds started scoring goals in big numbers and were swatting away opponents in a fashion that suggested even better things were to come.

That was the key thing. The hype, the expectation, the excitement. It was being felt keenly by us as fans, but it was very much out there in neutral land too. We were the team all were talking about.

What differentiated and gave it a sense of its own persona was that it wasn't just about Liverpool getting it on and winning a few games at the start of a season, it was the gelling of crucial new signings. They were refreshing and galvanised an already solid core.

There are echoes of this in Liverpool's here and now. We've added five new men this calendar year. Three already look and feel not just like mainstays, but essential components of an all-new and fearsome Liverpool team.

The big goalie – Alisson Becker – he's a lovely, big lad. As strapping as it gets. We've waited what might as well be a lifetime for him. But he's here now, like a whopping, great-bearded, handsome prince in our goal.

At Crystal Palace on Monday night, there he was. Throwing himself about, kicking short, arrowing balls long, chucking it out overarm like a world-class bowler. Everything done with decisiveness and confidence, with purpose and accuracy.

Then there's Virgil van Dijk, a veritable one-man defence. He makes men around him feel like men again. He completes our defence. He completes me. In South London he was arguably the stand-out performer in a Liverpool team of performers.

Running the colossus close as man of that match was another new boy, Naby Keita. We've waited a long year for Naby, but he's proving worth it.

Eighteen months ago, I doubt any/many of us would have known him had we crashed into him on a Leipzig street corner. Our manager knew about him, though. The impression is that it must have been love at first sight for Jürgen Klopp. Here was a midfielder he could build a team around. An all-purpose running, dribbling, tackling, shooting machine.

That Alisson, Virgil and Naby seem hellbent on fulfilling their Anfield destinies in such a rush, combined with the obvious wider functionality of an already legendary attack, an impressive pre-season and a bold start to the actual campaign, are allying to bolster the burgeoning impression that we're watching a Liverpool team on a mission.

Momentum can be all in football. The risk of a false dawn remains omnipresent, but if Klopp can harness all the positive forces working in Liverpool's favour at the moment then a truly special era can be beckoned in sooner rather than later.

Fitness issues notwithstanding, I think we all expect Klopp to go again with the same side for Brighton. We might have expected to be seeing a midfield of Jordan Henderson, Naby Keita and Adam Lallana a couple of months ago, but Gini Wijnaldum and James Milner simply refuse to be cast off as bit-part actors.

Expect the skipper, Hendo, to again be left kicking his heels, and other big names such as Daniel Sturridge, Xherdan Shaqiri, Fabinho and Lallana to be sweating on even making the matchday squad.

The Reds may not deliver the football fiesta and banquet of goals that Anfield now routinely craves, but this all-new, eyes on the prize red wrecking ball should still have enough quality and components to make relatively short work of those plucky and in-form Seasiders.

Take the next step, Reds.

Liverpool 1 Brighton & Hove Albion 0
NEIL ATKINSON'S REVIEW

JAMES Milner tackles their lad.

James Milner tackles their lad this morning when he has his breakfast.

James Milner tackles their lad while he packs his oversized wash bag.

James Milner tackles their lad from the minute he was born to the second the freekick is given. He has lived his whole life to just tackle their lad at that moment. He has pictured tackling their lad for eternities. Galaxies have exploded, all human life has evolved and become extinct and James Milner is both tackling their lad and picturing doing so.

That moment was the moment where I was reflecting on Brighton home and away against our rivals last season and how frustrating they could be. It was the moment I was beginning to think we could be in for the longest possible afternoon.

James Milner tackles their lad and Liverpool score. From the minute he wins his tackle there is an inevitability about events. For the tackle James Milner should be given:

· The assist.
· The freedom of the city.
· His Sunday dinner in a choice of Liverpool restaurants.
· The right to decide what the dressing room listens to for the next week.
· Maghull. If he wants it.

Flash, flash and there it is. Salah off the post or as near as dammit for it not to matter.

Then he celebrates. Then he prays. Then he pumps his fist staring at the Lower Kemlyn/Centenary/Kenny Dalglish Stand. He pumps his fist looking at me or as near as dammit and we lock eyes, or we don't, and we are thinking Manchester City drew. Liverpool lead. Everything is vital in every sense of the word.

Man City drew.

Listen, I do this thing. Two things. Both in my head.

Thing one: while I do day-to-day tasks, I do this thing where I have imaginary conversations with the Liverpool manager. It has never been as bad as this, not since 2008 with Rafa Benitez. Maybe never as bad.

I consult Jürgen Klopp. I wonder what he would make of x, y or z. Today we had a lovely big chat about how into Wolves/Man City I should be. We should be. Should we see it as an adjunct to our game? Should we focus on The Reds? Jürgen concluded that we should, for now, see this all as part of the season's rich tapestry, as the adventure.

Reader, I went berserk when Willy Boly scored. I kicked every ball of that last five. Manchester City have now dropped 1/7th of the points they dropped last season. That is bananas isn't our fault.

Thing two: I brush my teeth and think about the title. I hold a door open and think that is the behaviour of champions. I lie in bed and think about how it would be in May. If. If. If.

Everything is if. Nothing is when. If.

Send me on a night out and ask me what I would do if it happened. I have plans. Documents. A desk drawer full of contingencies. If. If. If.

Yearning on a large scale can make history. The yearning is palpable now and it isn't even September yet. But by Christ it is fun. It is vital. It is what it is to be alive. Yearning on a large scale can make great nights out.

We're going to have a lot of them.

I was umming and ahhing about whether or not I was going to go to town.

Then Virgil van Dijk rolled it back to Alisson Becker. And he dinked it, resplendent in yellow, over the onrushing player's head and controlled it, and you know what, nothing may ever be the same again.

On an evening where much was tinged beige – as it has to be from time to time – it was a technicolour dreamcoat of a moment. It was what it was to be alive.

Not long after, Trent Alexander-Arnold pinged it sweeter than you have ever seen. Earlier, Gini Wijnaldum dribbled past four doing keepy-ups. Liverpool never hit the heights while winning but they are such scamps. They fizzle. Your blood does the same.

Hero worship is a strange thing when you are 37. There was a point in the second half where two of their lads walloped Milner in close succession. The ground was incensed. How dare you hit our heroes like that?

The curve goes on for so many of these Liverpool players. Twelve months ago juries were out all over the shop. Now the question is which of them you love the most.

It needed graft. Because at times Liverpool hadn't quite gelled. Because Brighton are a well-organised outfit. Because you can't win 4-0 every week, it needed graft and it needed care and it needed seeing out. It needed love. Liverpool loved their three points James Milner's tackle and Mo Salah's whip-crack finish had given them.

They sailed those points home, held gentle between big hands. They understood the delicacy of the arrangement. They never sat back – the left back pops up inside right in the box with 10 left on the clock – but nor did they overcommit. They understood the best way to win 1-0 was to look like winning 2-0, something that has been true of football matches since the very dawn of time.

The love to work remains the best and finest thing about this Liverpool side. That and their sense of mischief. They know and believe that exuberance married to graft doesn't do the job. It is the job. It is vital. It is what it is to be alive. It underpins the worship and the imaginary conversations and the life lessons.

Three down and 35 to go.

Be scamps, Liverpool. The hardest working scamps we have ever seen.

Leicester City v Liverpool
Saturday September 1, 2018
ROB GUTMANN'S PREVIEW

UPON reflection, I think we can treat Brighton as a bit of a wake-up call.

The best kind. The kind where you are reminded that there's work still to be done, but learn the harsh lesson while still winning. Hopefully that, in itself, is a mark of progress.

Time may come to view the Leicester City team of this era as one of the strangest sides to have ever competed in the top tier. Their achievement in winning the league title three years ago remains – as near as dammit – the greatest sporting achievement of all time.

I'm not exaggerating. And I'm going back to the ancient Greeks here and assuming that, although some no-mark must have at some point emerged from the ether to star in the ancient games, that however Herculean that undertaking may have been, it could only, at best, have equalled Leicester City's crowning moment.

They'd been all but relegated the season before their title win, and after it they returned to the mediocrity that had been their default existence. As if it had all been a dream.

Since, though, they have stabilised, and although they never truly convince, they have an upper half of the table resident's-like ability to find wins, as and when they need them. At the very least, they're now consistent in being labelable as 'dangerous opponents'.

If we bring our second-half performance against Brighton, then we may be in for an uncomfortable Saturday. If we can find our first-half level, we will have few problems.

Klopp worried about the fade in 'intensity' in his team a week ago and hinted at a need for changes, despite the reasonably long recuperation period between games at this stage of the season.

Liverpool's bench has been a sight to behold in the early phase. Such reserve riches we haven't enjoyed for a very long time. Strange then that we were unable to truly benefit from fresh resources in the second half on Saturday. Perhaps, had Liverpool not been winning and had something to protect, we might have seen more bullish, and ultimately more productive, changes.

For Leicester, Jordan Henderson looks a solid bet to start his first game of the season. Who the captain replaces is harder to gauge. Does Klopp opt for a double defensive pivot – matching Hendo with Gini Wijnaldum – with Naby Keita foraging ahead of them, or does he stick with a singular number six, and retain Milner to augment Keita's attacking tendencies?

If there's to be a surprise selection it may come in the front three. Bobby Firmino hasn't quite caught fire yet and Klopp will surely have closely observed the likes of Daniel Sturridge and Xherdan Shaqiri in training, watching for signs that they may be ready to start, and rest the Brazilian.

Another possible is Adam Lallana, maybe at Milner's expense. Lallana has been all but written off by many supporters but the manager will recall that, pre injury, he had led the 'press' from the front throughout the 2016-17 campaign.

The Reds' three wins on the board so far give them room for breath, and although a point at Leicester would be far from a disaster, the head of steam and confidence that winning habit brings needs to ideally be sustained.

That is if this season is not merely to be another entertaining one, but the defining one we all so crave.

Leicester City 1 Liverpool 2
BEN JOHNSON'S RATINGS

I TELL you what. They fucking love Kasabian in Leicester, you know.

Like not just love them, proper freedom of the city shit. Like these are gods among men. The gods of the middle. Gods of skinny jeans, and silly sideys. The gods of pork chops. Fair doos to them.

They lash them on full whack, noise pollution levels to create an atmosphere and clap along with some silly fan things. I don't know what this fucking place is about, you know. But what I do know is that them fucking Kasabian mings were ringing round our lads' heads 20 minutes in and didn't go off until the end of the game.

We were shite, we won 2-1, is fucking right. Play something we can dance to, bellend.

Alisson: 6

Makes a great save and clutches one out the air when they fancy a goal first half. When he ran over to our end I wished I had an emoji button that I could press to turn my eyes into hearts. Hang on. Fucking hell, he's just been tackled in his own box. Fucking hell. Lad? Was Si Mig, the evil genius controlling him, there? Si Robot, the AI master? Robocop him, lad.

Trent: 6

Tried a bit of silliness with the ball when we went bananas first half for a bit. Thought he was poor today for the first time in a long time.

Virgil: 8

Immaculate there when everyone else bar him and his partner went to absolute shit for 20 first half. Had a whacky 10, including a shite backpass that led to their goal.

Joe Gomez: 10

Best game for The Reds by a mile. The goal-saving tackle was sublime, but he didn't put a foot wrong.

Andy Robbo: 8

Not at his best but better than most. I like that one. Showed bottle, and grafted like anything. Like his mates, wasn't the best on the ball but like his mates there wasn't a lot of options on when he had it.

Hendo: 7

Great first half when we were boss. Looked knackered there second half though, and couldn't impose himself on the game. Wasn't the only one.

Gini: 5

The Reds were great first 20. Almost perfect. Then Gini gives one away and we go to shit for the rest of the game. And for that, I'm out.

Milner: 8

Thought he was the vice man of the match, there. Ugly toes in, ugly boss challenges, sneaky time wasting, what a fella. Made out of rock.

Sadio: 8

Might end up with more goals than anyone this year, you know. A hero. Not all heroes wear capes. He had one on under his top.

Firmino: 6

Weirdly shite while being effectively effective. Thought he was absolutely last but then he scored. Thought he was absolutely last but then on 96 minutes he legs Harry Maguire, and his massive big mattress head, and makes him lash it out. I'll be honest, I could have cuddled him, there. Proper cuddle, mind you. Head right in there.

Salah: 7

Made some poor choices. But then, in fairness, we all do. I once ordered a prawn salad in a steak restaurant for fuck's sake. I was starving.

SUBS...

Shaqo: 7

Come on and absolutely barrelled his way to keeping the ball for The Reds. Go 'ed, you mad little fucker. Get to ours.

Naby: n/a

Come on, didn't he? Don't like that song, you know. Don't think it tracks right.

Matip: n/a

Come on and I nearly cried. Not sure why.

NEIL ATKINSON'S REVIEW

LIVERPOOL got away with murder at the King Power this afternoon.

Liverpool – top of the league.

Liverpool were poor.

Liverpool deserve their win. You get to defend well. You get to do the business without having the ball. That is the hardest thing at times to acknowledge – when you win the way you aren't accustomed to. Liverpool won in a way they aren't meant to.

They won.

They are top of the league.

Football doesn't have to make sense, but it does tend to work out.

Things that happen in the first half:

· Liverpool get behind Leicester four times and are worthy of two goals by 20.
· Liverpool score one goal.
· Gini Wijnaldum gives it away.
· Liverpool are abject for 20.
· Leicester create nothing.
· Liverpool make it 2-0.
· Half time.

The first half sort of makes sense as a game of football that Liverpool play. It was a firm reminder that football is sort of random and sort of not, and that you get what you deserve and what you don't.

Leicester had hard lines. But they didn't. For a vast swathe of the first half, they were firmly second best. For a vast swathe of the first half, they were on the verge of forcing an equaliser.

James Maddison aside, they lacked Liverpool's cunning, lacked Liverpool's incision. But they were very much in the ascendancy at home and so often that, in and of itself, can be enough.

And so it proved. And that is the 'but'. Many games have a but. In the second half, Liverpool were pushed right back by Leicester's desire to force the issue and they were rattled by it. Gone were Liverpool's creation of chances, they were hanging on for dear life, getting territory, forcing the ball into corners and looking to take time out of the game.

Liverpool were left to not be Liverpool, to be the side who you say 'but' about. That 'but' could prove positive or negative. They could find themselves being brilliant on the attack but able to hold sides out. They could find themselves being a side who promised a lot but ran out of gas.

Today, they were the side who weren't great but found a way.

Joe Gomez's performance was rolling a six on snakes and ladders and getting to 94. He went from supporting act to best defender on the pitch, a pitch with both Virgil van Dijk and Harry Maguire on. He went from boy to man before our very eyes. He was everything.

The list of things you want from central defenders: great on the ball, good in the air, brilliant on the turn, smartest man on the pitch, body on the line. Gomez's performance is one to walk around. There should be statues built off the back of it.

Elsewhere, there was a shortage of quality but a lot of heart and a fair amount of brain. James Milner the standout for that. He oscillated between infuriating to incendiary.

He won some tackles that should have meant more. He should be the man who launched Liverpool on a four on two which would have led to it being 3-0.

Instead, minutes later it was 2-1 through the goalkeeper making his first mistake of the season. He was rightly punished and he will be again. This is what we are bought into. There is no relief from this. The rough with all his smooth. I love his smooth. He will do for me.

He wasn't punished. Roberto Firmino was dreadful but – another but – my God did he work. Did he give us everything. Did he hunt Maguire down after 90 passed. Did he make it a nightmare to have the ball around him.

Against this Liverpool side what is striking is they can keep a good side at arm's length. Leicester hurt Liverpool but – but, but, but – they couldn't punish them. That's testament to a Liverpool side who went from excellent to poor in the blink of an eye but who remained switched on. They kept their shape, kept talking and kept working.

Football is the best of the sports because it makes you make peace with the random while addressing a set-piece situation while tending towards allowing class to prevail.

When our shape goes wrong it can be like a clock that can't tick. But it can still do the business occasionally.

Class prevailed, he types as he grins to camera. Class prevails. Liverpool prevail.

Four down. Twelve from 12. Thirty-four to go. Good lord. Thanks for the break…

CHAPTER TWO - THE WELCOME BREAK

THE thing with a title race is that for a large portion of the time you can't be certain you're in one.

The nature of the 24/7 coverage which surrounds football in the modern-day means that a team is just as quickly the champions elect as they are 'bottlers'.

Some title races have been over as fast as they've started, some have ebbed and flowed as teams drop in and out, and some have rumbled on and on every single step of the way.

As we all know by now, this season's title race can very much be categorised as the latter. But, if you were a fan of Liverpool or Manchester City, you'd have known you were in one almost immediately.

The first run of games before the international break started at break-neck pace for Liverpool. Like a freight train that you couldn't be certain would ever stop while being absolutely certain of the direction it was heading in. It wouldn't veer off even though the scale of the challenge we faced was immediately apparent.

Little did we know those first few games would come to form a microcosm, of sorts, of Liverpool's season. At least Liverpool's season in the context of games played against sides outside the top six.

It was an example of how much Liverpool had adapted their style; from a devastating 4-0 home win, to a hard-fought away performance resulting in a fairly comfortable scoreline, a home game which didn't exactly go how we hoped except that we won and another tough away narrowly navigated despite some setbacks.

Liverpool showed they could win every which way. They showed Manchester City they'd have to be at their best to pip them to this league title. But most importantly, they laid a marker down.

Liverpool were back at the top table. And it would take an awful lot for them to be moved.

Josh Sexton

Tottenham Hotspur v Liverpool
Saturday September 15, 2018
ROB GUTMANN'S PREVIEW

THERE are no cup finals in September. No title was ever decided on game five. So why does this feel like a game of monumental importance?

History may well cast this encounter into the ether, but in the here and now it's hard to fathom a more pivotal moment. Of course, this sounds irrational and a little bit hysterical, but stay with me.

I'm a title-winning veteran. There are less of us around these days. Cherish us and enjoy us while you still can. We know what winning the league feels like. Age is sure as hell withering us, and our recollections are hazing by the year, but no one will ever steal those treasured trophy-winning memories from us. More than the memories, the feelings, the sensations in the gut, will never fade.

I used to 'sense' titles. Smell them coming. Liverpool were very, very good in my youth – late '70s and the '80s – and we'd start every season feeling it was a God-given right to win the league. But we'd never feel certain, though. That was part of the fun. We were frequently asked if it got boring, winning year on year. It never got old. In fact, each passing triumph just heightened the anxiety that at some point this must all come to an end.

The story of each season would have its own unique character and narrative. Some of the best were those where we had to come up on the rails to win. To prevail in adversity. Like 1981-82 – mid table at Christmas and floundering, top of the pile in May and all conquering.

My favourites, though, were the ones where we looked right from the off. Yes, there'd be a twist or a turn along the way, but early on there would be that sense that winning the league was our destiny. The pivotal moment would often come around now.

Liverpool have a tough month of fixtures ahead, but this impending matchup, with as good a Spurs team as there's been in my lifetime, feels like it could be a make or break point. I'm being melodramatic because I think we all need to be. Me, you, the manager, the team, all of us. Because – to channel Jürgen Klopp – it's essential that we believe.

League titles are won by confident teams. Sides that can banish doubt. Those Liverpool teams of my youth turned up to win each and every match. I almost can't remember when we ever spoke of an English league fixture and said to ourselves 'a draw would be a decent result today'.

We're too battle scarred these days from 28 title-less years to be counting any chickens yet, or so naive as to not know that a draw away to Tottenham is never a bad result. These tonked us 4-1 at Wembley a year ago. But… We have to win this. We just do. Or at least near die trying.

Last year in this fixture, we were beaten inside the first 25 minutes. Dejan Lovren and Simon Mignolet had nightmares, and Spurs played like demons. Liverpool will have some different players to parade at Wembley this year, some in particularly key positions.

No crap goalie this time. This time we bring Alisson Becker. The greatest keeper of all time. That's the fantasy he's nurturing at least and the blotting of his copybook at Leicester doesn't change that, although he could do with not soiling his own cage again any time soon.

We also bring new centre backs. Lovren and Joel Matip stunk out Wembley last October but they won't get to reprieve themselves this time round. Virgil van Dijk and Joe Gomez look and feel like the present and future of Liverpool's defence. Other newbies are the full backs Trent Alexander-Arnold and Andy Robbo. That's four new faces in the back five.

In midfield, I hope we recall Naby Keita. He was rested against Leicester and we missed him. He'd had moments in his first three outings that suggested he wouldn't be long in fulfilling the prophecy for him. A red nation craves a midfield messiah and an heir to Steven Gerrard's legacy. No one has a better chance of being our saviour than Naby.

Klopp's ultimate selection will be much predicated on the fitness and freshness of his international break returnees. Mercifully, our front three have only had to play a solitary game apiece.

The Dutch lads – van Dijk and Gini Wijnaldum – have the relative respite of a near full week's training ahead of Wembley. So by the standards of these things, we might arrive in West London on Saturday morning in relatively good fettle.

If there's to be changes from the winning side at Leicester, expect Keita to replace Wijnaldum or James Milner. There might also be a surprise omission, if Roberto Firmino is deemed too weary to start after his exertions for Brazil. Might this enable a first start of this campaign for either Xherdan Shaqiri or Daniel Sturridge?

The Spurs were jolted by defeat at Watford two weeks ago. They were quietly motoring and purring in the wake of their demolition of Man United. Then reality caught up with them. It may well catch up with us soon too.

Tottenham are a very good but very strange side. There's a mental strength there, that seems to emanate from the stoic Mauricio Pochettino, that has ensured their place as *one of* this hugely competitive league's very best teams, for a number of seasons now.

The *one of* is key though. It's not that they 'need to win a trophy', they're bigger than that – they need to take the next step and be the actual best team. A bit like Liverpool.

Those of us travelling down to London at the crack of dawn on Saturday will do so with stout hearts and bagfuls of optimism. As we did about a year ago. Lightning often does strike twice in football. Be arsed with having to go through that trauma again, mind.

Have them focused from the get go, Jürgen. This isn't quite a cup final, regardless of Wembley, but it is on the level of some sort of semi final.

Win it – and that's no small ask – and take a giant step forward.

Tottenham Hotspur 1 Liverpool 2
BEN JOHNSON'S RATINGS

IT'S glorious winning at Wembley, isn't it?

We used to do it all the while, you know. Let's do it all the while again, aye?

Alisson: 8

Back to making his shit look easy, isn't he? Loved it when that 1945 fella upfront for them tried to lob him with a header and he just caught it and told him to shut his mouth.

Trent: 8

He's probably the best centre mid in the world and we play him right back for a laugh.

Virgil: 9

Lashed the afterburners on to bail Joe Gomez out there second half. Loved his dialogue with him after it.

'Lad.'

'I know, lad.'

Marked that blue whale-mouthed fucker right out of it there, didn't he? Imagine the shite he collects in his throat. He needs a filter fitting, him. Probably gets half his calories off spiders and flies, and that.

Joe Gomez: 8

Had an Igor whacky 10 minutes second half when he went shite for a bit, but then clobbered their best player. Virgil loves him, I reckon.

Andy Robbo: 9

Captain. My captain. He's boss, isn't he? Juicing on Irn Bru, him.

Gini: 8

Thought he struggled first half but bosses it second half. Loved it when he twatted it into their Kryton lad who plays centre mid. No fucking way that hurt him, mate. Probably just endangered his oil supply or something. He's like Pinocchio him, lad. I'm a real boy. Look, it hurts. No you're not, now get up.

Milner: 8

Like all the midfield thought he struggled first half weirdly, but was glorious second half. Twatted it against the robot to prove a point, had a load of lovely chats with the ref and managed us through the game.

Naby: 7

Thought he was alright. Looks like he's just figuring us out. Him and Mane are going to wound people back end of the season down that left, you know.

Mo: 8

Not at his best but could have scored four. Fancied a goal late on, reckon he's getting a bollocking for that as we speak.

Sadio: 8

Looked like he forgot how to run for a bit there and still set up the second. Like he'd been spinning a brush over his head. His legs were a show. Loved it when he got a cob on with Lamela.

Firmino: 9

Thought he was our best attacker, you know. Till that slow crab gouged his eye out. Hope he hasn't been Momo'd.

SUBS...

Henderson: 8

Come on and looked bigger and harder than everyone else.

Sturridge: 7

Freekick winner these days. Like Didi Hamann upfront.

Blue-Whale Grid:

Two celebration goal.

Harry Winks:

The last cockney.

NEIL ATKINSON'S REVIEW

BATTERED them 2-1.

No idea how well we played.

Mad this sport of ours, at times.

Quick things:

First half, I was livid with our midfield. Couldn't see what they were about, what they were doing. Felt all three of them looked just off, but felt the Wembley pitch – in terms of both how it was underfoot and the sheer size of it – wasn't helping.

Thought Spurs were alehouse. Really direct for reasons I couldn't pinpoint. Who did they think they were turning round? Liverpool are not last season's Liverpool. I understand escaping the press but there has to be better ways than that.

Second half I was delighted with our midfield. Loved everything, could see everything. James Milner tackles their lad, and tackles their lad, and tackles their lad.

But the thing is this.

I was not in the ground. There are things you can see better on television and things you see better in the ground. What your centre mids are doing is very much among that. Passing lanes are a thing and you can block them without pressuring the ball, intercepting or tackling. You can play well without being visible. That could have been happening first half.

I have no idea how well Liverpool played.

Our knowledge has limits, our emotions don't. We feel the game. We feel the kicking of the ball, we feel Milner tackling their lad. We feel it, they feel it as they play and our opponents feel it. They feel the ball going out tamely for a throw in. They feel their shortcomings.

I have no idea how well Liverpool played.

But Tottenham were abject. It was a crumble of a performance. Liverpool should have scored four, five, six. Tottenham had lads not digging each other out, centre halves exposed and left for dead, midfielders missing.

Eric Dier was dreadful. Tottenham looked a mile away from the consistent point-grinding machine of the last four seasons. They looked a side at a crossroads, a side who have been well managed but where the manager can do little more. He needed his players to stand up and be counted.

The game was spiky for an hour. It was unpleasant and, while Spurs didn't deserve to go in level at the break, did Liverpool deserve to lead? You tell me. All I could feel was what wasn't right until Gini Wijnaldum nodded it back at goal.

Has he given it?

Has he?

Has he given it?

It is football's record scratch of a question. Has he given it? Has he given it? He *has* given it. Mixmaster Mike letting loose the party, inviting the carnage. He has given it and The Reds in the ground, The Reds in Motel, the diaspora finds itself in *excelsis deo*. Finds itself beside itself. Knows what it means.

It means everything. It was a first goal game and it was a Liverpool goal that was given.

The second, if anything, scruffier but back to what we can't know. There, in that second, we see Liverpool play well. We see Andy Robertson, we see Sadio Mane, we see quality. And while it is a dog's dinner, we see Roberto Firmino convert from all the expected goals you will ever need. We see the facts. The facts were 2-0. The facts were undeniable and the feelings were irresistible.

Liverpool on the march. But I have no idea how well Liverpool played.

Until the close, the question wasn't will Liverpool crumble? Instead it was, will Liverpool punish Spurs? Will they take them to the cleaners? Will they put them out of their misery?

Virgil van Dijk was majestic. Joe Gomez scrambled but survived; was fortunate, perhaps at key times, but excellent at others. This is the game when it becomes alehouse, the game in its essence. Some waves you ride and ride well.

Across the contest, Robertson was the game's outstanding performer. He never dipped from his seven and extended towards his 10. He showed himself to be marvellous yet again, to be in the conversation about being the best in his position in the league. He was streets ahead of his opposite number in Danny Rose, a player who has often looked the part.

Firmino was the best he has been this season. He showed the best and battled through the game. He deserved his goal and didn't deserve to come off the pitch bleeding from the eye. He was holding the ball brilliantly.

I have no idea how well Liverpool played.

The Liverpool manager kept going berserk. He will have all sorts to bollock great footballers about. Loads to go spare about. But loads to bounce off, loads to be proud of. Loads of courage and presumably organisation. But he will be talking about decision making and final ball. Final ball.

What do we know? Right now, only how it feels. Only that Liverpool scored two when they should have scored five. Only that they saw out the game after the late goal. Only that they deserve three points and Spurs deserve none. Only that, in the blood and bone, Liverpool have 15 from 15 and they are determined to make it a joy to be alive this season. They want to make you feel.

I am out right now. We know this. I am out. Liverpool have won away at a top-six rival. This is what it is when they make it a joy to be alive.

Just don't ask me how good they were.

Five down, 33 to go.

Battered them 2-1.

Liverpool v Paris Saint-Germain

Tuesday September 18, 2018

GARETH ROBERTS

ONE of the theories for Liverpool's current run of form under Jürgen Klopp is that the core group of players understand what is expected of it.

They know where to play, when to go, when to stay – what their responsibilities are. And The Reds are reaping the benefits, even when they're not at their best.

With Anfield gearing itself up for the return of European football tomorrow night, there's an argument to say it isn't just the players who are in the right place to influence the club's destiny at the moment.

Not so long ago, it seemed like the Anfield atmosphere debate was never far away. There were genuine theories that it was dead and gone – a figment of a collective imagination that could never be rekindled, a golden age gobbled up by modern football.

While some aspects of that debate remain – the price of, and accessibility to, tickets; trying to get like-minded supporters who want to create an atmosphere together in the ground, and so on – we are no longer digging into ancient history to find an Anfield atmosphere that we can be proud of, and one that we can genuinely claim spurred the players on to more.

It helps that from the get go Klopp has publicly placed value on the power of supporters in the stand to influence the players on the pitch. It was clear he was lured by the romance of the club, and from his programme notes to his press conferences, atmosphere and support has been a recurring theme throughout his near three-year reign.

Best remembered in the wider football world is when Klopp, just a month into the job, pointed to those making an early exit from Anfield as he suffered his first defeat as Liverpool manager, a 2-1 loss to Crystal Palace.

'After the goal on 82 minutes, with 12 minutes to go, I saw many people leaving the stadium,' he said. 'I felt pretty alone at this moment. We decide when it is over. Between 82 and 94 you can make eight goals if you like.'

His point then was not only aimed at supporters, it was about the players too – that they had to show, through their play, their mentality, their spirit, that they were a team that could be trusted to fight for every point.

This team now is just that. And whomever the opponent, Klopp can point to the muscle memory of past conquests in his reign that mean they should fear no one, particularly in Europe. Think Manchester United, Borussia Dortmund, Manchester City and Roma.

In those very same games, plus the match with Villarreal, supporters played a part. The atmosphere was again the envy of all around. It spurred Liverpool on. Team, manager, us supporters – all of us felt it in the ground and talked about it afterwards.

A less-heralded Klopp soundbite on the issue comes from a time when things didn't go to plan for his side. When Liverpool raced to a 3-0 lead away in Seville, it looked like game over. It wasn't. And a second-half fightback saw the Spaniards claim a point, the equaliser arriving in the 93rd minute.

That night, the home crowd sensed blood. It bayed and booed and their players reacted to it. Liverpool did something similar – something better – to Borussia Dortmund.

In a press conference that followed shortly after that Sevilla game, Klopp said: 'They can make all the difference, that's how it is.

'We felt it a week ago in Seville. At Anfield, if we were 3-0 up, I don't think it would have happened. Football only really works, in my understanding, when we all play together, when we all work together, and that involves the crowd, 100 per cent.

'We do it only because people are interested, when they leave it feels strange. Players don't stand in the stadium going "Oh, people are going home", but they feel it. It's a big difference, we can perform better when the atmosphere is there.'

Liverpool supporters have demonstrated during Klopp's reign that they can still do European nights better than the rest in England.

Anfield doesn't need club-coloured foil or club-issue flags for nights that are owned by the most passionate of supporters, those who devote their own time, energy and money to decorating the ground as it should be for continental competition.

The ground too has fizzed with the electric of old when once tales of doom said it was gone for good. Klopp came from a club famed for its atmosphere and found one that can do it even better.

After the Dortmund game at Anfield he said: 'The atmosphere was the best I have ever experienced. It should serve as an example to everyone about how supporters can influence a team and influence a game.'

Tomorrow, we get to do it again. It's the first day back, time again to experience the edge of a European match, and it's a suitably tasty tie too.

Paris Saint-Germain have money, superstars and short odds to win the Champions League. Yet their European pedigree pales in comparison to Liverpool's with just one Cup Winners' Cup and an Intertoto Cup to their name. They need reminding of that.

As supporters we know our contribution is valued – the manager and the players have said so. These are the nights when we show it best.

Anfield, 8pm, you know what to do. It's another adventure, another big night and another indicator that Gary Neville talks shite.

Forget about Europe? No chance. We'll leave that to those less equipped.

Liverpool 3 Paris Saint-Germain 2
BEN JOHNSON'S RATINGS

PARIS.

Have you ever been? Romantic capital of the world, apparently. I've never been, but my bird's auld fella lived there for a bit. Said there is dog shit everywhere and you can't lift your head off the floor. Jib it.

Alisson: 7

He's massive, you know. Watched him from The Kop for most of the second half stretch his legs. Nothing to do, really. Gave it away in the buildup to their goal but you know, in the context of the game, so fucking what?

Trent: 9

Best game of the season. Seriously. Imagine if he played for them, every cunt would be crying after him. Glorious.

Virgil: 8

He can pass the ball better than our keeper and he can pass it better than Xabi Alonso. Made a great block from that mad fella from Stoke just before the winner. Unlucky for their goal as well, mind you. Scruffy cunts.

Joe Gomez: 8

Somehow in the top five centre halves in the world. Footy is mad, isn't it? Our fan base were swallowing their undies because we didn't sign anyone to play next to Virg and he steps up and just starts taking the piss.

Andy Robbo: 9

Up against Mbappe. Sound. Give him it. Beat me, you prick. Thanks and thanks again. The epitome of this side. Greater than the sum of his own parts by willpower, attitude and desire. A fucking star. Double up with Neymar on him in your gaff, lads.

Henderson: 8

You say the earth's flat. I say it's curvy as fuck.

You say climate change is bollocks. I say it's fucking roasting.

You say Henderson is shit and passes backwards. I say you have probably never played footy in your life. You say he isn't good enough to play for Liverpool, but spend your time tweeting how boss Rabiot is and how much of a semi on you have got for The Reds being linked with him instead, eh?

I say the majority of the ground appreciates him more than he could know. You say 'can I have my tea'.

Milner: 9

Best player on the pitch. Seriously. I was as wrong about him not being able to play centre mid for The Reds as these Henderson fuckers at the minute.

Gini: 8

Part of a midfield that was instrumental for The Reds tonight. Maybe this midfield needs to play against absolute quality to make sense. Use of the ball perfect, there.

Sadio: 9

Brighter than the brightest spark, there. Thought he was our best attacker by a mile. What a fella. Give him whatever he wants to sign a contract.

Mo Mo: 7

Not at his best, but you know what? He had about 50 fellas marking him every time he got it. Didn't help that he forgot how to pass it for a minute, but fuck it.

Dan Sturridge: 8

Contradiction in terms, isn't he? Is he? Hasn't got the graft of Firmino but then scores off his only chance first half. Should score second half but, in a normal side, what more do you want?

SUBS...

Firmino: 8

Comes on and I'm busy telling myself he is shite when he comes on as a sub and then he does that. Bat on, lad. The best one-eyed performance since Jenny Brown got a rubber in the grid by accident in second year seniors. Her glass eye fell out, and she still got on the bus home. Well in.

The Rest: 7

I don't know.

NEIL ATKINSON'S REVIEW

WHAT about that? What about it? Go fuck yourselves, you fucking cowards.

They are good, you know. They are good Paris Saint-Germain. Better than good. I will remember watching Angel Di Maria tonight. I will remember being impressed.

I will remember being more impressed by James Milner.

We have been conditioned to defer to our betters. We have been conditioned to defer to these names. But elsewhere our names are their names. Our names ring out. Tonight Paris talk about Milner, talk about Jordan Henderson. Our name is Liverpool.

All the best.

That is the point. Just to watch that game of football, that is a joy. That is a privilege. That is what playing Champions League football is about. It was truly something, a sight to behold. On the pitch were a load of footballers who are top five in their position in the whole wide world.

Take Andy Robertson. Robertson played brilliantly against Kylian Mbappe. Let's be clear about how good Mbappe is. He is the business. But only when he got inside did he get any joy. Liverpool's left back is among the world's very best. Imagine being among the best in the world at your job.

These lads show over and over again our own shortcomings in rating them. They are among the very best in their position on the planet. These are the facts. And beyond that they are more, much more.

The Reds showed more courage and conviction there than most manage across the course of a campaign. They stood up and were counted when a bundle manage neither.

I have new glasses. The lenses are bigger. The frames are bigger. Here's a thing – when I smile widely my cheekbones push the glasses up.

I discovered this tonight. I discovered this after Daniel Sturridge scored.

Anfield Wrap contributor Steve Graves says this: 'Yes I have favourites. I have 11 favourites. They wear Red and they play for Liverpool. The lads on the pitch are my favourites.'

It is something always worth remembering, worth clinging to. A first principle. A seemingly difficult sentiment for some in an era where, for instance, sniping at the Liverpool captain is in vogue when he has barely played.

But there is also something that Steve would echo. There is something different, and marvellous, and tragic, and flawed, and incredible about Sturridge.

Sturridge scored on his first Champions League start.

He scored and we all celebrated, and I smiled and I smiled so widely my glasses peaked. They fell off my nose. What a thing. What a smile. I am among the most handsome on the planet. These are the facts.

Sturridge is something shiny. Maybe something special but more something worn. I like that. He isn't pure, more something muddled. He is a bit broken. He isn't alone. Who among us isn't these days?

He may not be Liverpool's best. He may not be in Liverpool's best 11. It is his tragedy, and his humanity, and his ongoing quality why he is the most marvellous. What a footballer. What a man.

These get to be our heroes. They get to be our champions. They get to be everything unfettered. I know how hard this game is by virtue of being shite at it. I get to understand leadership and organisation.

After 13 minutes Robertson puts his foot on the ball and all I want to scream is: 'You know the courage this takes?'

Do you? Do you get what it is to be these Reds? To play the game in such a sense, under such pressure? Do we understand what we are looking for from our footballers?

Tonight Jürgen Klopp asked his players to be the best in Europe, the best in the world right now. Tonight's game is that unquantifiable question. Tonight's game is never clean answer. What have we got that they haven't?

That answer could be the core thing. We made the final. We talk ourselves down far too much. We have such marvellous players. Our front three is allegedly among the best in the world. So our back eight could also be, yes?

Yes. We're tidy. We are good. Milner, Henderson, Gini Wijnaldum. These are our lads. Our best. What a thing.

This is your match report with a thousand question marks. Your match report with a thousand units of love. These are our lads. And that matters when it is continent wide. Don't you dare not love our lads.

There is no one more loveable.

These Reds, Queen.

Reds Continue To Capitalise On Post-Kyiv Positivity

Wednesday September 19, 2018

PAUL COPE

I'VE developed a new app that's going to be bigger than Facebook, Instagram and Twitter combined.

As with all of the best inventions, it's dead simple. It just allows fans of other football clubs to prevent any element of Liverpool supporters enjoying themselves from seeping into their lives.

No tweets, no messages, no photos. No videos of our happy faces bouncing around the place singing songs and letting off flares.

The rest of the world is desperate for it, Reds. They can't stand it. Can't stand watching us having a laugh because our football team is so fucking good.

We'll sell it for a fiver a pop and reinvest all of the money back in the team, basically just buying Bobby Firmino whatever mad clothes he wants because The Reds don't need any more players, they're already too good and it's not fair on everyone else.

I can't wait to flick through non-Liverpool Twitter today, just to see all of the cryarsing from the rest of them having to watch us have so much fun.

I'm still not sure why they hate it so much – it's meant to be fun, isn't it? Isn't it meant to be a laugh, something that takes us away from the mundanity of daily life?

I'm not really arsed if they think it's not, because unless they can get my new app up and running within the next few months, I'm concerned for them that they're going to have to get used to watching our grinning faces peering out at them from every nook and cranny of the internet for a while.

Thought you were checking how your nan is on Facebook? Unlucky mate, there we are, sitting next to her at the bingo, teaching her the words to Allez, Allez, Allez. And she fucking loves it. She'll be calling you soon to ask why you don't support Liverpool, and telling you how this Firmino seems to be an absolutely lovely lad. Smashing white teeth.

Wanted to see how Theresa May is getting on with her latest dance on Twitter? Never mind, sunshine. There's a gaggle of tweets for you to get through first, every one of them showing happy faces of Liverpool supporters enjoying their fucking faces off.

I've talked before about walking and talking the way you want to be before it actually happens. Walk the walk and talk the talk, and sooner or later the universe will catch up. Well we've been singing about taking over Europe for months now. We've been telling them we're never going to stop.

They can't say we didn't give them plenty of warning.

The first game in the group stages of the Champions League isn't met with such excitement in many places around Europe. But they made a mistake again, didn't they? They made sure that whatever group Liverpool entered would be the group of death by putting them in pot three.

The pot that Manchester City have moaned about being in for years. Crying their eyes out about how the whole thing is rigged and it's not fair.

CHAPTER TWO - THE WELCOME BREAK

They didn't realise we're not like them, though, did they? We love it. Send us your big boys. Send the biggest you've got. We've all been taught since we were kids that if you're getting picked on by a group of bullies just knock out the biggest one and the rest will take care of themselves. We're not frightened of you.

You and all your money, and your second (third?) best front three on the continent. They're no match for ours. No match for The Reds' ferocity. No match for our belief. No match for James Milner, Gini Wijnaldum and Jordan Henderson.

Jordan fucking Henderson.

If you watched that game and still think he's shite you need your head testing. I don't often use the line 'you don't know what you're talking about' in football conversations, because none of us really know what we're talking about.

But if you watched our captain smash into their show ponies time and again and come out with the ball, if you watched our leader regain possession for fun and ping one-touch passes off spinning balls like he was strolling around the local park with his kids, if you watched all of that and still think he's fucking shit then you don't know what you're talking about.

He was immense alongside his unfashionable teammates in the middle of the pitch. A midfield three that the oil barons wouldn't be interested in, but one which Jürgen Klopp has turned into a powerhouse of energy, shape and gegenpressing mastery.

I think my favourite thing in the world now is watching Milner get to the ball just a split second late so that he can smash it as hard as he can into his opponent. I can picture him practising it on the training pitch for hours. Sparring partners brought in one after the other while he boots the ball into their nether regions from a yard away through a disguised tackle.

The show-pony jibe aside, we shouldn't overlook the fact that Paris Saint-Germain are a quality football team. After dominating the early stages of the first half, those of us in the ground could slowly feel that creeping sensation that only happens when you're watching world-class players knocking the ball around for the opposition.

When they get anywhere near the edge of your box and you feel the muscles in your back tense just a little bit more. The relief flooding through your body every time they're dispossessed without even a shot materialising.

They're good, make no mistake. They're good, but Liverpool are absolutely fucking mustard.

For all of those fans of other clubs dreading accessing the internet whenever The Reds have won, there isn't much good news to report. It's now six wins out of six, including two tough-looking away games to Crystal Palace and Leicester, a win away at Spurs and a home victory against the champions of France.

And all of that still without the front three clicking into gear and with the biggest weakness being that they haven't been clinical enough. Liverpool could have scored 10 goals against Spurs and PSG combined without batting an eyelid.

The statistics look good, but they still don't have any stats to show how often The Reds could have scored if one of their attackers had chosen a better option than they did, or if Sadio Mane and Mo Salah could regain their finishing composure from the end of last season rather than the 'hit it as hard as you can' technique that the rest of us deploy.

As soon as that rectifies itself and they all get back in the groove they were in during the second half of last season, it's unlikely that Liverpool will get worse than they currently are.

What a position to be in. Six out of six with some obvious improvements that can be made by the coaching staff on the training pitch. A £40million centre midfielder not yet able to get any more than a couple of minutes in the first team. A back five that is still getting used to playing together, with two of the five being brand new to their positions in that setup under this manager, one of the five being a teenager and the other being the greatest left back the world has ever seen.

I'm sure Liverpool will lose a game again sooner or later. At this rate, I think it's likely to be some time in 2028 when Milner needs a rest after playing 587 consecutive games.

The bad news for everyone else is that the feeling running around this football club is as we all hoped and expected after last season's Champions League final defeat, when they all started to get worried.

When they saw us come away from that laughing, singing and telling stories about how much fun we'd had, they knew it was a bad sign. They realised that instead of imploding like Liverpool have so many times in the past, we were all settling in for the start of an exciting journey, not the end of a disappointing one.

And they were right. The Reds have started exactly where they left off, except this time there's a hunger to go one step further. A desire to put the finishing touches to all of the hard work that's gone before.

Whisper it quietly, but there are echoes of Manchester City at the start of last season, winning tight games with last-minute goals to keep momentum going. Building a fear factor that puts them ahead in games before they even kick off. Everyone glancing at the fixture lists to check when they have to face this red machine.

No one fancies taking The Reds on when they're in this mood. Meanwhile, we can't wait for the next game, hungry for another opponent to swallow up and spit out, churning through them one after the next, discarding their carcasses over our shoulders as we plough forward to whatever challenge lies ahead.

Send whoever you've got. Send your biggest and your best.

We're not frightened anymore.

But they should be. This is only going in one direction.

Liverpool v Southampton

Saturday September 22, 2018

ROB GUTMANN'S PREVIEW

THIS is the type of game I look forward to most.

Following a team involves so much tense anticipation and trepidation. Who really relishes the prospect of a derby or watching us go to Old Trafford? Yes, there's excitement at just how important a result could be secured, but equally there's nothing to be savoured about living on nerves for the best part of two hours.

These sort of games, though – the ones that pitch us against the, let's not be coy, shittier teams in the league – I look forward to as a real treat. Liverpool, bang in form, full of goals, matched up against a bottom-half side, at Anfield, 3pm on a Saturday. It doesn't get more retro than that.

My happiest memories are of the Saturday mornings before the Anfield afternoons against this kind of opposition. I've lived for most of my time for one thing, and one thing only – Liverpool wins. Nothing more, nothing less.

There are two modes of enjoying those wins – luxuriating in them once they've happened, and then there's the relishing of the prospect of them. I almost enjoy the latter more. It's as though you have a window into your own future. You say to yourself 'by 5pm on Saturday night I know I'm going to be truly content'. At peace with everyone and everything.

Of course, these prophecies so often prove false. Default post-1990 Liverpool have not been a team to be entirely trusted to blow inferior opposition away at Anfield. In this knowledge, I'm more excited about Southampton than I have been about a home game for a while.

We have nothing to fear and all to look forward to, because of a truth, namely, that Liverpool now, 2018 Liverpool, are a very, very good football team. We saw major indicators of this last season, but opening the current campaign with a salvo of six straight wins, confirms it.

My bravado notwithstanding, Southampton is actually a disproportionately important game for Liverpool. It is the filler fixture in a harsh batch of seven that commenced with Tottenham last weekend and ends with Manchester City. By then, we'll have also played Paris Saint-Germain, Chelsea twice and Napoli. All in this schedule, bar Southampton, are sides that can properly hurt us if we're not sharp about our business.

We must beat Southampton at home at the weekend simply because all of our title rivals will, at some juncture. Additionally, a win would take our opening sequence of league victories to six and provide us with something of a buffer when we play Chelsea, before the early 'decider' against Man City in October. A draw or defeat would represent an undoing of the fantastic work done at Wembley a week ago.

We'll be sending out a very hungry Liverpool team. We played like rabid dogs for much of the midweek win over those Parisian big shots. Klopp talks about needing to keep his team 'angry'. On Tuesday night, his Reds looked positively livid. And PSG paid the price.

In this first cluttered phase of the season, rotation has obviously become the order of the day for the Liverpool manager. In the week, he made two changes from the side that had seen off Spurs. It was satisfying to see that he could change two of his front four and not noticeably weaken the team in any way. For Southampton's visit to Anfield expect him to again make a couple of switches.

The smart money will be on Bobby Firmino returning as number nine, ahead of midweek goalscorer Daniel Sturridge. It may also be deemed time to rest one of Milner or Wijnaldum, who have both played a lot of football already this season.

Henderson most likely keeps his place, Naby Keita returns surely. There's an outside chance that summer signing Fabinho earns his first start, but Klopp will probably be more inclined to hold the likes of him and Sturridge back for the League Cup clash with Chelsea next Wednesday night.

Having comprehensively written off Southampton's chances I'll U-turn mildly in the interests of not entirely jinxing the outcome of the game, by caveating that 'there are no easy games at this level' and by stressing that we need to retain the fierceness and hunger we demonstrated in the Champions League.

The Saints won't exactly be bringing Neymar and Kylian Mbappe down ours, but their scalps in our current context are equally if not more important.

Liverpool 3 Southampton 0
BEN JOHNSON'S RATINGS

THERE'S Mark Hughes there, looking like yer nan got dressed in the wrong wardrobe again.

Alisson: 8

Nothing to do, nothing to do, nothing to do, bang, 92 minutes, smart save down to his right. I love a smart save. Suit and tie.

Trent: 8

Running out of things to say here, really. He is a brilliant, brilliant footballer. *L'Equipe* rated him the other night and them fuckers don't give points to anyone. Who the fuck am I to disagree?

Big Joel: 8

He's a mad fella him. He literally oscillates between really good and shite in the space of a minute. Like a big really good/shite metronome. Passed it to their lad on the edge of our box, Big Virg got him out the shit, the metronome banged across to the really good side and he won the ball, marched up the pitch, set Salah up and then nodded in the corner, just in the nick of time. That said, we were a bit mad first half, once we boxed our shape he was sound.

Looks like his body was made by playing Boy Girl. Remember Boy Girl? Someone drew his sink feet, folded the page over, and passed it on to someone else who drew a giant's legs, folded it over and passed it on to yer man, who drew a skinny fella's long body, and so on until we end up with his pea head.

Big Virg: 8

Sweet Jesus, Mary and Joseph, thank fuck for that. Bruised ribs. You can have mine lad, if you need them. Like Prince, I'll get shut of them bottom ones. Not worth a carrot. Give him some cotton wool clobber la, and let him sleep on a cloud.

Andy Robbo: 8

See Trent above. The two best full backs in the league.

Henderson: 8

Think I'll give everyone an eight today. Suck it up.

Gini: 8

In loads of space. Overrun a little first half but that was more to do with the shape than anything else.

Sheridan: 8

Can't half find space, can he? Loved the formation first half. Imagine being Nan Head, working all week to plan to close our front three down, when he goes there, you drop here, you block this space, you close there. And then Klopp plays a diamond with this mad little head case at its tip, like a 1920s explorer and your plans are in the bin.

Bit harsh to take him off, but then imagine being Nan Head, spending all half creating another plan to deal with the diamond, and Klopp legs Shaqiri and goes back to the three upfront. Go and lash some Oil of Olay on, lad.

Mo: 8

Scratching for a goal even though he keeps scoring. Was unlucky there today, could have scored six.

Sadio: 8

Horrible to play against. Hard as iron, fast as anything, tricky as fuck. Was great today without hitting top whack.

Firmino: 8

Played well in them little pockets drifting in from the left. Couple of lovely little one twos. Unlucky not to score. Can see with both his eyes. Would love him to have to wear them gigs for the rest of his days.

SUBS...

Milner: 8

Come on and was boss.

Naby: 8

Come on and was boss.

Joe Gomez: 8

Come on and was boss.

NEIL ATKINSON'S REVIEW

LAST season Liverpool came back from this international break and lost heavily away to rivals Manchester City.

In midweek, they drew a home European game they had dominated against Sevilla after Roberto Firmino missed a key penalty which drove his form into the doldrums. They then drew a home game against Burnley they would have been expected to win comfortably.

The comparison brings its own conclusions with this season. There is a greater sense of purpose about Liverpool but also a greater level of performance. The former adds to the latter, but Liverpool are just a better football team now.

It is worth remembering, though, that Liverpool then included Philippe Coutinho and Emre Can. The development of this side as both individuals and as a collective is testament to these players, their coaches and their manager.

This week this season, like that week last season, has had every type of test this Liverpool side will face this season. It has had all the flavours and Liverpool have stood up to them all and come away with three wins, each of which was impressive.

Today's was the most underwhelming of the games, but for the consummate professionals in the dressing room it may prove the most pleasing. Liverpool didn't rest on their laurels, didn't reflect on victory and lose themselves, Narcissus in the water. Liverpool, instead, dived in and had a lovely swim.

It was perhaps too easy at times. Liverpool could have knuckled further down. But they had eased themselves through the water and constantly had the other side in view. They won the game in a quick 45 minutes, making the second half redundant as a contest.

In every sense, Xherdan Shaqiri made a mundane win fascinating. Pre match: How would he fit in? During the game: Can Liverpool get him on it more? Second Half: Why was he taken off? Shaqiri is another of Jürgen Klopp's footballers with a redemption arc. Daniel Sturridge was our romantic hero against Paris Saint-Germain. Today was Shaqiri's turn to emphasise his seriousness of purpose during his third turn at a big club.

He did that. He was the first 45's compelling performer with no stats to his name. The record should show a brace. Instead they show diddly squat, but he was a pleasure to watch.

And then he wasn't there.

We will discover why. The question will be asked, and it will be answered, and it will be reasonable. The manager felt that he wanted a change and the easiest way to change was to revert.

He had spent much of the first half shouting at Mohamed Salah, demanding something – perhaps something around how he arcs his runs or something around where he positions himself when Liverpool were in their back third. There was something.

Salah was, for this observer, fine. He had a good 90 minutes, scoring one, nearly scoring another and having a goal disallowed. He wasn't a joy to watch, but this analysis overlooks the fact he very often wasn't last season. Last season he wasn't in games as much as his colleagues but he was scoring in them. His penalty box instincts were crystal clear today.

Given Klopp's response first half though, the thought occurs that it may well be a side where there is more pleasure and more joy to play wide. Your life may well not be an easy one being Jürgen's number nine. He demands the world.

Joel Matip returned too and marked it with a goal. It was a lovely header, the sort which should be acclaimed but also be more regularly seen. Liverpool have delivery. They have height. They have quality. That Matip has probably been our highest-scoring centre back during his tenure is cause for annoyance.

On the whole pitch, he was at times rusty but at others he offered a reminder of his ability. It was lovely to see him burst forward and be part of Liverpool's attack, but fab to see him be unflustered on the whole. He is too good for this opposition and that is exactly what you want from your fourth centre back. Not since Sami Hyypia in 2008-09 have Liverpool been able to boast of similar.

Virgil van Dijk's substitution will be a concern. Gini Wijnaldum's ovation as much for efforts in times past as today. Jordan Henderson shouted at all his teammates almost as much as his manager. Southampton looked a better side than they have in recent memory, but ran into Liverpool; different class to last season, top of the league and deservedly so.

Liverpool improved from September 17 to be one of the best in Europe. They are now one of the best in Europe. The more you improve the tougher the next improvement will become, but Liverpool are not finished. It has been a fabulous week for the club, a brilliant start to September adding to a marvellous August.

This is what it is to be on the march.

Six down, 32 to go.

These Reds. These days.

Shaqiri's Substitution A Sign Of Klopp's Growing Pragmatism

Monday September 24, 2018

GARETH ROBERTS

SUM up Jürgen Klopp's approach to football and the likelihood is you will quickly start to lean on the well-worn phrases that litter any attempt to characterise his work.

Whether it's 'heavy metal football', 'Gegenpressing' or the idea that a team under this manager will ruthlessly undress the opposition through lightning quick counter attacks to win its battles, there is an accepted impression of his approach in the general football psyche.

Klopp himself has added much meat to the bones on this score, saying only this year: 'Entertainment is the most important part of football. There are too many serious problems in the world to make football boring too.

'I want to see happiness with my players, passion in their eyes and a desire to fight. I want to see them bursting, to surprise me, to look what's on their right, to try and make a pass to their left, that sort of thing.'

And yet, while Liverpool sit pretty at the top of the Premier League with a perfect record of six wins from six games, and now two points clear after Chelsea's failure to beat West Ham, there are hints at an increasing lean on pragmatism as hopes and dreams of a successful season continue to grow.

Saturday's win over Southampton was a prime example.

For the fans in the stands, caught in the moment of a Saturday 3pm packed with positivity after a perfect start to the season, Xherdan Shaqiri had tore it up on his first start for the club.

A key contribution to the first goal, an eye-popping freekick that cannoned off the bar and led to the third, and in general a willingness to get on the ball, to join in and to make things happen, led many underneath The Kop to toast his opening contributions as a first-team starter in red.

It was with some surprise then that the man that had beamed his broad smile all over L4 didn't re-emerge after the break. Surely a player that had been so key to two of the goals had done enough to stay on, especially given how long he had waited for his chance from the get go?

Not for Klopp. A half-time substitution for tactical reasons was always going to upset the pros, and so it proved – the move much under the microscope as the weekend analysis poured in post match.

The argument coming from the *Match of the Day* pundits on Saturday was the message it sends out to the man in the 23 shirt; that a player would feel slighted being treated that way by his manager; that it was seen as being 'hooked' and that you had done something wrong to deserve it.

Klopp, though, is in a position to do things differently now. There doesn't need to be a sell. He doesn't have to be a salesman through his football. He just has to win. And he is. Every player wants to be a part of that.

In the second half, generally speaking, hardly a thing happened at Anfield on Saturday. Southampton – who had their moments first half – finally mustered a shot in the 91st minute, Charlie Austin's shot easily saved by Alisson Becker.

Liverpool dominated the ball, and while it wasn't Gung Ho, all energy, or high octane, it was effective in closing out the game.

Further, while many saw the introduction of James Milner for the box of tricks bagged from Stoke as a negative switch, there is evidence for the contrary.

It's Milner who has Liverpool's two efforts of note in the second half. And it's Milner who ends the game second only to Andy Robertson as the match's top contributor in terms of passes in the attacking third (21 to Robertson's 25).

Klopp explained that it was new ground for him. That never before had he pulled a player who had contributed so clearly in the first half. He also made it clear that he explained his reasons to the player and that he was happy with them.

Ultimately, Liverpool comfortably saw out the game, clocked up another three points, and now sit top of the league – an improvement of seven points on this stage of the season last year.

And for Shaqiri, how will he feel after the supposed ignominy of a half-time substitution?

Perhaps, just maybe, he will be even more determined to deliver on what the manager wants from him. If, as some have speculated, he reneged on some of the defensive work expected of him, perhaps he works harder next time out to put that right.

It was clear Shaqiri didn't lack in any confidence on Saturday. He was all flicks, tricks, demanding of ball, an oozing of a man desperate to impress. The freekick was a genuine open-mouth moment.

This isn't a player who will sink into his shell Stewart Downing-style, and already he has shown he is comfortable in the company he is in. As his previous clubs include Bayern Munich and Inter Milan, this should really come as no surprise.

Perhaps, though, he is a player who needs reminding it is team over individual at Liverpool (now more than ever before under Klopp), the many over the few. And again – perhaps – this move from Klopp helps with all that.

Liverpool – as we are constantly reminded by some sections of those in the football media – are in the middle of a 'nightmare run'. The squad is now being utilised, minutes are being managed, and Shaqiri will soon get another chance, possibly on Wednesday when Chelsea come to town in the League Cup.

If selected, he has no choice but to try to impress again, to continue to be high energy, positive and looking to impress. And if he isn't, as he has already experienced, the manager isn't afraid to make what are perceived as being traditionally tough decisions.

Shouldn't a manager be playing expensive summer acquisitions in midfield? Why is he hooking players at half time?

Who writes the rules when you're top of the league?

Liverpool this season have look well drilled, well organised and with added steel. It comes from the top.

The manager means business, and so do The Reds. And that can only be a positive thing as the fixtures continue to flow thick and fast.

Chelsea 1 Liverpool 1
Saturday September 29, 2018
BEN JOHNSON'S RATINGS

LAD. I know, lad.

The wrigglies are back.

Alisson: 7

Made three great saves there dressed as a massive big pink fella. What a kit. Might be at fault for theirs, maybe? I don't know. Can do what he wants in that kit in fairness, can't he?

Trent: 7

Few sloppy balls in. But, The Reds, let's be honest, were the better side, and Trent is on ours, isn't he?

Virgil: 7

Better than any of their lads, didn't do much wrong there, deserved to be in the winning team, settled for a glorious draw.

Joe Gomez: 8

Thought he was exceptional, you know. Our best defender.

Andy Robbo: 7

Was he sound? I think he was sound. Hard one to judge really 'cause The Reds were great, then shite for a bit, and then probably deserved to win.

Henderson: 6

Thought he struggled today, you know. His use of the ball was poor, his positional sense wasn't great.

Gini: 8

Best midfielder on the pitch. Linked up the right of the side really well, got us playing, deserved to be on the winning side.

Milner: 7

Like the whole of The Reds, played well and didn't really get his rewards.

Mo Salah: 8

Our most dangerous player. Don't care if he wasn't firing on all fronts, we were worse when he went off. I wouldn't worry about him, you know. He's going to be sound.

Sadio: 7

Simultaneous threat coupled with being not at his best. I don't really even know anymore, to be honest. The front three were great and shite in the same breath.

Imagine when they are great.

Firmino: 9

Was sound. Forgot about him there, didn't I?

SUBS...

Dan Sturridge: 10

Come on and just twatted one right in the top bin there, didn't he? The wrigglies are back. Wrigglies forever. What a fella.

NEIL ATKINSON'S REVIEW

'DON'T shoot,' says Ben Johno.

The ball goes to Daniel Sturridge.

'Don't you fucking shoot either,' I say.

The 'r' of either leaves my mouth as the ball hits the back of the net and even in Head of Steam in town everything is pandemonium. All I can say is 'Oh my God.'

Oh my God.

What a goal that is. What a goal. It is hard to imagine anything quite like it. Right now it is my favourite Liverpool goal ever. Come next May it could well be one of our most important.

The beats. The story:

2012. He turns up. He's a football genius.

2013-14. He's so important to us, it is just that Luis Suarez is Luis Suarez-ing.

2014-15. He gets injured and is never the same again.

It never quite takes flight for him since the Europa League final when he scores one of the great lost Liverpool goals.

He goes to West Brom last January. He is done as a Liverpool player. Everyone knows it.

He comes back in July.

He does the summer. He does the pre-season. He looks his manager in the eye. His manager looks him in the eye. And they know.

He scores first day.

He scores first Champions League game.

He scores midweek.

And then he does that. He does that. He knows, and he knows, and he knows, and he does that then. He makes it 1-1 from a million miles. He strikes that not as a shot in the dark, but because he knows he is capable of it.

It is one of the great Liverpool goals. It is Sturridge and, as discussed before, we shouldn't have favourites. The 11 should be our favourite. But he is my favourite, my very finest, the man I go to the ends of the earth for.

The most marvellous, broken man who reminds us of our own humanity, our kindness and brilliance. When he does that he is the biggest star in the whole wide world. He is Beyonce in Lemonade. I would always get in formation.

The whole wide world is a thing. What a game of football that was. Tonight there is every chance we watched two of the best six sides on the continent. More things. More beats. More sheer adrenaline.

There is this thing where we know one of the reasons we watch the best footballers on the planet is the television money. And the coverage is phenomenal. Look me in the eye and tell me that BT and Sky aren't adding to our knowledge and understanding of the game in both tactical and human terms and I will call you a liar.

We are brilliant at The Anfield Wrap, we're the best. But they still find ways to take your breath away, these people. They find ways to make you think and reason and feel, that stun me and I am *good* at this, I assure you.

But. But, but, but. But part of me wanted our run last season on terrestrial television. I wanted the country at large to watch this Liverpool team, the country at large to appreciate their brilliance. I wanted the neutral to become the opposite, to become a

Liverpool supporter. I wanted the neutral to appreciate the speed Liverpool play at, to appreciate what this game is.

Tonight. Tonight was the greatest imaginable advertisement for the game as it is now imaginable. Tonight's first half was one of the quickest I have ever seen, but at no point did the technical ability drop. These were the two best in the world knocking lumps out of each other in a manner which prompted and brought about brilliance.

The moment at the final whistle when Jürgen Klopp smiles at Maurizio Sarri is because he knows what that just was. What a thing, what a game. The country should get to see that not just as highlights but to understand it was all highlights, all potential highlights. Every snapshot we were 10 seconds away from a would be highlight.

David Luiz was brilliant. It was his game, all speed, all activity, all ragged edge. He pinged it and won it. He strode forward with the ball and niggled away without it. He lived just there, just in the place where marvellous, maverick footballers live. It couldn't be too fast for Luiz. You make it faster and he stands up.

Gini Wijnaldum, one backpass aside, is not dissimilar. He wants the big game and the stage. He wants the challenge and the speed. He wasn't backwards about coming forwards.

These teams reinvent what we want from holding midfielders every week and remind us how limited our perception is of the game's evolution. Every now and again we see that leap forward that managers see, have planned for. They work out what the next dimension looks like with their players and then they enact it. I mean, wow. We trail in their wake.

Joe Gomez and Virgil van Dijk showed the needs and wants of centre backs for this Liverpool side. They showed the pace and presence. They were impressive throughout.

I hope I sound overwhelmed. I hope I sound so hopelessly in love with this game of ours. I hope I sound like I think footballers are the very best of us. I hope you hear me here, not some neutral voice, not some dispassionate thing.

All this is is passion and all there is is love. All there is is what is brilliant about the round thing on the green thing and aiming for the rectangular thing. All there is is 22 men who tend to be between 20 and 30, and everything else is fluff and nonsense. All there is is our game played so quickly and brilliantly.

But there is also a league table which Liverpool are jointly at the top of. There is the idea that not losing next week means Liverpool finish their first eight level on points, at worst, with last season's marvellous champions. That is what Sturridge's finish means – it means Liverpool have the opportunity of succeeding in phase one of this season's mission.

In the end, Liverpool salvage a draw that has the value of a win. In the end we are spent, exhausted, impressed by their heroes, delighted by ours.

In the end, all was Sturridge. Our most remarkable human from all the best of us. All was Sturridge. All was resplendent. All was our broken magnificent wonder. Hot sauce in his bag.

Deus nobis haec otia fecit.
He did.

The Worrying Trend For Jordan Henderson
Thursday October 4, 2018
JOHN GIBBONS

LAST night wasn't good, was it?

Why couldn't anyone in a red shirt pass to anyone else in a red shirt? I know Napoli's pitch looked like it had been dug up, but still. We should have managed at least one shot on target. It's really hard to score without them.

It rounds off a rather disappointing week or so for Liverpool. Out of the Carabao Cup, beaten in the Champions League and losing their 100 per cent record in the Premier League – albeit in a game where we rescued a decent point.

Even in a frustrating run, some players have come out with credit. Daniel Sturridge has scored twice, Alisson Becker has proved he can make big saves at big times and Joe Gomez continues to grow every game.

For others, form is starting to become a concern. It has been a particularly worrying eight days if you are Jordan Henderson.

That's not to say Henderson is to blame specifically for any of the last three results. Blaming any one player in a team game is daft, unless it is a goalkeeper throwing the ball in the goal. (Hiya Loris, mate. Glad you are enjoying Turkey.) But the facts aren't great at all.

Not including stoppage time, Henderson has spent 179 minutes on the pitch in the last three games. In that time, Liverpool have scored zero goals and conceded four. In the same games Henderson has spent 91 minutes on the bench, and Liverpool have scored two goals and conceded zero.

Again, saying Liverpool's fortunes or otherwise are down to one player is daft. In two of those games Henderson isn't in the first 11 and Liverpool start dreadfully. He also can't do anything about Sturridge hitting the bar with one shot and scoring with another.

However, if you're the captain of a football team, the above should worry you. As a leader he should be a positive influence on the team, yet the opposite seems to be true. Given the fact that he also doesn't start Liverpool's biggest win of the Premier League so far (4-0 against West Ham) or their most eye catching (2-1 at Spurs), you would worry a pattern was emerging.

Is it Jordan himself or the balance of the midfield with him in it? Naby Keita hasn't set the world alight yet, but he does offer something different, and crucially James Milner and Gini Wjinaldum seem much more sure of themselves and their roles in that three.

With Henderson in for Keita, regardless of their respective abilities, it all looks a bit samey and a little bit too safe. Wjinaldum and Henderson managed just 12 forward passes between them last night. No wonder the front three looked frustrated. They haven't been in great form either, but you could imagine they would really benefit from someone passing the ball forward.

Crucially, the manager's faith in Henderson seems to be wavering a bit too. While Gini and Milner have been largely ever present, it is Henderson who has been in and out. He had a much busier summer so that might be a factor, but at crucial times this season, like 1-0 down at Chelsea, there have been on-pitch lieutenants Jürgen Klopp seems to trust more.

I'm not writing Henderson off by any means. He's got shares in The Anfield Wrap after all. But with Keita potentially unavailable and Fabinho seemingly way off the pace, we could really do with Henderson imposing himself on games sooner rather than later. In fact, definitely sooner, Jordan, to be honest.

Manchester City on Sunday. They've got about seven lads who play number 10, and we are really going to need him at his best.

Liverpool v Manchester City

Sunday October 7, 2018

ROB GUTMANN'S PREVIEW

I DON'T take defeat well. I don't take not winning well.

Three games of only this makes me blue. Like a Blue.

They're calling Liverpool v Manchester City a 'title decider in October'. Actually, I might be the first to have dubbed it this, but what the heck.

The Liverpool results of the past week and a half have only served to ratchet up my personal football-related anxiety levels to, as yet, unforeseen heights. I'm not in a good place right now. This season has hardly begun and I'm already a man mess.

Ilkay Gundogan is out of this game with an injury. Kevin De Bruyne definitely won't be making the cut either. These are both good things. These are helping restore some equilibrium to my fragile mentality.

I'll be sweating on Naby Keita's fitness a while longer it seems, and although he was by no means a guaranteed starter, even if in perfect health, he has a quality that you feel we'd like to be able to call on at some stage over the course of Sunday afternoon.

Just right now, I'm more in love with Liverpool's potential substitutes bench than the lads in the first 11. At Chelsea, a week ago, Naby, Daniel Sturridge and Xherdan Shaqiri leapt from the sidelines into the fray and saved us from what would've represented a very damaging defeat. Those boys fired from the off, where the main men had floundered.

We've seen quality already this campaign from Mo Salah, Sadio Mane, and Bobby Firmino. But only glimpses of it, and usually on a man-to-man basis, not harnessed, not in tandem, in the way we were so used to seeing last season.

Liverpool's front three are fantastic, supremely gifted individuals, yet remarkably, they still managed – in 2017-18 – to be greater than the sum of their substantial parts. A summer apart has not suited them though. They were all at the World Cup, but in different camps. It was only for a few weeks but it seems to have served to break that magical spell between them.

The offset has been the emergence of a Liverpool defensive unit to be reckoned with. Sure, the new supreme back five are due a combined bad day at the office, but it is upon their rock-like solidity that Liverpool have built such a strong start to the 2018-19 season. Few would have predicted that back in early August.

The bonus has been Joe Gomez. We knew Virgil van Dijk was becoming our man main in every sense, that our young full backs were on a stellar trajectory, and that we'd signed the world's best goalie, but we didn't see Gomez adapting to the all new requirements of becoming a centre back with such consummate ease.

Joe is a very mentally strong young player. He was an incredible prospect at 18, then dealt with a career-threatening injury that saw him through to 19, before fighting back from being all but written off as an under-23 league player, to establishing himself at right back.

Further injury saw him lose his place to Trent Arnold, and consequently few saw anything but a bit-part role lying ahead for the player this season.

But here we are. Here he is. The mighty Joe Gomez.

He's got a long way to go, but he already looks like he's built for the distance. Man City remain the country's best team until we, or others, prove otherwise. They will represent a massive test of the resolve of Gomez and our all-new, often near impregnable line of defence.

In beating City three times last season we did well at keeping them away from our goal. That was because we were able to overwhelm them with our energy and hunger. Flailing in our storm, they were there for the taking by our front three. Those lovely boys who stop Pep Guardiola from sleeping as soundly as he should.

We've managed ourselves through games well this season, more often than not, but without the intensity in performances that became a hallmark last season. I'm hoping that the collective muscle memory of those three wins over City serve to remind us just who we are. The identity we looked to have lost in periods this term can be rediscovered in the face of the challenge presented by City.

City will want revenge. 'Revenge' gets talked about around football, but within the game itself you suspect it's not a factor. Revenge is an intangible. Sport is not about intangibles. It's about results. Apart from when it isn't, and this is very much one of those moments.

The desire for revenge can work two ways. It can fire, it can motivate, it can fuel, but equally it is imbued with fear. In their lust for revenge over Liverpool also rests City's fear of Liverpool. Those light blue lads are scared shitless of what we can do to them. They know that we are singularly the only side they have faced who have looked equipped to rip them apart, to order. They also know that knowing this has not served them well in the recent past.

Liverpool raced into a 4-1 Anfield lead over them in January. Guardiola was therefore ready for Liverpool when the sides were paired in the Champions league in April. Liverpool win again. 3-0. They saw it coming, but only in the sense that rabbits in headlights do.

My hope is that the importance of this fixture, and the adrenaline it will stimulate, will serve to truly galvanise what remains a potentially awesome Liverpool team. None of Salah, Mane or Firmino are content with their seasons to date. All are looking to properly kick start.

Liverpool have won six out of seven league games, the club's best opening sequence since when, but the abiding feeling is that we need to get into gear and soon.

As golden opportunities come, they don't come more glittering than this.

Liverpool 0 Manchester City 0
NEIL ATKINSON'S REVIEW

NINETY minutes of sheer hell, John Barnes said years ago.

The words echoed through today. Liverpool 0 Manchester City 0. Unbelievable we pay good money to be made to feel like that.

If it wasn't hell it was purgatory. The prospect of losing loomed large, the stick bigger and more powerful than the carrot for both sides, and that dominated the whole contest. For Manchester City's 100-point heroes, it was a trial to get through.

Could they see off Liverpool? Could they see off the cauldron, the eye of the storm? This was to be an examination and they can feel like they passed. Aymeric Laporte was particularly excellent but their wonderful, clever manager can look his players in the eye tonight and feel like he has helped them and they have shown him something new.

They turned up like Brighton or like Leicester away, taking significant risks to stop Liverpool's passing shapes from working. The football from neither side was cowardly, indeed to play as both did takes an awful lot of bravery and even more trust.

Out of possession, you have to take up odd positions and hope your teammates have done the same. In possession, you have to play an awful lot of passes along a tightrope just to get out.

The first half was just that. Two sides trying to get out, having to work hard as anything just to get to halfway and have a breather. Everything you can normally rely upon gone, because Bernardo Silva stands just there, and Gini Wijnaldum just there, and now you can't see anyone. Let no one say these aren't serious football teams. There were no jokes on show, no flourishes. There were brains, bravery and brawn.

It was astonishing to see them time waste, dawdle over every restart and take time out of the game. They stole yards from throw ins during what would normally be a comic three minutes during the first half, but throw ins like everything else became too serious to laugh about. They mattered and they took up time and time was on everybody's mind, going by so slowly.

It was unbelievable when it was 58 minutes on the clock. More than enough football had been played but there was to be over 30 minutes more. Football does things to time and scientists should look into it. Repeatedly Ederson Moraes was Ben Foster, no goal kick could handle enough contemplation, the ball spotted and re-spotted.

The City players loved a row, nothing takes time out of the game like a good row, whereas Liverpool captain Jordan Henderson kept up an ongoing conversation with the official.

He could have given us more, but he was right to give the penalty, one of the few breaks in the attrition, though wrong not to give us a freekick on halfway in the build up. It was a game of marginal decisions, marginal positioning, marginal passing. That he perhaps struggled shows that neither side rose above him. He was not to become irrelevant.

The second half saw Liverpool shade it in general play, but City were constantly dangerous on the break. It's not meant to be that way but that was the way it was, and everybody took their medicine. Liverpool got around City's box a lot, but City got in Liverpool's more often than their opponents.

Kyle Walker sat in a similar position to his for England, Andy Robertson broke out in fits and starts, Joe Gomez was ignored first half but integral second, Benjamin Mendy was more desire than quality.

Sergio Aguero's main contribution was to block lanes and get himself booked, Gabriel Jesus gave The Big Dog the chance to remind everybody it can still be his yard. All of Liverpool's front three toiled but none could both escape attention and make themselves available. Instead they scrapped in areas.

Words will be written about them but this was another game where Liverpool missed Alex Oxlade-Chamberlain and would have liked to have seen more from Naby Keita.

He's a new signing, the fixtures have been a nightmare and it will take time, but when lanes are blocked everywhere it helps having someone run beyond them, someone creating new realities. Keita never quite did that and we could do with him finding his mojo soon. Huddersfield Town, Red Star Belgrade and Cardiff City should be easier.

Gini Wijnaldum excelled again. It was his sort of game – a challenge just to keep it. He was in his element. Riyad Mahrez spurned the chance to win it. Liverpool and Manchester City instead settled to have 20 points from eight games. That extrapolates to a 95-point season. Ninety-five points.

The thing is this: these are really, really good football teams. Our starting point and our end point should be the same. Amazing that these young men made it this hard for one another and that tells the story. The stick was greater than the carrot. The examination was everything. Everyone passed.

Eight hurdles passed for both these sides, 30 more to go. Few will feel like that.

Has Naby Keita's Form Affected Liverpool's Attack?

Tuesday October 9, 2018

DAVID SEGAR

IT was a big weekend on Merseyside.

The Giants from the French arts company Royal de Luxe were drawing the crowds in the city centre of Liverpool, while two giants of the Premier League were ready to clash at Anfield.

The hostile welcome Manchester City were expecting as their Super Grassbus 3000 made its way to the ground was almost as badly misjudged as Virgil van Dijk's late challenge on Leroy Sane that gifted the visitors a penalty, but in both cases, it came to absolutely nothing.

Both sides cancelled one another out in what was a much higher quality game than the average observer seemed to give it credit for.

No win in four isn't an ideal end to what has been an incredibly tough run of fixtures for Liverpool, but nor is it all that bad, particularly when you consider this… Chelsea have 20 points and their best players are on fire, especially Eden Hazard. City have 20 points and they very much look like they've picked up where they left off from last season.

Liverpool have 20 points, and all anyone can talk about is how meek they look up top.

There would be justified concern if The Reds had been electric but were only level on points with City at a time when Sergio Aguero, Raheem Sterling and Hazard were having a bad patch.

Liverpool have clear gears to go up, while Chelsea look like they're at full throttle, and though City have Kevin De Bruyne coming back, they didn't seem to miss him much when he was gone thanks to the performances of their spare Silva.

It is fair to say though that Jürgen Klopp needs his front three firing again before long, in particular Mo Salah, but there's one other area that has been identified by some as a hole in the Liverpool team at the moment.

The Reds' midfield has largely performed well this season, at least in terms of individual showings. James Milner is deservedly earning all sorts of plaudits, Gini Wijnaldum has thrived in a deeper role than usual and Jordan Henderson has mainly been impressive (or terrible, depending on which part of Twitter you happen to be).

As a unit though, they don't offer quite as much thrust going forward as they did when Phil Coutinho or Alex Oxlade-Chamberlain were around. The front three of Sadio Mane, Mo Salah and Roberto Firmino have all been short of form lately, but the supply line to them also doesn't feel as potent as it was last season.

With Coutinho gone and Oxlade-Chamberlain out for the majority of the campaign, Klopp needed another to step up into the role of midfield creator this season. A lot of people, myself included, assumed that 'another' would be new boy Naby Keita. However, the £52m signing from RB Leipzig is yet to live up to the hype that followed him from Germany.

It seemed to be a good sign that Klopp, a manager famed for allowing his signings – no matter how expensive – time to settle, decided to throw Keita in straight away by starting him in the first game of the season against West Ham.

The diminutive firecracker was impressive, and gave a glimpse of what fans could expect. The following week he produced THAT turn against Crystal Palace and in an instant, Reds seemed to fall in love once again.

Shortly after that turn, Keita was in a similar area of the field and gave a loose pass to van Dijk that nearly handed Palace a run on goal. Ever since then his confidence and form seems to have dipped.

Klopp has understandably rotated him more than others, but it's difficult to tell whether it is down to allowing his new signing a gradual introduction, or if it's because he's noticed how much the 23-year-old has struggled (or both).

Having taken to the French second division as a teenager at FC Istres seamlessly, and then the Austrian Bundesliga with Red Bull Salzburg, and the German Bundesliga with RB Leipzig without any struggle whatsoever, it appears that for the first time in his career, Keita has found a league that might just take a bit longer to master.

Some concerns have started to creep into the fan base (let's face it, it doesn't usually take long) that Keita perhaps isn't quite as good as advertised when he arrived, which would be a concern given the needs that Liverpool have if they are to maintain the pace in the Premier League and progress in the Champions League.

His sub appearance at Chelsea gave hope as his energy late in the game at Stamford Bridge did have a positive influence, and as a result, he was given a start in Naples a few days later, only to spend 15 minutes giving the ball away time and again before ultimately going down with a back injury and having to come off.

It could be that the injury was the reason for his iffy touches, and he was far from the only one who had a bad night in the 1-0 defeat, but it was an alarming – albeit short – cameo.

Then on Sunday, in the biggest game of the season, he was on the other side of it, having to replace a teammate unexpectedly in the first half, and he struggled to get up to the pace of the game.

It wasn't a bad performance per se, he showed some nice touches and produced some good dribbles. He also misplaced some simple balls though and didn't show the usual energy not only expected of a Liverpool player, but also of him after the levels he showed in Germany.

And that's the thing. The Keita we have seen since the Palace game has been practically unrecognisable from the Keita who dominated the Bundesliga. All the plaudits he received in Germany were fully deserved.

He was a phenomenon in his first season at Leipzig, comfortably the best player in the league outside of Bayern Munich's squad, which is why Liverpool made the deal for him a year in advance, and why Barcelona tried to usurp them at the last minute.

It's also why Leipzig sporting director Ralf Rangnick insisted time and again after the deal was done that he was worth more, and that if it wasn't for his release clause, they would have rejected any and every offer for him.

You could tell from the effusive words used by Klopp when the signing was confirmed that this was a signing that the manager was particularly excited by. It was almost like interviewing a 10-year-old at Christmas to see what he thought of his new puppy, games console and remote-controlled Ferrari.

'Naby was two years ago, together with maybe Thiago Alcantara of Bayern, for sure the best player in the Bundesliga by far,' Klopp told the *Liverpool Echo* in pre season.

'It was unbelievable how he played and then we wanted to get him in, but Leipzig didn't think that was the best idea in the world so they kept him.

'And then last season he was still good. Not as good as the year before but still good. He is young, he is full of football skills, very stable, very good in small spaces, endurance wise fantastic, quick, good finishes, good runs in the box.'

The thing that struck me most about watching Keita in the Bundesliga was his decision making. Whether it was something simple or something intricate, he almost always did the right thing for any situation.

That is something that he has struggled to replicate so far in England, probably due to the increased speed of the Premier League, and is therefore likely to be something he improves on, even if it's gradually.

His teammates have seen Keita's talents up close as well, with Daniel Sturridge telling the club's website, when asked about his new teammate in July, 'I love that guy. I'm surprised how good he is actually, if I'm honest. I knew he was good but I don't watch German football too often.

'I haven't seen a midfielder like him for a while, he is something different. It's crazy. The things he can do with the ball, he can defend, he can pass, he can dribble, he is fast, he is strong. He has got everything. I'm excited to see what he does.'

Those who have seen enough of Keita know just how good he is once he gets going, and trying to build up form in a new team, a new system and a new league is hard enough, but more so when you're playing the likes of Chelsea, PSG and Manchester City every few days.

However, after this international break, Liverpool have a run of games that could be an ideal opportunity to give Keita plenty of starts and allow him to get up and running. The sort of teams The Reds are set to come up against will be more like West Ham in the first game of the season when he had more time on the ball, less pressure on him and could put things together to build up his confidence.

With Milner out for a few weeks, now is the time for him to step up and show everyone exactly what he's about.

Once Keita is up to full speed his link ups with Salah, Firmino and his mate Mane, it has the potential to be game changing, and exactly what has been missing from the team so far this campaign. Just ask Leipzig stars Emil Forsberg and Timo Werner what playing with him was like when he was in form.

In 2015, I wrote an article for this very website about how exciting it was to be signing Bundesliga hipsters' favourite Roberto Firmino from Hoffenheim. A few months later I had to write another article reassuring everyone that he wasn't anywhere near as bad as he appeared to be from his first few games, and that with a bit of patience, he'd come good.

Admittedly, Bobby had to go through the end of the Brendan Rodgers era which couldn't have been easy, but he came through it to become a key part of Klopp's team, and just yesterday made it to the 30-man shortlist for the *Ballon d'Or* award.

Consider this my article on Naby's behalf. He'll be fine and will come good. As with Bobby, he's too talented and determined not to.

Like the giants, once Keita rises from his slumber and starts marching through midfields, kids and grownups alike will look on in awe. Great swathes of onlookers will gather to gaze on his cultured magnificence.

And they'll probably stop the bloody trains again.

CHAPTER THREE – THE GRIT AND GRIND

Huddersfield Town v Liverpool
Saturday October 20, 2018

WOULD you like a trade secret?

Of course you would. Who wouldn't?

Well, keep it to yourself, but every year in October and November the numbers drop. Numbers of people reading articles, engaging with our social media, listening or watching our free shows, subscribing to our premium content, every October and November the numbers drop.

We're assured we aren't alone in this. Assured that the same happens industry wide and there are suggestions it is more pronounced in World Cup years. It begs the question, why? Why does this happen?

We're talking about football diehards here, not just the casual fan who loves a bit of *Match Of The Day*. People who are prepared to pay cold, hard-earned cash for much of the year to see their teams and others find it suddenly a tiny bit harder to immerse themselves. It's worldwide as well.

It's there around tickets, too; not just home but away tickets too. Away game tickets are harder to come by in August and September than in mid-November. The psychology of it is everything feels harder, everything is more of an effort.

Even when Liverpool are winning a load of games, which they were last October and November, this is true. Suddenly, football has mounted up. Suddenly, there is too much of it and there are other things to do.

What's also true is there is a mystery of what the impact of winning those games actually is. Had Liverpool been nine points clear after winning against Huddersfield Town in a grubby little 0-1 after an international break then the response could have been different. Liverpool are on the march to the promised land.

Instead Liverpool were just matching Manchester City stride for stride and people don't want to get their hopes up – the bubble will burst at some point. At some stage City just pull away. This was the psyche.

October and November is when we all begin, up and down the country, whether you support Liverpool or Hartlepool, as autumn turns to winter we work out what our seasons actually are, what our seasons will mean. We don't know mid October, we hope to know first weekend of advent.

Therefore, Liverpool win a game they should win playing badly (this is probably Huddersfield's best performance of the season, by the way) and riding their luck and the supporter body as a whole is left none the wiser. What actually is this season? What are we buying into? What can we expect from Liverpool?

CHAPTER THREE – THE GRIT AND GRIND

The truth of the matter is this: the point of Huddersfield Town away is that you eventually get Mo Salah from 30 yards against Chelsea at home.

You can't have one without the other. And however uninspiring and however flat it may feel at the time, however mucky the experience and however it leaves your Saturday night feeling, you need this to get that.

Every journey starts with a single step. Every journey continues with a bumbling step in the middle of nowhere when you are a bit lost.

Huddersfield Town away, ladies and gentlemen.

Neil Atkinson

Huddersfield Town 0 Liverpool 1

BEN JOHNSON'S RATINGS

FAITH is a funny thing, isn't it?

The Reds are the best Reds I have seen in probably my whole adult life and here I am as the team news drops, with my undies in my throat, wishing I was one of them grey fellas who liked nothing.

I mean, the team has the look of one that could get legged all over the gaff. Adam Lallana playing his first game since last year, Dan Sturridge starting his first game since Luis Suarez was banging them in or something, Divock Origi, fresh from getting flashed to all and sundry for a couple of bob, is on the bench.

But it's fine, isn't it? I mean Huddersfield are shite, aren't they? But then The Reds, The Reds get beat against the bottom three away from home, don't we? That's one of our things, isn't it? Weirdly?

That said, I've just come across these words in one of my notes. It was my motivational speech to a nervous karaoker. It's probably going to end up on mugs and headstones all over the world: 'Believe in yourself and fucking give it bifters.'

Can someone make some T-shirts with that on it please, and sell them for me?

Alisson: 8

That kit really is wondrous. Glorious. Like a massive big wondrous vagina, with arms, that saves everything it should, and loves a touch on the ball. Venus fly trap. Fucking big pink magnet.

Joe Gomez: 8

Mad the way he has completed centre half so is just titting about at right back for a laugh. The ball to Shaqiri for the goal is the pass of the match, mind you. And there we were thinking we should have played the more attacking Trent.

Virgil: 8

That image of him with the armband, mate. Adam Melia had a vision before The Reds bought him that whoever ended up buying him would end up with him as captain lifting the league trophy. When it looked like it was Man City we were very down. When he signed for The Reds, mate... God's plan, lad.

Degsi: 7

Was great in that he did everything he needed to, but still had the chance to buzz about like a Jack Russell for a bit. There was a Jack Russell that used to live next door to me nan's in Fazakerley, little fucker it was, fucking couldn't stand me nan. Mad that.

Andy Robbo: 7

Part of the defence that has literally got the greatest defensive record for the start of a season in The Reds' history. Give them all an extra point to what I have written your own selves. Like a handicap in golf.

Henderson: 8

Thought he was really good, you know, not in a 'Henderson is sound' needle way either. Hope he only has a knock, rather than something that's gonna keep him out.

Milner: 8

Made out of fucking rock, mate. Could conceivably knock about with Deadpool there, knocking shit out of people with his granite arms.

Ad Lallana: 7

For someone who hasn't played for two years or some shit he was sound, you know. Got a lovely half turn, hasn't he? Forgot how good it was. Looked like he'd aged 15 years by the end of the game, mind you. Like yer man out the end of Indiana Jones who has a swig out of the jarg cup.

Mo Salah: 8

Reckon he was back to his best, you know. Two chances, slots one, just misses the second. Linked up well with Sturridge, his touch was great, his movement was great, he was great.

Dan Sturridge: 7

Lasted a whole game there without snapping his banjo. Thought he linked the forwards and the midfield well, looked stronger than he has for years. Well in, lad.

Shaqiri: 8

Mad little fucker played centre mid there, just stood still finding space all day. Movement for the goal is perfection. First touch for the goal is perfection. Pass for the goal is perfection. Mo literally doesn't have to touch it. Boss.

SUBS...

Gini:

Come on, looked fucked.

Firmino:

Come on played centre mid or the top of a diamond or some shit, played the worst pass I've ever seen, probably could have scored or set up three.

Fabinho:

Made some tackles, won some tackles. Done alright. Well in.

Liverpool v Cardiff City

Saturday October 27, 2018

ROB GUTMANN'S PREVIEW

MOHAMED Salah. Sadio Mane. Bobby Firmino. Three hearts beating as one. Once again.

Liverpool bounced back from a slump that has seen them win seven in nine league games, conceding just three goals. If Carlsberg did slumps they'd do them like the rampant Reds.

Against Red Star Belgrade on Wednesday night, Liverpool looked like Liverpool once more. In truth, they looked like something a touch better. Yes, the opponents were hardly European royalty, but you can only demolish what's in front of you with an orgy of goals while simultaneously looking like defensive perfection.

It is taken for granted that Liverpool must now forever and always be the side that will score four goals or more. Prior to midweek though, they had only put four past an opponent (West Ham) on the opening matchday of the season.

Lost in mumbled conversations about the front three having lost their mojo and around Salah's exploits perhaps being just a one-season phenomenon, was the reality of Liverpool's fixture schedule thus far.

In 12 games we'd been paired with Manchester City, Chelsea twice, Paris Saint-Germain, as well as Napoli, Spurs, Leicester and Crystal Palace away. These were not games, in the main, where Liverpool were able to exactly cut loose last term.

In this sample (looking at just the league games) during 2017-18, Liverpool won three times, lost twice, scoring 10 times, conceding 10 times. This time out, we've won three times, but haven't lost, scoring seven times, conceding just three times. The unbeaten Reds are improving. The data don't lie.

A home banker weekend represents rare respite for Liverpool in recent times. That it coincides with title rivals Man City matching up against fellow hopefuls Spurs, is significant. We simply must make hay and hope that Spurs can stay resolute enough not to be beaten at home by City. Breathing space is everything in this league.

We travel to flying Arsenal next week. A win would be golden but a draw an entirely reasonable result. The chances of us pulling away from City, or even the likes of Chelsea or Spurs aren't great in the near present, but every week we can look at a table and see no other side with more points than us takes us another step closer to our nirvana. I'd happily see us nip and tucking this close to fellow challengers right up until May.

Liverpool have the relative luxury of a seven-day lull until the Arsenal game, and barring the after effects of the Champions League game, Jürgen Klopp will see no reason not to go full strength. What that actually manifests itself as in midfield is unclear, with Jordan Henderson out, and James Milner being eased in out of games following his thigh strain injury.

There's some talk of an early return for Naby Keita from a hamstring problem, but my guess is that Klopp will challenge Wednesday night's new look, and impressive midfield to go again. Expect Fabinho to push on, Gini Wijnaldum to control, and Xherdan Shaqiri to continue banging against all doors, open or otherwise.

Liverpool 4 Cardiff City 1
NEIL ATKINSON'S REVIEW

MO SALAH scores.

Gambles and scores. Cardiff City have thrown their bodies on the line, done everything they can to stop the goal and yet the ball is in the back of the net, Anfield is in raptures, Cardiff in shreds and there isn't yet 10 minutes on the clock.

Three outfield Cardiff players are lying on the deck, one with a knock, but all three looking at each other, all three knowing the worst thing that could happen has, all three just done in as were the whole team at that stage. They knew how hard the afternoon was going to be.

Cardiff then should have either conceded a penalty or gone down to 10 men immediately from where I sat. Liverpool perhaps should have scored. Cardiff an absolute mess. And just when the game should have been swept away from... Nothing.

Liverpool allowed their domination to become completely sterile. It was almost as though Cardiff rope-a-doped Liverpool. Nothing worked for Liverpool but that was fine as they didn't try much. They forced very few issues and lacked urgency in all areas of the pitch. The centre backs seemingly became Liverpool's most progressive players. It all added up to the most frustrating 4-1 victory I can remember.

This frustration isn't anything about goal difference. I can't worry about that yet. Those who can are fine to do so. I get it, but for now I can think about March but not May. The frustration is much about Liverpool yet again failing to have other ideas, Liverpool yet again acquiescing to play at the opposition's tempo.

Having other ideas is my favourite thing in football. 'But Liverpool had other ideas,' is my favourite sentence. Today the other ideas never seemed to come. Instead Cardiff set a pattern, a horrible pattern, an entirely passive pattern, and Liverpool were alright about it.

At least it seemed that way. But the manager had three warming up at half time and made his first change bang on 60. That change was Adam Lallana for Xherdan Shaqiri. Lallana had very much struggled and had lacked the spark required. Shaqiri was the opposite. He was lively and demanded the ball. James Milner came on and did exactly the same. Two footballers suddenly had other ideas, two wanted the ball. The difference was marked.

Shaqiri got the goal his performances had deserved and in this frustrating game is probably MOM given that he wanted to be MOM. He slalomed through the box and rolled the ball calmly into the corner. Milner was worthy of an assist, but instead terrible things happened behind and Liverpool conceded their first league goal at Anfield since either February or 1993.

Sadio Mane ends the game with a brace and his opener was very much about him forcing the issue. He ought to have ended with a hat trick but Mo Salah decided to shoot from the halfway line instead.

It's important not to overstate Liverpool's performance, not to labour the point. Fury inducing frustration is not the same as deep under performance, but there is something concerning or contradictory about The Reds. There is something grown up about them on the one hand, something measured and calm, but on the other that isn't shots from the halfway.

If Liverpool want to be a crushing machine, commit to it wholeheartedly, but that means crushing Cardiff when they want to be crushed, when three of them lie on the deck, the game taken from them in the 15 minutes that follow before relaxing through the game. Score goals and finish them.

Liverpool, though, are top of the league because they are playing some of the best football and have some of the best footballers.

There are 28 more hurdles and some of them soon will need other ideas.

Arsenal v Liverpool
Saturday November 3, 2018
ROB GUTMANN'S PREVIEW

THERE are good times to play teams.

When they've won 11 on the spin isn't one of them. When they've ended that run, regardless of the manner in which it ground to halt, that is the sweet spot moment.

Arsenal conceded late and drew at Crystal Palace last weekend. They are ripe for the taking.

Three weeks ago, we'd stopped winning. In fact, we'd taken to losing. Two defeats (to Chelsea and Napoli) in a week preceded the visit of Manchester City. We were vulnerable and City were/are good.

We navigated our way to a draw the afternoon City came to Anfield. And despite Riyad Mahrez's late penalty miss, we were worth our point. I think that single point will come to be seen as worth something more within the context of the totality of our season. It was a good time for City to play us. We were there for the beating but resisted. The gods were thwarted.

I always look ahead to derbies, weeks ahead, and track Everton's form. I'm broadly happy if they're doing well and feel good about themselves with a month to go. It's just enough time for their latest revival to peak and then inevitably peter out. Just in time for The Reds. Timing is everything.

Liverpool are in the right place at the right time. Two four-goal wins in the past week have served to correct a needlessly growing misapprehension that our world-acclaimed front three were a flash in the pan phenomenon. Between them, they've plundered seven goals in two matches. A further bonus is that their primary understudy, Xherdan Shaqiri, is also at last in on the act, slaloming his way to a first Liverpool goal against Cardiff last Saturday.

The two wins halted a mini slide that had seen Liverpool winless in four, albeit four of the hardest fixtures imaginable (Chelsea twice, Man City and Napoli away). While we were stuttering, Arsenal kept on winning and before last weekend, had reigned the table-topping Reds into within just two points. Unai Emery's new-look Gooners were the league's latest insurgency.

Although Emery's team were delighting Arsenal's Arsene Wenger-weary following with goals, acute observers noted that the wins being amassed were largely against the cannon fodder of the Premier and Europa leagues. Sterner tests clearly lay ahead.

Crystal Palace, rocking and creaking under Roy Hodgson, didn't appear to be one of those tests as the fixture approached. Palace roughed up Arsenal though, and made them look every inch their former-life selves of whom it was routinely declared 'don't like it up 'em'.

Then in the space of minutes, Arsenal turned the game around and looked on course for straight win number 12. But they conceded again near the end and the run, and I suspect also the spell, were suddenly broken.

Jürgen Klopp was able to express himself via his team selections for the Red Star Belgrade and Cardiff fixtures. With Liverpool billed as strong favourites going into both encounters, he was able to experiment with formation and personnel. I suspect he'll not indulge himself further for Arsenal, although injury concerns mean that his final 11 is hard to call, certainly for the midfield.

All being healthy, he'd go for a midfield trio of Jordan Henderson, Gini Wijnaldum and James Milner. In concert, they've served him well this season. Henderson hasn't kicked a ball in anger for two weeks though and remains an unlikely option for the weekend.

If Wijnaldum and Milner are near certainties then, who gets the captain's berth? It could be a game in which to make or break Fabinho. Maybe it comes just a touch too early to risk the latter. Fabinho is acclimatising nicely, but he's only started starting games in the past 10 days.

Klopp may choose to be very bold, and start Shaqiri, matching Wijnaldum and Milner as double pivots in a 4-2-3-1 formation. It is also a system Emery has defaulted too more often than not, and it may suit us to effectively go like for like with Arsenal, on the premise that we're better than they are, across the pitch.

Manchester City went to Spurs on Monday night and to the chagrin of the chasing pack, failed to drop points. That puts the ball firmly back in our court.

A draw at the Emirates would represent no shame for us, but my God, a win feels like it could elevate us to yet another higher plane.

Our time is now.

Arsenal 1 Liverpool 1

BEN JOHNSON'S RATINGS

Alisson: 7

The save in the first minute is really good, you know. Like, really good. Doesn't do anything wrong for their goal.

Trent: 5

Struggled like fuck. Touch was off, legs were off, head was off. Off. That said, their whole tactical plan first half was to get after that wing. Could have done with some help.

Virgil: 8

Literally could have had a hat trick. Sublime at the back. Not really sure what went on with their goal, there. Think it just might have been a good finish that the lads couldn't do much about. Great defensive line all day.

Joe Gomez: 7

See above. Faultless but then conceded a goal which was no one's fault. Faultless?

Andy Robbo: 7

Played well, up and down, consistent option.

Fabinho: 4

Fuck me, looked like he'd run the ground straight from The Paradox. Anyone fancy telling me Henderson is shite in comparison to him? Reckon I might hunt you down and fucking burst you, to be honest. Had to change our formation to protect him, which literally impacted on our ability to win the match. A problem.

James Milner: 7

Scored a great goal there, in that he hit it and it went in and all hell broke loose. Felt sorry for him playing next to someone probably three or four levels below what was required. Plugging holes, choosing passes that he wouldn't need to do if he had a proper fella playing next to him.

Gini: 7

Had a lot to do. Like a lot. Like two fellas' work. Possibly three fellas' work. I don't fucking know. Played well though, Gini. Played well.

Mo Salah: 7

Dangerous, weren't he? He's not as good when he plays upfront as opposed to on the left of a three. We need to fuck that off, really.

Sadio Mane: 7

Thought he was poor, first half. Had opportunities time and again to get after them, but didn't. Poor touch, poor decision. Whatever. Better second half.

Firmino: 7

Gets an extra point for playing centre mid second half to look after his mate.

SUBS...

Henderson: 9

Fuck off.

Shaqiri: 6

Legged it, gave it away once. That is all.

Matip: n/a

Big giant purple one. Got a hazelnut inside him.

NEIL ATKINSON'S REVIEW

IT'S dead hard playing centre mid for Liverpool.

Been saying it for a while and today that hopefully has been made crystal clear. I say 'hopefully' because there have been people refusing to accept this for an astonishing length of time. I say 'hopefully' because I do hope. I genuinely think that people desperate to talk about football should acknowledge this.

There is an argument the hardest job in football could well be playing centre mid for Jürgen Klopp's Liverpool. That he asks so much. That he wants the lad in the middle of his three to do about five jobs, to be almost everything, to be the three things you can be in a 4-2-3-1. It could be that that is unfair.

Liverpool spent £40m on a really good midfielder in the summer but today it was all too much for him. Fabinho looked like he wasn't fit enough, sharp enough, smart enough. Like his touch wasn't good enough. He looked absent while present. He looked a million miles off.

For years this column, your correspondent, has found himself criticised for being too kind about Jordan Henderson. For being too upbeat about Liverpool's captain. The truth of the matter is that for an age Henderson has had the world asked of him and has been too harshly criticised.

And this will extend to Fabinho. He scraps and works. He never shirks and I bet he would have liked to. I would have in his shoes. But he shows and is keen. The truth is that it is dead hard playing centre mid for Liverpool.

The hope and expectation is that Fabinho learns from tonight. He watches the video. He has a think about it. He redoubles efforts around being 10 per cent fitter. He takes it on the chin. He recognises the size and scope of the challenge. Because while this manager made it easier for him for a half, that will not happen again.

There should be no doubt about two things:

· Fabinho has the talent to become the starting centre mid for Liverpool.
· Being the starting centre mid for Liverpool could be the hardest job in football.

The Reds were the better side for much of the first half. They were the side most likely, but this Arsenal is worth watching and liking. They are in the business of being in business. They are a migration of a football team, an avian swoop and shift. They are the boys and are enjoying being the boys.

There is a chance that no team in the country could be more fun to support this season than them. They are effervescent and teeming with brio. They want a bit of it. Whatever it is. Their manager has looked at his squad and backed them not to find glory but to be glorious. Fair play to them.

But The Reds should still have beaten them. Virgil van Dijk should have had a hat trick. Andy Robertson could have had three assists. Sadio Mane spent his evening just being in vain. Everything nearly there, nothing quite right. Liverpool, even while poor, even while not functioning or while accommodating in central midfield, were the better side at all the football that matters.

We can have 10,000 words on the James Milner finish for the opener. Its values were Yorkshire and Protestant, the ball fell to the most ideal man to make sure what had to happen did without a flourish. He roared at the crowd because he knows what it means.

He is a man you would follow to the very jaws of Hell or beyond. He is the best and the finest of us yeoman. An artisan better than most artists. He should never be damned with faint praise, he should be overwhelmed with adoration. He is the business. The footballer you would call upon.

It was 90 minutes of Mo Salah almost getting in. God I love him. The less he succeeds the more he becomes ours. He is a man of so much brain. Talk about his speed or his touch by all means. But he outthinks you three times before he even has the ball under his spell. He will have the finest season.

A point isn't a shame. Klopp's Reds remain unbeaten having faced four of their six closest rivals by this stage – and three of them away from Anfield. A point only feels it because of Manchester City's class.

The bigger issue is perhaps what we ask of our boys time and again, but you know what lads? We're all in this together, for better or worse. They are our lads. They always were. They always will be. Let's encourage them and understand the scale of the challenge in both micro and macro senses.

Eleven down, 27 to go. They are our Reds and they have very hard jobs.

Watford v Liverpool
Saturday November 24, 2018
ROB GUTMANN'S PREVIEW

I LIKE a bit of Watford.

It's a no-nonsense away. Not so close that you barely feel you've had a day out but far enough that it feels like going on a mission.

I'm becoming fonder of aways the older I'm getting. When I was young it was all about Anfield. That was going to church, entering the temple. Other grounds, other towns felt like paler equivalents. Hostile non-homes from home.

I've improved the away experience as the years have past, by elongating it. My mates always laughed at me for how early I wanted to get them all out of bed to begin an away day journey. Slowly but surely though, I've won over hearts and minds.

The actual football element of the away trip can be trying. Over the last 30 years let's guesstimate that Liverpool win an average of about eight away league games per campaign. That's eight happy endings out of 19. That in turn necessitates that there are 11 other occasions where you're walking away from a ground, having had a long, often fairly expensive, day end in frustration, if not downright bitter disappointment.

My remedy, of sorts, for this is to ensure there are other wins to be had. Hence the early departures. A brisk start facilitates a champion's breakfast en route. I like to get us to our last pit stop before the ground at least three hours before kick off. Bedding in for food and booze.

Select a venue that's ticking boxes. The scran must be edible, the ale preferably real, and the environment ideally similar to that described in George Orwell's seminal essay on the British pub, *The Moon Under Water*.

For Watford, we're targeting the sleepy home counties hamlet of St Albans. A town legendary for its sheer quantity of public houses. It's only a few miles from Watford but the distance is key.

Ale houses close to football grounds are not for me. I don't need pre-match terrace bonhomie. That will keep till we're in the ground. I'm after a civilised bolt hole with a bit of charm, a useable bog, somewhere to sit, and where you can easily get served. Pubs near away grounds have none of these things.

Preparation is everything. Jürgen Klopp will surely have planned as meticulously as I do. Perhaps with less alcohol involved, but you never know with Kloppo.

The news on the wires is that for once, our boys have returned from the international duties unscathed. Praise be. Most of our lads only played solitary games at most. Freshness should not be an issue.

I see no selection dilemmas for the Liverpool manager at the back, where his most trusted five should all reconvene. As this fixture is categorizable as 'a tough away', Klopp is likeliest to revert to his more compact 4-3-3 formation, saving the 4-2-3-1 for more yielding opposition.

The temptation to start the very much in-form Xherdan Shaqiri will be huge. Out of sorts Bobby Firmino could be the fall guy with Mo Salah asked to play as a number nine.

Jordan Henderson is not certain of a recall as he continues to be hampered by a niggling thigh injury. If Henderson isn't risked, expect Gini Wijnaldum to play at the base of the midfield with James Milner and Naby Keita ahead of him. It's been a frustrating start to a much-anticipated Liverpool career for Naby and he will be hoping for no more false starts.

It's a seven bells start for my team behind the team on Saturday morning, and I'll be urging for early nights all round on Friday.

This Watford adventure has taken a lot of planning and we can't afford any slip ups now, can we Reds?

Watford 0 Liverpool 3
BEN JOHNSON'S RATINGS

THEY fucking love getting their hair cut in Watford, you know.

I'm not sure I've ever seen so many barbers in one gaff in my life. About 10, in a row, all of them chocker. Mad that, isn't it?

Alisson: 7

Tried to pass one to Firmino at centre half first half but fucked it up because, like everyone else in the ground, he was like, 'what the fuck are you doing at centre half, you bellend?' Makes a great save when Degsi falls over. Nothing else to do apart from fill the goal.

Trent: 8

The freekick, mate. Right behind that. Half crying that Shaqiri had gone off, then he just bins it, like it's dead easy. Needs a song, you know. Wish his name rhymed with Ronnie Whelan. Been singing Ronnie Whelan songs all day. Dead easy.

Virgil: 8

He's our centre half, he's our number four.

Troy Deeney got interviewed by the BBC or BT or someone and got asked who he hated playing against the most. His response…

Virgil van Dijk. Too big. Too fast. Loves fighting. Smells nice. He runs past you and you're like 'ooh' smelling him.

The best ever.

Degsi: 7

Did well first half considering he was playing with two boxes of fish fingers instead of boots. Fucking loves falling over, doesn't he? Last year, a Degsi fall over was a goal. This year he has lads to dig him out. Well in, Degs. Get your feet in front of the fire and warm them up, lid.

Andy Robbo: 7

Sets up Mane to set up Bobby for the third, at a time when arses are twitching. Boss.

Henderson: 4

Ticked it over and done alright, but in fairness the sending off was fucking ridiculous. Daft as a brush. If the game had gone the other way he might have been strangled, and rightly fucking so.

Gini: 7

Did some keeping hold of the ball for a bit. Can't remember much else. But The Reds won 3-0 and frankly I could hug all of them.

Shaqiri: 7

Feels like when he plays no-one else bothers there arse trying to create anything and just leave it to him. A little bit cursed, really. Did alright. Bright, can't half pick a pass, just needs everyone else to play their normal game around him.

Mo Salah: 8

Don't like him playing upfront, you know, but then he scores every time he does, and maybe I'm just a bellend who doesn't know his arse from his elbow. Did some jiggery to get that goal in. Not sure what it was. Just seen it trickle over the line.

Sadio: 7

Think he might be getting diddled a little with our mad 4-4-2 shape, but still dangerous at times. Signed a new contract. Frankly, if I could get away with it, I would wear my undies on my head for a week.

Firmino: 7

Another one who might be getting had off by being made to play centre mid/centre half/centre forward, basically anywhere centre. But then he scores second half and does an exaggerated bow celebration, and we should all just carry him on our shoulders until we die.

SUBS...

Matip:

Massive fan of the Big Joelly five-minute sub. The piano man. Love him to get a league medal based on 19 five-minute appearances.

NEIL ATKINSON'S REVIEW

IT'S a small away end at Watford.

I wish you could have been there with us, I wish it with all my heart. But that wasn't always the case. Surround me with songs of deliverance, oh lord. You know, it was purgatory at the break.

While Liverpool had finished the half broadly in control the game never felt likely to spark and a slight threat of dropped points began to loom. It was a game I had seen before, a 72nd minute goal from, say, Etienne Capoue, followed by an equaliser if we are lucky and some frustrating woodwork if we are not.

The atmosphere was flat in the whole ground, including the travelling contingent. There was no spark in sight, Xherdan Shaqiri doing his best but nothing quite there. All the way up the other end and Liverpool looked blunt.

Watford are clearly a good side. They do lots of good things and had a strong shape. They played well and looked like going nowhere.

Everything hurt. Then Gini Wijnaldum made an absolute pig's ear of something in the right-wing area, but he and Roberto Firmino redeemed the situation, Firmino doing so gorgeously, and Wijnaldum delivered a drilled cross into a defender's legs and won a corner.

He urged the crowd on, making big circles with his arms as if to say: 'Fucking hell, it is hard this, lads. Give us something.' The crowd responded and while the corner led to very little it felt like all this led to the opening goal.

From there Liverpool looked irresistible and irrepressible, Liverpool were not to be denied. Liverpool delivered the goods. Trent Alexander-Arnold scored a glorious freekick and let us know what it meant. The three points in the boot on the way back north.

Andy Robertson roars forward into space, sprinting, sprinting, my lungs burning watching him, him looking up, finding Sadio Mane who found Ben Foster in fine form, but Roberto Firmino found the net and checked, double checked and triple checked with the lino and then he gleamed towards us. His smile mischievous and beautiful, the best night out you will never have, the pint of pints, the king of kings. Hosanna in the highest.

It's the best all three of the front three have played his season in a league game. Mo Salah was constantly a threat but Firmino made more sense of what was asked of him, while Mane was probably your man of the match, an incredible football brain on springs, all loops and curves, every run arced with and without the ball.

To see the three of them doing their business with panache matters. It is the only pathway to glory for us this season. That's not to downplay what everyone else is doing, Virgil van Dijk and Alisson can be very proud of their afternoon's work.

However, the truth of the matter is that we were rightly delighted when the three forwards each signed new contracts. We know what they can do for Liverpool and when they click they know what they can do for each other. They become greater than the sum of their parts and those parts are pretty great in the first place, let me tell you.

The three goals were such a relief, such a delivery from the other reality, the one seen in so many seasons passed. Liverpool's forwards offered all of us such relief. The final whistle sounded and the Mighty Reds were shattered. They will not be letting anyone down this season. Not us, not themselves.

It was what we needed in every sense. The crowd defiant, delighted, delirious. Deservedly Dejan Lovren giving it the big one to the crowd after the final whistle, bookending the Wijnaldum roar. Surround me with songs of deliverance.

Liverpool survived the red card and delivered Jordan Henderson from his sins, the captain dug out after his daft sending off. His irresponsibility left his side in the lurch but they saved his day and ours. Liverpool sang and Liverpool delivered us from evil. What's a psalm without you? Every psalm I cite is about you.

For the first half, for the half time, I wanted to be anywhere else. For the second half, I wish you could have been there. But then you were in the sense that most matters. We're in this together. Liverpool's players made that crystal clear today. They made it self evident.

Thirteen hurdles cleared from us, from all The Reds. Twenty-five to go.

We're going nowhere.

Liverpool v Everton
Sunday December 2, 2018
ROB GUTMANN'S PREVIEW

THE Blues. The fucking Blues. And I guess that's why they call them The Blues.

I just cannot be arsed with them right now. And annoyingly, inevitably, they will be so invested in this weekend's derby.

Blues, blue men, blue people, you may well get your win, that win, this time, but you can't make us really care. Of course, we hugely need the points. But we don't need the spoils. You Blues are simply not our business.

I think this Everton team has enough to become the best Everton team in a generation. It's a team that, in the finest traditions of 21st century Everton, can, on their day, be 'a handful'. Liverpool will not get it easy on Sunday. I'd love easy, but nothing about this season feels care free.

I like this Everton side. I think Richarlison is a footballer. The rest are like a who's who of Liverpool dream signings from five years ago. We shouldn't sneer. We've come a long way. There, but for the grace of God, are we regarding Andre Gomes and Yerry Mina as game-changing acquisitions?

I'm just back from Paris and the experience has changed me. I've returned with all kinds of airs and graces. All the moules and escargot have gone to my head. I think I might be too good for Everton just right now. I'm ripe for some serious hubris.

League games post Europe are a phenomenon in Liverpool's history. We have conquered all of Europe, and in the process of doing so have played many subsequent bread and butter games at half cock. Bob Paisley knew it was impossible to reprise the fire and fervour of a season-defining midweek in Europe against the likes of Stoke and co back home.

A mid-80s Liverpool side limped to a forgettable 1-0 win over Sunderland at Anfield after a legendary European excursion. The Kop was fretful that afternoon, but Bob P was sanguine about it all. He expected 'flat', and flat was delivered.

He was so at peace with second gear that he even substituted Craig Johnston, who had not been exerted in the European game, for fear that his freshness and enthusiasm might over stretch his wearier teammates. Anfield booed the change that afternoon but wise Bob secured the precious three points.

Wily and wise Jürgen Klopp must do the same this Sunday. The Blues will be vibrant and straining at their leashes after a Liverpool-obsessed week of preparation at Finch Farm. Gylfi Sigurdsson et al have gone to sleep seeing only red. By contrast, Mo Salah, James Milner and Sadio Mane haven't thought about Everton. Not even once.

Part of me thinks (hopes) that our indifference will give us an edge. Not that we should need that edge. We are simply better than them. But our two-decade superiority over our blue cousins can partially be attributed to calmness in the face of their frenzy. We have remained productively distracted while they've whorled like hapless dervishes around us.

Things were far from perfect for Liverpool in Paris on Wednesday. Not for the first time this season, we failed to find the level that we seemed to rise to at will, last campaign. It could be down to our earnest midfield; then warrior like, now workman like. We need more from the engine room. Naby Keita was bought to provide that. There were hints in the French capital that he may be readying himself to step up to the plate.

The captain, Jordan Henderson, is suspended for this derby, so Keita will start. I'd also like to see Joe Gomez reunited with Virgil van Dijk in the centre of our defence. I'm not seeing what Klopp is in Dejan Lovren. A settled back five is the way forward.

In attack, Roberto Firmino continues to baffle. Last term, our heart and soul, but now too often a flailing passenger. He needs a break. I'd draft Shaqiri in and back him to do his worst. He's got Everton written all over him and I'd like to see the Swiss given the opportunity to write his name into derby folklore. Big time. In blood. Dripping, drained, blue blood.

Let's sink some teeth into these, Reds.

Liverpool 1 Everton 0
BEN JOHNSON'S RATINGS

HONEST to god, I've never seen anything like it in me life. That might have to do. Everyone gets 10.

Hahahahahahahahahahahaha.

Fucking hell.

We should have known. Three little mings dressed a bit like Father Christmas except in blue said 'Merry Christmas' to us in town about an hour before the game. The response. Go ed, lad. Merry Crimbo, gang. Let's do this again next year.

I mean flare on the pitch three seconds before we score because they thought it had finished. Hahaha.

Divock Origi getting the sausage in his first act in football since Ramiro Funes Mori did the most celebrated thing at Anfield by a Bluenose for pretty much 20 years. Their mad little keeper keeping it in. One of the lads here said he had on a shirt that was too tight, so he couldn't raise his arms. Like a jazzy Next work shirt your bird bought you.

Imagine being them, la. Hahaha. We will never see anything like that again in or lives. Might as well jib it, you know. We might have completed footy, there.

Alisson: 9

Two world-class saves and a hug from Jürgen Klopp. Hahahaha. Best I have seen.

Trent: 9

Played well, you know. But none of this matters. Because hahaha. Was it Trent involved in the little kick off at 95 minutes that led them to sing murderers, and lashing phones on the pitch, and the added time for our goal? Extra point if so.

Virgil: 9

I mean, I thought we had a deal whereby he scores in December at home against the Blueshite. But all day long, I'll take him slicing one up in the air and their keeper wafting at it with his fake arms. Hahaha.

Joey: 9

Hahaha. I don't even know. Richard's lad upfront for them was good but so was Joey. But you know, Pickford and that.

Andy Robbo: 8

Boss. We tried to get on the pitch when we scored. The steward was incredibly strong for a 70-year-old fella. Adam Melia gave everyone a hug as they left.

Gini: 8

Better second half from a virtually non-existent Gini first half. But if he had played any better that wouldn't have happened, so you know. The greatest thing these eyes have ever seen.

Fabinho: 8

Thought he was our best midfielder. Made a few good tackles, most involved midfielder says Adam Melia.

Shaqiri: 7

Missed that sitter first half but then you know the drill. Without that we wouldn't have had this. All of them should be carried around on our shoulders until they die. Twenty-four hour call out. What do you need, Shaqo lad.

Mo Salah: 7

When Klopp took him off I thought it was the worst decision ever made. Then he brought Divock on to run the channels and I thought it was even worse than that. What a bellend I am.

Sadio: 8

Best forward for The Reds. Pissed me off when he picked up his mate, instead of doing something else for The Reds.

Firmino: 7

Thought he struggled. Looked knackered, but then he went off for Divock and the rest is the best moment of all our lives.

SUBS...

Hahaha. I don't even know.

Divock: 10

So good he only needs two chances from point-blank range. Not my words. The words of the mercurial Adam Melia. The greatest thing I think I have ever seen at Anfield. Honest to God. He can move into ours, you know. I'm decorating the spare room at the minute, that will be lovely for me. A hero. Honestly. Keep him forever, play him once. Hahaha.

NEIL ATKINSON'S REVIEW

THIS is the greatest day of our lives.

There will be analysis and there will be chat, and there will be talk. But this is the greatest day of our lives.

There is a piece. It is the only piece I have written in advance. I wrote it three years ago. The piece is 800 words about Everton winning at Anfield. It sits there waiting to be shown, waiting to emerge. Because I couldn't imagine having to write about Everton winning at Anfield and so I have, and it sits, and when I was oddly furious around the 80th minute I started to think the piece may emerge.

I mean, up to 90+4, you could have been furious. Furious with the referee, furious with the old men in the crowd, furious with missed chances and brick-shithouse defenders trampling on Liverpool's goalscorers.

But on 90+5, let the heavens declare it: the city is all ours. Hosanna in the highest. He only has little arms and Divock Origi is the greatest footballer ever to play for Liverpool.

And whatever did it, we are rejoicing. Whether it is Jürgen Klopp's genius in the substitutions, whether it was the brutality of the 'murderers' chant that demanded an answer, or whether it was Jordan Pickford's arms that plucked the ball from its direction of travel out of the game and placed it in front of Divock Origi, who the fuck cares?

Hosanna. Divock owed them that. Divock owed them that for Ramiro Funes Mori derailing his career with a stinker of a challenge years ago. Origi's scored three goals against Everton but would probably have scored more goals against everyone if not for that challenge. The mentality that chants 'murderers' at Anfield celebrated that red card.

And all that is unfortunate. Because this is an excellent Everton side. They were great, you know. They showed character and aggression and quality in spades. It's their best performance since their last win at Anfield, their best performance since before then.

I'll tell you this now: Marco Silva is already, and will prove to be, a better Everton manager than David Moyes. It is spectacular the progress made from last season's cowardly showing at our place. Sam Allardyce got one more point but he had no future. This Everton team is all future, all impressive. They get to be good.

It's what makes the win all the sweeter, the day all the greater, what makes it a joy to be alive. The sheer happiness and the reason this is the greatest day of our lives is because they came to Anfield and deserved at least a point and then that.

Rejoice. Rejoice.

Rejoice in the smart and effective saves made by Alisson Becker. Rejoice in Virgil van Dijk's leadership (even if at times, Everton's press got to even him). And rejoice in last minute, throw caution to the fucking wind, decisions by our manager who demonstrates appetite for gambling that would make the mayor of Las Vegas blush.

Our gaffer is incredible. Our gaffer is the best of us, wants to be us, wants to enjoy in the blood and in the bone. Before Burnley away this year I will reflect on being lucky enough to talk to him about Burnley away last year, reflect on how much at heart he is a drinking, swearing, screaming football supporter.

His job is to make it a joy to be alive and he does so with aplomb. He believes in the joy. I loved that he took them to The Kop. I love he ran on the pitch to celebrate with the goalkeeper.

THE ANFIELD WRAP

It was pandemonium when it went in. It was bedlam. Remember this – these are young men in their 20s. Remember this – they are living their best life. They are getting to live large, live for us. Tonight we need to live for them.

They need to get the adrenaline out of their legs, get themselves in shape for Burnley. Be professional. We get to live the greatest day of our lives, the happiest day of theirs because this is the game. The blood and the bone.

Origi knows that I hope. Knows he is a hero. Knows he provoked screams, and pride, and delight, and a little cry from somewhere.

Fuck your hurdles. Fuck your league table at least for a day. Fuck your blue flares. This is the greatest day of our lives. Red resplendent.

See you in town, handsome. See you in town, gorgeous. Let's go dancing.

Burnley v Liverpool
Wednesday December 5, 2018
ROB GUTMANN'S PREVIEW

WE have a drill for Burnley away.

It's often felt like a rush to be getting there. It's close, but there's never quite enough time to fulfil all ambitions and expectations. This Wednesday will be a challenge. We've got to scoop my youngest, Rafael (Benitez) Gutmann out of school at 3.35pm and then hit the trail northwards.

'Raffy' will have to get changed out of his school uniform in the car. Into his club-branded clobber – like a crap, nine-year-old Superman. He's had to pull this off a few times and it doesn't please him but he does it for The Reds.

The established Burnley routine involves hitting up a posh pub 20 minutes outside the town. It's called The Fence. This boozer is sedate and faux classy, but oh that roaring fire, those comfy country gentry furnishings, and those sweet, sweet pies and selection of cask ales. It fortifies for cold a night in the away end singing lengthy songs about Virgil van Dijk.

With the fixtures coming so thick and fast now I can't tell good form from lame. There's no thinking time, just matches to be won. Performances mean nothing in the face of the need and greed for points.

The memory of the frenzy and mania of that last-gasp derby winner won't fade quickly, but there's little time for luxuriating in it. In a season of must wins, Wednesday's challenge now becomes the most important.

Despite points, clean sheets, and a fair few goals, Liverpool haven't looked quite right yet this season. Everton felt hard done by at the weekend. There was a consensus from all parties that they deserved more. What was lost within a bit of a forced rush to give The Blues credit was that, a couple of defensive lapses aside, a good Liverpool performance had been witnessed.

The vaunted pressing and counter pressing were at the levels of last season. Jürgen Klopp noted this in his post-match press conference but no one was really listening. The time-honoured drama of a derby day, the urge to discuss only the moments, distracted from the game's reality.

Watch back the preludes to the chances for Trent Alexander-Arnold, Sadio Mane and Xherdan Shaqiri in the first half. This was aggressive, incisive Liverpool at their very best.

Second half, the breaks that saw Roberto Firmino and Sadio Mane put in to one on ones with the goalie, and Divock Origi's burst down the right flank, reminded that, in the zone, there is no better counter-attacking team anywhere than Liverpool right now.

A cut on his foot should suffice as just cause for Mane to be given the night off. Firmino urgently needs to be rested for everyone's sake. His form hasn't been right all season. Andy Robertson has a dead leg and Gini Wijnaldum has played an exhausting amount of football. Expect these four to miss out, or at least be benched.

Klopp has the resources to freshen up strongly. Both Daniel Sturridge and derby hero Divock Origi made cases for taking Firmino's shirt, if only for Wednesday night. I'd give Divock the nod. His pace and energy on Sunday were reminders of gifts we'd thought had long deserted him. Post match, Klopp was keen to reassert faith in the player. His time might be now.

In midfield, the captain Henderson returns, probably for Gini. Then there's the need to get the potentially important Naby Keita on the pitch. He'd come in for Fabinho with James Milner due a recall, nominally filling Mane's berth. I think, given the personnel, that Klopp will play a 4-4-2 diamond, as he did at Stoke this time last year when juggling resources.

For Wednesday night I think Henderson will anchor with Milner and Keita advanced and wide of him. Shaqiri might be given the chance to play centrally as the attacking tip of the diamond. Mo Salah and Origi working, effectively, as twin strikers. Whatever team the manager goes with, it will be a stronger side than that which narrowly took down Burnley on New Year's Day 2018.

It's another must win, as they all will be, for a while longer yet.

Burnley 1 Liverpool 3

BEN JOHNSON'S RATINGS

ARE we still doing this footy watching thing? I mean, seriously?

I thought we all decided that it couldn't get any better than Sunday, for as long as we live, even if we find the pool off *Cocoon* and double bubble it with the magic mouse off *The Green Mile* and live till we are a million.

Make no mistake though, that is as impressive a Liverpool win as you will see. I honestly think that is up there with our best performances of the season. Didn't panic, got ourselves back in the game, backed ourselves, made some smart changes to bladder them on the break. These Reds are going to take some stopping, you know.

Alisson: 8

Had his hair cut. Looks like Superman now, as in how Superman was first imagined. Like an actual super man. Whereas, Joe Hart hasn't had his hair cut, but really looks like he has, right down the middle. Get shut Joe, your self-esteem will go through the roof, lad. Unless you have a weird head.

Has hard lines for the goal, doesn't he? I mean, how's that lad who goes for the first not offside? He's offside, isn't he? Unreal for the third goal there, you know. Does he save that one onto the post? Who's arsed? Keeps it in, stops a corner, gets The Reds on the march with a great throw, 10 seconds later its 3-1, pressure off, undies on head, under me hat as I'm in a restaurant, and that.

Joey Gomez: n/a

Got whacked there, didn't he? Need to keep your wits about you up them ways Joe, even when its going out for a corner. They'd kick a dead dog just to make sure. And when I say dead I mean fucking buried.

Joel: 8

Thought his passing was shite there in the first half an hour. Ridiculous foul for the disallowed pearler. Part of a great line, though. That's great defending holding a line like that. So well in, everyone. Defended really well in fairness. These are horrible to play against. Big, ugly and horrible.

Virgil: 8

They got in behind a few times first 30 minutes, but then in fairness they were legging themselves into the ground and we still managed to recover every time. Funny when teams try and rough him up, isn't it? That rugby league lad for them didn't get a sausage out of him. Brilliant for the goal.

Albie: 7

Thought he was actually pretty good first half. Then they scored and he went berserk a bit, giving it away for a laugh. Does well for our first though, in fairness.

Milner: 8

Scores a great goal, only place he can score, nestles it in the bottom corner. Goes left back and shows who Andy Robbo has been learning from. One of Jürgen's best subs in a while, that.

Stretched the game, let us play from full back in a way that Albie and possibly Robbo can't; mainly because he can play side on and use his right. Not great when you need to break down the line, but boss when you want to stretch the play and keep the ball.

Henderson: 7

Does all the horrible bits that you don't see unless you want to. Like filling in for Virgil when he lost the ball, and closing space. Not at his best but was part of a functioning midfield which was nice.

Remember that game years ago, where the ball bounced around everywhere and you had to get your little platform at the bottom of the screen to bounce it back up in the air to get the things in the sky? That's Henderson, that. Acts as a mirror to open up passing lanes. Does it well.

Naby: 9

Excellent first half. Popping it off, always on the half turn. Doing that thing where he blags he's in trouble and then legs past you, picking your pocket on the way. Like Bubs and his mate in *The Wire*. Picked up where he left off second half. Really unlucky for the save from auld, baldy Joe.

Could have scored a hat trick in about 10 seconds. (He couldn't really, like, because as soon as the first went in he wouldn't have got any of the other chances, but you know what I mean.) Tired a little bit but that looked a hell of a lot like the fella we've been batting one out over on YouTube for the last two years.

Shaqiri: 8

Sharp when he got on it in and around the box but miscontrolled the one that mattered when he was in at the end of the first half. Feel like I want more out of him, to be honest. Not sure he offered enough. Hang on, he just give us more and offered the third goal. Shut up, bellend.

Dan Sturridge: 7

Another one where you feel like you might want more, but then he pieced it together lovely at times and the ball for the third is brilliant.

Divock: 8

Does it really matter? Didn't offer much, but then sets up the first, in a way, by not being silly after a bit of a poor touch. To be honest, reckon he could sit in our house on the couch like fucking Jim Royle and I would pay him £500 a week for the privilege.

SUBS...

Trent: 7

Puts a ball and a half in for the second. Shifts the angle, lashes it in the corridor. Scenes.

Firmino: 7

First touch, goal. Looked sharp. Probably because they looked bladdered by the time he come on. Not a bad plan all told. Linked up well, tried to boot their fella in the chest. All for that, to be fair.

Mo Salah: 8

Mad how sharp he looked when he come on. Almost like the rest and coming on against fellas with 70 minutes of trying the hardest they have in six months might have done him good. Great for the third, unlucky for a couple of others.

Honourable Mention:

Sean Dyche's tie. Mad the way he only has one. Reckon he puts it back in the plastic wrapper about 10 minutes after full time every week. Had it 10 years.

NEIL ATKINSON'S REVIEW

VITALITY and purpose.

Nothing other than the title is our business.

Our business is nothing other than the title.

There is a purity to that.

Tonight told you that story and told you how much it matters to this club, this manager and his players, and what everyone is prepared to do.

Sunday was a local skirmish, a bit of internal business. Something you have to get through and Liverpool did so with class and élan. Brio some may say.

But tonight was back to the job in hand, the matter that matters. Tonight was about our title hopes.

There was a moment they wobbled. A moment when a big selection looked a wrong selection, when rolling the boulder up the hill looked beyond us. The task may prove to be Sisyphean but not tonight, not today. No way on earth.

Liverpool heaved, James Milner shoved and then the manager showed the courage of his convictions and got all his footballers on the pitch and backed them to box it for the remaining time in the game.

They boxed it. They repaid that backing. Naby Keita and Jordan Henderson were excellent in the middle of the park in the second half in different ways. The former all chorus, the latter all verse. Keita had been Liverpool's most likely first half.

Milner went to left back and reminded us he may well be the second best left back in the country, behind only the absent Andy Robertson; all sense on toast along with his galvanising, fantastic goal. Milner loved the battle, roaring at the away end, scrapping with purpose.

Xherdan Shaqiri spent much of the game struggling to get himself on the ball. The first half especially graft but the second anonymous too. But when he gets himself on it he can be sumptuous, scrumptious and finally, ultimately, victorious. I'd say I loved his finish but I didn't see it. I saw him, though. Wheeling away. Never in doubt.

Daniel, oh Daniel. Daniel Sturridge grew into the game like ivy up an exterior wall. At times in the first half he was completely unable to assert himself. By 80 minutes he had the game in a headlock and walked it round the playground, rubbing its head. The game curved back towards him.

He truly is the best of us, eventually finding Mo Salah who found Shaqiri who finished. Sturridge came right towards us at the end. I thought of him, of you, of us. You got light in your eyes, and you are standing here beside me.

But the save, the magnificent save at 1-2, then keeping it in, then finding Daniel who found etc. Alisson Becker isn't currently the best of us, he's the best of them, the best full stop. He's galactic, fantastic. He's magic and constant and certain throughout. He's winning points and creating goals.

Roberto Firmino and Salah end the game the most super of subs, leading a charge. Firmino bags to make it 1-2 after brilliant work from Virgil van Dijk. They pressed Burnley right back.

It was clear after Sunday our manager had serious courage, more so than his opposite number that day. Sean Dyche today sent his lads out to be absolute warriors. They left their foot in everywhere.

This isn't a moan, it is what going to Burnley should be. That the refereeing should be better is the bigger issue. Dyche should be concerned; his lads tired before our eyes and there is a massive challenge ahead. Are they ready for it?

But their challenge is nothing to ours. Liverpool are ready, willing and able. They aren't going anywhere these Reds of ours. They are in this until the bitter end, whether they are his footballers or not.

Fifteen hurdles surmounted. The Reds have 12 wins and three draws. This is what it is to be alive. This is what it is to be vital. This is what it is to have purpose.

Nothing other than the title is our business.

Our business is nothing other than the title.

CHAPTER FOUR – THE WINTER RUSH

Jürgen Klopp was stunned by his first English winter.

Not the weather, just the number of games. Every year since has been a learning curve. Liverpool have improved markedly in December.

It's a hugely entertaining thought, him firstly being shocked and secondly sitting down and deciding how to defeat it, like a particularly frustrating crossword puzzle.

Every manager who comes in from overseas has one. Rafa Benitez couldn't believe the way goalkeepers were treated in this country. Klopp has December and the wind. He talks endlessly about the weather. He clearly believes it makes a difference in football games and he is arguably right.

Liverpool played in some strange climates in 2018-19. Burnley at home was four seasons in one day. Leicester at home had hailstones like marbles falling from the sky. That glorious day in June saw Liverpool arguably play the conditions better than Tottenham having had a week with the Spanish heat prior to the final.

The weather matters but the fact he wants to talk about it matters, too. For some inside the Liverpudlian tent it became annoying but it is part of how Klopp sees the whole game, sees it as a contest between two sets of 11 lads who are all just doing their best. The contest in part comes against the elements.

The weather and how he discusses it is almost at the heart of how Klopp, for some Liverpool supporters, is too centred on football being a game rather than a Shankly-style way of life. He has often been at pains since he arrived to remind us this is a game, not a sentence, not an obligation. It occasionally jars with everything we have had our whole lives but it is central to his view. This is to be enjoyed not endured.

And that is where he reached with December. Enjoy it, don't endure it. Don't let it grind you down. December matters most; Liverpool hustle harder. This season it was when Liverpool went up a level, a side who had been conditioned to peak when the conditions deteriorated and when the games came thickest and fastest.

Klopp had worked long and hard on his crossword puzzle, had engaged with his reality and had his players in that rhythm he craves.

Liverpool didn't just walk on through the wind and the rain. They pushed on.

Neil Atkinson

Liverpool v Napoli

Tuesday December 11, 2018

ROB GUTMANN'S PREVIEW

IT'S an odd competition at times, the Champions League.

Its group phase is unsettling. The matches are all obviously very important. They must be, as teams – especially those in the Premier League – have sweated nine long months to qualify for them. Yet the reality is often anti climatic.

The level of contest is often a touch mediocre. Even the fixtures against elite clubs have more of a showpiece feel about them. Then it throws up a Liverpool v Napoli.

The phoney war definitely ends here. All we worked for last season, and all that we define ourselves by this term, comes down to a game. At least in our immediate reality, it appears this way.

Timely then that the fixture arrives at a peak moment of beauty for us. Beating Bournemouth in style and then retaining top spot in the league has put smiles on faces and calmed nerves. Crazy as it sounds, the pressure of maintaining a winning run just to keep on City's coattails was more stressful than gratifying.

Had Liverpool faced up to the Napoli challenge a week ago, I suspect that we'd have been worse placed to deal with disappointment. We can go out of the Champions League this week, and it will be a major blow if we do so but at least on Wednesday morning the team will be able to remind itself that it still sits top of the pile in our fearsome domestic league.

That knowledge alone should keep the black dog from the door for a squad showing signs not just that they can compete for the Premier League title but push on to actually claim it.

I hope that, safe in the knowledge that Napoli cannot end our season, our lads will be less encumbered and play with some of the freedom that saw them maraud to last campaign's Champions League final. In our muscle memory is the near conquering of all of Europe.

Jürgen Klopp rested his entire first-choice front three last week at Burnley so that his team could arrive in this pivotal week in fresh fettle. Sadio Mane has even enjoyed two games off. In his absence, Xherdan Shaqiri continues to impress. Likewise Naby Keita is back on the scene and providing food for thought every time he plays.

Others have plenty of miles still in them due to enforced absences. Jordan Henderson hasn't started every single game and nor has James Milner. Adam Lallana is also returning and providing his manager with options.

It's tricky to call the Liverpool team for Tuesday night. Even at the back there are limited certainties. Of course, the keeper, Alisson Becker, Virgil van Dijk and Andy Robbo start. But who claims the right-back berth? It should be Trent Alexander-Arnold but then Milner is the last man to have played there and played there with great efficiency (at Bournemouth on Sunday).

At centre back, Dejan Lovren will believe that he is first in the pecking order to partner van Dijk but Joel Matip was singled out for praise from Klopp for his weekend performance. He may very well retain his place.

While we'd all guess at the front three being a combo of Mane, Roberto Firmino and Mo Salah, selecting the midfield to back them up is no simple task. Having been rested at the weekend it seems reasonably likely that Henderson will be recalled and will anchor that midfield.

Klopp's Liverpool have been a much more patient model of late. They have not sought to throw the kitchen sink at opponents from the off, preferring at times sterile domination before applying the accelerator. That may suit a Napoli side who come to Anfield knowing that a draw is their win.

Liverpool must beat the Italians 1-0 or by at least a two-goal margin. Given this challenge, Napoli can afford to be more patient than we can be. Carlo Ancelotti's team will force nothing, safe in the knowledge that they have attacking players to punish a Liverpool side who may tend towards over stretching themselves at times.

Jürgen Klopp may sense that the only way for The Reds to prevail will be if they harness all of Anfield's power. That would require Liverpool to be at their most swashbuckling.

Napoli are a really good team and a formidable challenge, but so too were their peers Roma in April. Bobby, Sadio and Mo will fancy this.

Expect no tiptoeing from Liverpool. Expect war.

Liverpool 1 Napoli 0
BEN JOHNSON'S RATINGS

Alisson: 9

What can you say about this fucker? I'm fairly sure he is the best keeper I have seen play for Liverpool. Seriously. Pepe Reina was good and that – first few seasons, till his hands disappeared like a *Back To The Future* photo – but this fella is unreal. His passing, his starting position, his movement, his footwork, the save at the end, everything about him. Untouchable. The best there ever was.

Trent: 8

Was sound, weren't he? You try thinking of something new to say every week. He is one of our best players and is probably going to be up there with Gerrard by the time he finishes. Will that do?

Virgil: 8

Was indignantly slaughtering the referee for the absolute tackle there first half, looking at it back mind you, it was possibly a foul, and possibly a great tackle that somehow bent their lad's leg in half. If he was a normal human centre half you would worry about him getting sent off, but then, he is Virg, and he danced his way through the rest of the game.

Joel: 8

Thought he was excellent again, in fairness. I didn't think he had it in him. And maybe he doesn't, but he's absolutely doing a belter impression of a good centre half at the minute.

Andy Robbo: 8

Imagine him chasing you through the woods. You flicked him the Vs and he clocked you, lashed the handbrake on, opened the door and was on you like a wolf. Reckon with a minute headstart you would last four minutes before he caught you.

Gutted, you're literally left spluttering on your own blood, before he lashes mud on your head, and empties your pockets, walks back to his car muttering something about cheeky English cunts, and then lashes on ABBA's greatest hits.

Henderson: 7

Thought he was shite there first 20 minutes but the crowd were fucking worse. Slaughtering him for not playing the ball forward, even when it wasn't on. That said, he looked like a man whose hips had been locked together when he was trying to turn. Much better second half. On the front foot, not as exposed, linking and starting attacks.

Gini: 8

Kept the ball for about eight minutes of the five added on at the end of the game. Could have carried him around for a month on me shoulders when he just kept rolling them. Another performance to add to the catalogue of evidence that suggests that he plays better against better teams.

Milner: 8

Always available for the ball, always willing to take it, keep his shape, legged them all over the gaff. A James Milner-type performance, really.

Mo Salah: 9

Didn't see his goal there, so mark it yourself. Was discussing Henderson's ability, or lack thereof, to pass the ball forward with the fella behind me. Amazing what happens when you keep the ball, isn't it?

Looks well stronger than last season, doesn't he? Looking forward to him getting Sergio Ramos in a million dollar dream and lashing a 20p price in his grid when he lays him out.

Sadio: 7

Probably could have scored six, didn't fancy it as it wouldn't have been decisive. Saving himself for Sunday, you know.

Firmino: 7

Back upfront, part of the pack who were relentless on the break. Not quite hitting his stride but there or thereabouts.

SUBS...

Brought a load of lads on. Degsi went right back and everyone's undies disappeared down their throats. All worked out though didn't it, lad?

NEIL ATKINSON'S REVIEW

I WHISPER things, the city sings them back to you.

Evening gorgeous. Evening handsome. I thought of you throughout. What a win. What progression.

Four things:
- That is the greatest save I have seen in my whole life.
- The game was mad.
- Mo Salah wants to be the best player in the world.
- Liverpool are the business.

Shall we do them in order?

That is the greatest save I have seen in me whole life.

It was spectacular but it crowned the last 10 days. The footballer who has announced himself most for Liverpool in the last five isn't Naby Keita or Fabinho. It is the goalkeeper.

Alisson has won points, been the pass before the pass for goals and has now provided Champions League progression. It's been underscored by phenomenal charisma. You can taste the pheromones.

He's the first lad to hit puberty, he's Rihanna walking out the restaurant with a wine glass, Rihanna in the red thing with her legs spread letting you know. He's more gorgeous than you, gorgeous. More handsome than you, handsome. Soz.

I mean come on. It is like cheating. But it is like cheating on ours. Cheating on ours is allowed. This cat is the cat. That Liverpool should have been over the hill and far away doesn't matter because Liverpool have the cat. You've got the cat, winning is far easier. Five-a-side rules, lads. And soz, he is on ours. So we win.

The game was mad.

The clock in games like this is a strange thing. A seesaw Liverpool, broadly speaking, managed well but my God it skewed the game.

My guess is 77:43. That's the moment when holding 1-0 overtakes wanting to get the second, to get the third. This isn't a science but that was it for me. Start time wasting.

It wasn't the same as a two-legged encounter then, all of a sudden. But through the whole match it was chaos. The poor fella who sits in front of me in his 60s spent most of it stood. I think he hates me but we had quite the moment when Jose Callejon missed.

Across from me there was beef about standing. The younger lads were bang into The Reds. The older fella bang into sitting down. You know where my loyalties lay in advance, really.

It was huge this game. I barely sat second half, not least because of my man in his 60s. He got it, he understood it. Sitting down was just not an option. My point would always be this:

This is what we are in it for.

This is what it is to be alive.

The fella in his 60s who I think hates me, I now love him. Because he loves The Reds. Because he loves to be alive. Lord, let me always be him, not the lad having murder with younger people having a good time.

Lord, let Liverpool always win mad games.

Lord, let me always see the 94th minute with my heart pounding. Let me feel alive.

Mo Salah wants to be the best player in the world.

I loved Koulibaly tonight. Because he decided he was giving Mo Salah a tough test.

All the best.

All the best when you win seven from seven of the first battles and he just makes an absolute show of you. All the best when he decimates you. Because – this is important – you can be the best and be destroyed. You can win seven from seven and lose the eighth, and there it is.

Leo Messi is the best anyone has ever been at football but he is getting on. Cristiano Ronaldo is the second best anyone has ever been at football, but he is over a hill, though still irresistible in bursts. There is about to be a vacancy.

The thing about those two was you could stop them, but keeping stopping them was the thing that was almost impossible. They won't be denied over and over, whoever you are. Mo Salah is in this category now. He is irresistible and he is getting better. He is the best in the country. And the country is a good one.

Someone will be the next best player in the world. He might play for Liverpool.

Liverpool are the business.

I wanted him to play Keita. I wanted him to play Matip. I wanted him to play 4-4-2, you know.

Henderson has a bad 10 and a shaky half, but then runs the second. Milner constantly likely without quite producing. Wijnaldum the best he can be. This team is astonishing and we take it lightly.

The facts:

They are won 13, drawn three from 16 league games.

This is the fourth best since association football started in the top flight in this country. Not since 1992 or since Shankly or since World War II. But since it began.

AND: They have progressed from a group with Napoli and Paris Saint-Germain.

Both Napoli and Paris Saint-Germain are really good.

It hasn't been perfect but then that is the point. Liverpool are being brilliantly managed and are able to ride their luck and are the absolute business. And it is possible they may now be coming to the boil.

Let's not pull our punches, they deserved to win 5-1 tonight. Sadio Mane missed a hat trick. Salah should have scored two, won a pen and got two assists. They didn't manage that but Liverpool still won, still prevailed.

These midfielders aren't clowns. These defenders aren't just Virgil van Dijk. Liverpool are excellent. They are an astonishing football team.

Walk around them, Reds. Green light, Reds. Let's be alive in February. Let's be alive now.

Liverpool v Manchester United

Sunday December 16, 2018

ROB GUTMANN'S PREVIEW

YOU know what I love about Anfield? Every time I go there I feel like a child.

I was a kid when I first went there. I'm far from one now, but in that place, I will be forever.

As Liverpool summoned the gods and overwhelmed Napoli on a chilled Tuesday December night, I was a jack in a box in my seat. I couldn't settle myself the whole night long. I'd occasionally glance leftwards to catch the eyes of my two sons and sensed their embarrassment and mirth at my immaturity. 'What's that dickhead doing now?' Oh, the things that we do when watching The Reds.

I was ready to lose the Champions League, our beloved Champions League. I've said it before, no English club more defines themselves by that competition than us. But then again, no other side from this country is more about winning the league, about being the champions, the best team in England. We are truly a club torn between two great endless loves.

Our wild night with the European Cup, in midweek, must now be filed and the next challenge prepared for. Europe will be there for us again in February. We haven't lost our cup just yet. It's back to league action this weekend and a matchup with the nasty neighbours.

Manchester United remind us, more than most, about who we are and where we've come from. Our rivalry with them seems to defy contexts. It's never mattered whether we were shit and they were top dogs, or vice versa, the aching to beat them never goes away.

They're not in a good place at the moment, while we're flying. The opportunity to check us though, will motivate and focus Jose Mourinho like nothing else can. I think we hold a special place in his heart. I suspect we are his great lost love, the one that got away. I could be completely wrong, but we just seem to affect him.

Anfield certainly affected him on that night in May 2005, when his champions Chelsea fell to European Cup semi-final defeat. The apparent illogicity of the outcome has always vexed him. They were much better than us, but we were Liverpool and we had Anfield. Jose has always wanted to possess Anfield.

I'll never forgive him for the way he almost spitefully set up a Chelsea team to do nothing more than frustrate us as we stood on the crest of a league title win in 2014. Of course, he was entitled to be conservative in the face of our attacking machine that year, but he seemed to take the challenge more personally than was necessary. His team had virtually nothing to play for, yet it remained his mission to hurt us. You most hurt the one you love.

The world is criticising and pointing fingers at Man United at the moment. They are perennially football's favourite story. Mourinho will be seething with envy at Liverpool's progression and will savour an opportunity to remind that he is not the spent force football wants him to be.

We all expect him to set up this mediocre United outfit to simply park the Jose bus and stifle the existence out of the game. That's probably exactly what he will attempt but you never know with Mourinho. His sense of the theatrical is never ending. Maybe he'll simply attack us, just for shits and giggles.

Mourinho will appreciate that this current Liverpool side are not daunted by teams that low block. If anything, they relish it. I think Klopp will treat United like the mid-table team they have become. He will not show them the respect he showed Napoli in the week.

To this end, expect him to revert to his recently favoured 4-2-3-1 formation. Xherdan Shaqiri could well come back in, as well as Naby Keita. Both were pivotal in the demolition of Bournemouth last weekend.

Given that the squad will enjoy the rare respite of six game-less days following United, there shouldn't be any rotation for its own sake. The main front three should go again. From the midfield pool, Gini Wijnaldum and Fabinho may all find themselves benched to facilitate returns for Shaqiri and Keita. James Milner may again stoically deputise at right back.

Liverpool are brimming with confidence. I want this bubble to stay unburst indefinitely. Good things can come to good people. The Reds are delivering us Christmas after Christmas and we've not even put our stockings out yet.

If you don't feel like a child again in the midst of all this you're doing it wrong. I just want to always feel this way.

Forever young.

Liverpool 3 Manchester United 1
BEN JOHNSON'S RATINGS

HAHAHA. They are worse than us under Hodgson.

Alisson: 7

Oh for fuck's sake. Had hard lines for the goal, there. Catches it and hits his own legs and bobbles out. That said if that was Miggy I'd currently probably still be strangling him. In the changies, as Jürgen is giving his team talk. 'Don't mind me lad, I'll be finished in a minute.' Nothing else to do there for the rest of the match, did he?

Clyne: 7

Actually did alright for a fella who has been on gardening leave for six months. First start back, tough ask to play 90.

'Getting picked up for footy. Doing 90 today, Johno.'

'Fucking hell lad, I thought I was getting the last 10. Just had three eggs on toast and a Wispa, for fuck's sake.'

Degsi: 7

First half, 2015 Degsi was back. Couldn't pass the fucking thing 10 yards. Looked like a massive, big accident waiting to happen. Absolute piano at the top of a hill. He was playing like a chicken after a Gary. I couldn't believe the shot. I thought we had fucking waterboarded that out of him after that one against Aston Villa in the FA Cup. Extra point for the overhead kick.

Virgil: 8

Didn't give Lukaku a sniff, first half. Exceptional as per. That said, he's had some dinners there Lukaku, hasn't he? Got legs like a postie. Addicted to Yazoo him, mate.

Andy Robbo: 8

That lad playing for them, who no fucker has ever heard of, reckons he has got the beating of him. Robbo swatted him away like he was playing against kids. Surging runs going forward, intelligent use of the ball. Ran like a man possessed. Reckon that Young Fathers' track from the Apple advert just plays in his head. Non stop. The loop.

Fabinho: 8

Front foot with everything there first half. Acres of space, used it well. Needs to not bother shooting I reckon, but that aside was boss.

Absolutely made up to be wrong about him. Thought he was too slow to play centre mid for us. I am so jam packed full of shit it is unbelievable, you know. It really is incredible that these dopey fuckers let me mark people out of 10. Bananas.

Gini: 8

Ticked it over and found space all day long. He'd go far on *Love Island*, I reckon.

Naby: 7

Does well to get out of the way of Lukaku, there. Twenty stone of strawberry milkshake landing on your leg doesn't end well. Feels like he needs to do more when he is getting it with them squared up on the edge. On the edge of setting the world on fire.

Firmino: 8

Bright, there. Picking up space, using it well. Great foul when he gave it away. Was absolutely fantastic second half. The megs on Rashford was horrible, la.

Sadio Mane: 8

Best player first half. Great movement all day long. Cool as fuck for the goal. Better than any of their players by a mile.

Mo Salah: 8

He's so strong now, you know. Their grocks were practically wrestling him but he just bounced them. Unlucky not to score, really.

SUBS...

Shaqiri: 10

What can you say? He's like someone has sprinkled angel dust on a gnome. The absolute best fella I have ever seen. Magic. Was absolutely, obviously always going to get the winner there, wasn't he? Glorious.

Hendo: n/a

Done well when he come on, there.

NEIL ATKINSON'S REVIEW

IT was almost mundane. It was simultaneously magic. Manchester United tragic.

The form book didn't go out of the window. It rarely does. Since Rafa Benitez arrived at Anfield, broadly speaking, Liverpool have got the results they should against Everton and Manchester United. This season Liverpool have done that at Anfield in back-to-back home games.

The win against United was in part forged against Everton. The victory against Everton has settled The Reds into the moment. It has given them the fillip they needed. Since then it has been nothing but league wins, strong performances and last 16 qualification in Europe. But it has been assurance.

And Liverpool were assured against Manchester United, they were as certain of victory as it is reasonable to be. In fact, complacency was more likely to undermine them than anything Jose Mourinho or his players could do. Liverpool would find a way. Liverpool dismissed their opponents. It was almost mundane.

There was dominance everywhere. There wasn't a Liverpool player who didn't win their battle. Nathaniel Clyne was theoretically the weakest link, but he didn't play like it. The only question mark wasn't his quality but his energy. It is one hell of an ask off so little match fitness.

Andy Robertson on the other side was the opposite. His energy is incredible and his certainty when Alisson played out to him was repeatedly brilliant. He starts the move that leads to the second goal taking the ball under insane pressure before arrowing a diagonal into the midfield.

Fabinho had a whale of a time. He was in his pomp, enjoying space and picking his time to win his battles. His selection part of the manager doing his business well.

He picked a side which was very fluid and started Sadio Mane from the right with Mo Salah through the middle. But the best first-half performance in attack was Roberto Firmino who similarly had a whale of a time. What was difficult in general for The Reds a few weeks back suddenly looks a joy.

Jürgen Klopp brings on a sub and that player scores two. When that happens a manager will be acclaimed but the player himself deserves massive credit.

Xherdan Shaqiri finds his spaces like a man watching on from the sidelines and visualising how he helps the side win. He picks his moments brilliantly and shows all the time. His shots, while deflected, were sensible and it is his sense which has surprised far more than anything else – dancing on the light-up floor.

Liverpool had 36 shots. It is an astonishing fact and, while it is arguably 10 too many (hiya, Dejan), it shows just how dominant they were. How easy it was. It shows they battered Manchester United 'til kingdom come.

They are coming to the boil as the decorations go up. They are aiming to be top of the pops while we hit the turkey. Seasons have seasons, have rhythms, seasons wax and wane, and right now this feels like the time of Jürgen Klopp's mighty boys in red. Hang onto our coattails if you can.

The new normal being seeing off Manchester United mundanely is sound, long may it continue. But the new normal in terms of what Liverpool are doing to the Premier League cannot be dismissed as easily.

Liverpool have now played 17, won 14 and drawn three. This is simply incredible. It isn't championship form; it is beyond championship form, while simultaneously there are no guaranteed championships.

But there are no guaranteed championships for anyone right now. Manchester City will again have been watching on, again hoping, again disappointed. Liverpool are going at a rate only they can cope with, perhaps performing in a way only they can cope with, and both red and blue Mancunian stomachs will have fluttered today.

For now we bask. Top of the league, the ultimate form book. Seventeen hurdles down, 21 to go. Liverpool's dismissal of Manchester United in our back pocket.

It's fabulous. And it is also just one of them.

What The Win Over
Manchester United Represented

Monday December 17, 2018

GARETH ROBERTS

ULTIMATELY it was only three points.

However, it was also much more than three points as the smiles, the hugs and The Kop's impromptu rendition of Wonderful Christmastime proved.

Manchester United – and Jose Mourinho – had long since cemented a place in the pain-in-the-arse category for Liverpool.

They're a side that has traditionally put sticks in the spokes of The Reds, winning more than they've lost historically, and seemingly doing it plenty when victory hasn't always been deserved.

Any Red can recall Liverpool hard-luck stories against Manchester United, while victory has always tasted sweet.

Despite their current problems, Mourinho's issues, and the general vibe around the team and squad, fears that they would turn up at Anfield and rip up the odds that had them as wide as 5-1 to win, weren't totally unfounded.

When Jesse Lingard pounced on a rare error from Alisson Becker to level the scores on 33 minutes, there was a palpable pin-drop moment at Anfield.

Everyone of a Liverpool persuasion looked around Anfield for a flag, waited for a whistle – after the utter domination from Jürgen Klopp's side up to that point in the match, how could a side as poor as United had been possibly have scored, and scored like that?

But they had. And the celebrations in the Anfield Road said it all – they knew they had nicked one and gave it the big one accordingly. A draw in those circumstances would have been celebrated like a win on the coaches heading back to Manchester.

For us, in that moment, it was easy to worry. This is what they do. This is what happens when we play them and play him.

We'd waited since Daniel Sturridge's winner under Brendan Rodgers for a league win against Manchester United on home soil. Was the wait to go on even longer, with a side as good as this against a side as bad as that?

Then there was the Manchester City aspect. From players and supporters through to the manager Pep Guardiola, you know they were watching, waiting and hoping.

As Liverpool's defence was decimated by injury pre match, those hopes were surely raised another notch.

After doing their job against an obliging Everton, City wanted a favour from their Salfordian friends. In any race, any fight, any battle, you look for a sign of weakness. United's psychological voodoo – and any inability to overcome it – could have been just that.

A draw against Manchester United wouldn't have been the worst result given the context mentioned above. Yet Liverpool showed hunger for more. Klopp and the players will always say publicly they care little for what City are doing – it's exactly the right message.

Yet it can't have gone amiss that, having nosed in front at the top of the table last weekend, to fail to maintain that advantage just a week later would have been a boost to City – and a blow for The Reds.

Instead, the reverse is true. Liverpool aren't going away. And if 'luck' is playing a part, as Mourinho suggested, then all the better. If that's the story, and the story helps us, then keep that story alive.

For years we witnessed Manchester United benefit from 'luck' – the late winners, the dodgy penalties, the substitute turning the match that looked over and done. It became an art form under Alex Ferguson, much to our misery. 'We never lose, we just run out of time,' was their mantra.

And here's Liverpool doing the same. Divock Origi winning the derby. Nathaniel Clyne in from the cold to contribute and contribute well. And Xherdan Shaqiri winning it on Sunday, after arriving from the bench like a football superhero ready to unleash his powers.

There's belief, desire and confidence coursing through The Reds now – all of them. And what about in the stands?

While, yes, there was a little wobble post goal, what was noticeable was that it was shortly followed by a collective shrug.

Twitter's 'banter' accounts might have been enjoying themselves slaughtering Alisson for the goal but there was very little of that inside Anfield. Two mistakes in 17 league games? Where's the fire? What he has brought to Liverpool is obvious to anyone who has watched the side regularly and a split-second slip up changes nothing.

Equally, where was the fire conceding an equaliser? Liverpool would come again and come good. The mid-table mediocrity suggested United were a busted flush. The performance on Sunday proved it. Surely Liverpool would prevail. There was little panic in the performance or the support.

A win over Manchester United, however poor and crisis-ridden they might be, is another tick in the box for the title credentials of this Liverpool team, as is bouncing back from an equaliser in such unfortunate circumstances.

In the past, not so long ago, we have seen Liverpool lack the requisite mental fortitude in similar circumstances. We have seen fans file out the stadium. We've witnessed body language that is all wrong. There is none of that now.

Outside our bubble, there will be more talk of 'luck'. Inside it, we can add Shaqiri to the front three as a man who can now be looked upon as a bona fide match-winner, from the start or from the bench. From talk of a player with an attitude problem, we're instead watching a star that looks determined to make an impact every time he takes to the pitch.

Next up, it's Wolves in a tough-looking Friday night fixture. Tough or not, it's also an opportunity to further underline those title credentials. A win where City could only draw, a four-point lead before City next kick a ball and a cementing of a position that has been too alien to Liverpool since the last title party. The motivation is clear.

Every three points feels huge now, every game matters. And this is exactly how we want it. The same must surely apply to the players and the performances say so.

After 17 games last year The Reds were fifth, trailing leaders City by 18 points. This year they lead them by one having beaten Guardiola's side three times in 2018.

It has to be in their heads, it should definitely be in ours. This Liverpool is the real deal and is ready to tick more boxes between now and May.

A Wonderful Christmastime awaits.

Wolves v Liverpool

Friday December 21, 2018

ROB GUTMANN'S PREVIEW

THERE'S something about a game on the edge of Christmas. Tensions are heightened in the best way.

The seasonal context inexplicably enhances the sense of excitement. Maybe it's because we allow ourselves to be lovingly brainwashed from a young age to associate everything about this time of year with the most glorious sense of anticipation.

We aren't just going to Molineux this Friday night to get three points, we're on a mission to win Christmas. And there's a league title being chased down too.

Right now, Liverpool are champions elect. We're being allowed to savour this mantle for a good period. We took it at Bournemouth nearly two weeks ago, and we're looking increasingly equipped to fulfil our destiny.

I want us to beat Wolves on Friday night, and then Newcastle next Wednesday so that we can all feel this way for yet another full week.

Kids often say to me: 'Hey old timer, what was it like to be a Red and see them win all those league titles?' Well, funny thing is young 'uns, I don't really remember the exact moments we were crowned – when the winning of the league became a fact. I do recall the mood of the seasons, though.

I remember times of year when things felt that they were moving our way. I had a sixth sense in certain campaigns that it was our time. Those ancient great Liverpool teams had moments in seasons when they'd truly click into gear. We could sense it, we could see it.

A month or so ago we were a good team having a good season. There was a sense, though, that we were moving towards a turning point of sorts. Would we fall back from our trajectory and come to expect merely mortal rewards for this season, or would we 'click', find our true greater selves and push on?

Jürgen Klopp's Reds have been emphatic in their response to these ponderings. Six straight league wins and Champions League knockout qualification tells its own story. Drill down deeper and there's been so much to savour.

The renaissance of Mo Salah, the ebullience of Xherdan Shaqiri, the relentlessness of Andy Robbo, the majesty of Virgil van Dijk, the coming of Fabinho. All across the park, throughout the squad, individual after individual is writing his own history. No one accepting being passenger.

None shall keep down Joel Matip, Divock Origi or Nathaniel Clyne. Liverpool are a bandwagon all are now clinging to for dear life.

The spacing of fixtures around Christmas is something that shocked Klopp when he first started working in England. Mere 48-hour gaps between games forced him into some extreme line up choices. This winter, things are a little different.

Liverpool will have 'rested' for six days by the time they face Wolves. There's five days respite, then to Newcastle. Arsenal arrive at Anfield four days after that. By English football scheduling standards, this is as relaxed a programme as a manager could wish for.

Regardless, I think the manager will look to give each player at least one game's respite over the period. For instance, I'll predict that Salah will be benched for Newcastle on Boxing Day.

Wolves, though, Klopp may view differently. It's the gateway fixture to the Christmas bundle. He will want this game won and dusted. That means he sends Liverpool out as strong as possible.

Wolves, with three straight wins and an enviable record against the league's top six will be a serious test for the potential champions of England. That will not deter Klopp from reverting to his long-time favoured 4-2-3-1 formation. That will necessitate a recall for Shaqiri, and boy does Xherdan deserve it.

His two goals that served to get a Manchester United manager sacked ensure him a place forever in our folklore. But Xherdan isn't content with cult-hero status. He wants to push on and show that he's the real deal.

Klopp will likely pick four of the back five that played against United. He must decide between fit again James Milner and a reborn Clyne for the right-back position. Both have durability issues at the moment (Milner back from injury, Clyne possibly match rusty) and the Liverpool manager will make his decision based on what he sees in training this week.

If Klopp does recall Shaqiri and go 4-2-3-1, it will mean at least one of his central midfielders having to make do with bench duty. My hunch is that we'll see Gini Wijnaldum and Fabinho given another chance to develop a partnership, with Jordan Henderson saved for Newcastle on Boxing Day and possibly beyond.

Wolves may be feeling buoyant and very much at home in the top half of the league right now, but they have not had to face the country's in form and most irrepressible front four yet.

It's the most wonderful time of the year. It's been the most wonderful year. Happy Christmas, everyone.

Wolves 0 Liverpool 2
BEN JOHNSON'S RATINGS

Alisson: 8

Makes a good save that looked like a shite save first 15 there, sneaky little deflection. Makes everything look a piece of piss. That chance where Robbo backheeled their lad in with five to go; he doesn't save it, doesn't need to, closed him down like a fucking massive big dust storm. Fucking score now, shit head.

James Milner: 7

Took loads of time out of the game when it was needed first half. Kept it well.

Degsi: 7

First 10 minutes. Chasing their lad down the line. Three men in the boozer at the same time say 'Stand up, Degsi'. Degsi fell over, somehow. Fancies himself as a reverse Nostradamus there based on that first-half performance. Crying it in. Better second half.

Virgil: 9

Their fast lad tried getting after him for a bit, and then fucked him off for the easier prey of Degsi. We had a conversation there at 1-0 about him being better than any of our best ever centre halves put together, but come to the conclusion he needs to score more. Then he bangs like fucking Aldo. Sublime.

Andy Robbo: 6

Unusually gave it away every time he touched it in the first 10 minutes. Struggled first half. The only Scottish fella who doesn't like the rain. Them fuckers dry their fucking clobber in it.

Give their lad a backheel for a laugh in the last minute to keep our goalie on his toes. The Albie Moreno run-out clock has about three days left on it.

Fabinho: 8

Still in the changies in the first minute when he played their sprinter in. Then looks front foot for fun, fancies overlapping and getting The Reds on the march with a belter ball to Mo for the first.

Mad the way he is better than Souness, Gerrard, Alonso and Didi Hamann put together, and I was calling him a crab a month ago. Drifted out of it a bit second half but then so fucking what.

Henderson: 7

Played well in tandem with Fabinho. Does well second half breaking it up. Played Mo in a few times down the channel really well.

Naby: 7

Bright at times. Got wellied all over the place at times. Is going to be amazing at some stage, probably for the last month of the season to win us the treble. Had a mad patch on his stomach there when he was going off. Could be a nicotine patch.

Ciggies are boss. Vapes are the pits – end of the world. Think of all the bad shit going on in the world. Coincides with ciggies going out of fashion. Get them down your neck, la. World peace.

Mo Salah: 9

Movement for his goal was fucking ridiculously good. Then for a laugh, just flicked it over their defender. Yer, I'll just flick this over there. Like Subbuteo. Such a threat. Legged them second half, could have scored 15. Our mate had him first goal and 3-0, made up he never scored again. Well in, lad.

Firmino: 8

Was excellent there, first half. Link play, touch, vision, workfare, muzzy. Not in it as much second half.

Sadio: 7

Looked like he was doing that Mickey Finn thing, where he pretends he can't be arsed but then legs someone, except he didn't really leg anyone.

SUBS...

Lallana:

Forgot about him there, you know. Did alright.

Gini: 9

Cost our mate £300 with that miss last minute. Tremendous.

NEIL ATKINSON'S REVIEW

IT teemed down. It bounced down. It danced down. And you're damn right we danced.

Fucking hell, that was glorious. And fucking hell it was. Mad Friday and a mad Friday night in Wolverhampton, possibly the best night out in Wolverhampton that has ever been had. A crazy night out in the driving rain when you could have seen Liverpool players slide all over the show and make a mess.

Even through torrential, pouring, biblical rain, Liverpool's class shone through. Liverpool stood tall as it bounced, as it danced. Liverpool soaking and resplendent. What a gang of lads. What a set of heroes.

Mo Salah's speed, right until the 95th minute was immense. Wolves weren't even that bad. They were just left in the cold by a man whose gift from God cannot be beaten. You might think it would be impossible to control the ball in such a storm, but Salah has skill, control and precision, even while lashed by water from every direction.

However, the travelling pilgrims who had come from Liverpool to the West Midlands had the most hymns for the man not leading the charge for The Reds, but for the big fella at the back.

Both Salah and Virgil van Dijk scored at Molineux. Both played brilliantly through the bouncing rain, but Virgil's control of every aspect of the game probably gives him the stronger claim for man of the match. It was lovely watching him burn off Adama Traore, a siege weapon of a footballer. More rugby league than association football, but no less dangerous for it.

Honestly, let me tell you, lad. Honestly, let me tell you, queen. Let me tell you what it was to watch that game in those conditions. The potential for it to go wrong was everywhere, but Liverpool found their way through everywhere. This was the essence of managing imperfection.

There is this thing – our rivals for the big one are better than us at perfection, better at purity. Occasionally we crave purity, but our boys are brilliant at imperfection. Brilliant at the chaos, and the filth, and the mud and the driving, pissing rain. The driving, pissing rain defined a contest in Wolverhampton and while Wolves are a good side, Liverpool were better.

While there is something around the Liverpudlian tradition of pitching teammates against one another, Jordan Henderson and Fabinho complemented each other gorgeously in the middle of the park. They locked so much down and propelled so much forward. They looked a lovely two, all size and certainty. Walk around them.

Possession wise, Liverpool's 60-plus per cent tells the usual story. While the ball was heavy and – like in the recent derby – the football was never going to be as attractive as in dry conditions, neither Liverpool nor Wolverhampton gave up the attempt to pass the ball with grace.

It just happens The Reds are at least 10 per cent better at it. It just happens Liverpool have more cutting edge, have better players in every position. It just happens that however good Willy Boly does, Liverpool can do that bit better.

I feel a bit sorry for their lads. Firstly, they whacked some absolute bangers on pre match which was great of them because it set the whole night up marvellously. Then they played well. They have loads of football players doing odd things. It's not easy in that side but when it works it finds unexpected space. They are a board game you aren't quite sure of the rules too.

But Liverpool are great at dice and great at working out what to do with good throws and bad throws. Liverpool are irresistible. Liverpool are played 18, won 15 and lost sweet fuck all.

Salah caps a lovely move, van Dijk stands up to his song, 10 men give everything and James Milner keeps it in the corner so long he has squatter's right by the time it is over. He keeps it in our corner.

They are all out Liverpool. All out for each other and their manager and for us. Liverpool's players and manager and staff can't go to town. We can. We will.

And it is Mad Friday. Black Friday before the other black Friday gegged in. It's a night to savour, and enjoy, and get stuck into.

Eighteen down, 20 to go. Dancing in the rain. You are damn right we danced.

Liverpool v Newcastle United
Wednesday December 26, 2018
ROB GUTMANN'S PREVIEW

I HOPE you're reading my preview a bit pissed and soaked with Christmas cheer.

That way you'll be kinder with me and my flow. I'm not sure exactly where I'm going with this other than to say it will be off somewhere near the deep end. Keeping it together at the moment is no easy ask. The Reds are on fire and setting our worlds ablaze.

There have been moments in this season, a season of moments, where it feels like Liverpool haven't so much 'passed tests' as reached markers.

Early on I'd said here that I thought we needed to go to Wembley and beat Tottenham to plant the first flag in this season's title race. That was done, with minimum fuss. More recently it's been about facing the challenges of the upper-middle rankers; Watford, Everton, Bournemouth, Manchester United (yeah, I know) and Wolves.

Draws in any one of those games would have been no disgrace. In fact, two or three draws and a couple of wins from those four would have represented a solid return, given that three of the games were away at difficult grounds.

But Liverpool are better than that. Liverpool have won all of these games.

Seven straight wins now, Champions League knockout stage qualification, 48 points from 54 on offer. These are not the things we took for granted in August. A league title challenge was, if not exactly demanded, politely expected.

Ordinarily, a team with around 40 points at this stage would consider themselves worthy of topping the table. Had the gods told us that we'd be looking towards 50 by the halfway point in the season we wouldn't have believed in them.

Manchester City, the greatest points-gathering machine in the history of title winners in England, are the yardstick for a Liverpool side who are on course to break the club points record in the top flight. It's wonderful and cruel in equal measure. That they've just recently shown fragility must only encourage us further.

Newcastle's arrival in the midst of the Christmas fixture mire is a tease of a game. The Geordies aren't a great side, but Rafa Benitez is such a redoubtable force that they'll ultimately prove too resilient to go down. That's not our concern though, we have the biggest fish to fry.

Jürgen Klopp knows that Arsenal come to ours just three days after Boxing Day and will be the feistiest of opponents. Liverpool will need to be at their freshest to equally be at their angriest and most aggressive.

If the manager makes the changes I think he'll make for the visit of Newcastle then, by the time Arsenal rock up on Saturday night, a few key lads could be as good as boxfresh.

They would be Andy Robertson, Fabinho, Naby Keita, Mo Salah and Bobby Firmino, who will all have played no more than a single game over the last week, IF the manager takes risks against Newcastle.

What do those risks look like? Is dropping Albie Moreno in at left back a gamble too far? If Liverpool fail to beat Rafa's team it will be viewed as such.

Keita was kicked from pillar to post at Wolves so resting him and bringing Adam Lallana into the team doesn't feel too much of a stretch.

The decision that may attract most attention would be the one to take Salah and possibly Firmino out of the fray. Not entirely out, mind. Both could be held back for late impact. They would represent some seriously sexy insurance policy.

It is inevitable that Shaqiri will get a much deserved start. I think Sadio Mane will dovetail with him and one of Daniel Sturridge or Divock Origi will complete the front three spearhead.

In midfield, perhaps the not overplayed Henderson and Wijnaldum will augment Lallana. Klopp believes – almost as an act of faith – that a manager must trust his squad. Without that trust, they will fail and he will go down with them. His belief system faces another test on Boxing Day, then. Ours too.

Jürgen Klopp promised that one day he would turn doubters into believers. Just right now, I'd drink any Kool-Aid type potion this man proffered towards me. I believe, boss. I really do.

Do what you know is best? Take us with you to where you're going. Take us to the promised land. Take us home.

Liverpool 4 Newcastle United 0
NEIL ATKINSON'S REVIEW

THE Title Truism…

'It's a marathon, not a sprint.'

It is a marathon and a sprint. It is an 800m race, two laps of the track where you run as fast as you can. It's long distance, it's dead fast. It's tactical, it's breakneck. It's momentum and it's momentous.

We saw both of those today. We saw Liverpool's irresistible momentum, when Newcastle United became powerless to resist, when having worked so hard to keep Mo Salah quiet they just had to foul him and give up, when there was nothing to do but take 2-0 and finally there wasn't even that.

Liverpool were both brilliant and grinding, and had the momentum with them. The momentum today was set from the back, from Virgil van Dijk and Jordan Henderson. The former all assurance, the latter all demands of his teammates, of the referee, of himself. It was never going to drop with van Dijk on the pitch, never going to slow with Henderson.

We watch Liverpool, we love The Reds but we struggle to see at times how hard they are to deal with. Newcastle played well for 45 minutes, they worked really hard, kept shape, blocked passing lanes and all round were solid. They were 1-0 down and grafting like nothing on earth to do it.

We ask so many questions. Stop the main man, deal with Sadio Mane. To have a Mane solution, you need to have thought about Xherdan Shaqiri and Roberto Firmino. Want to stop the ball getting to them? Get on Henderson and Gini Wijnaldum. But what about the full backs? Sorted that? OK. What about van Dijk?

Rafa Benitez shared with us the metaphor of the blanket in football. Your blanket can cover your head or your feet but never both. There is no blanket equipped to deal with the irrepressible Reds.

Today showcased momentum but was momentous. The rumble and roar from The Reds when the news spread that Leicester City had scored a second against Manchester City was spectacular. It showed how engaged this club is with the business in front of it. Anfield was suddenly red raw, adoring its heroes, screaming in defiance.

For weeks football's punditry class has wondered if Liverpool can continue to match Manchester City's pace. It was looking in the wrong place.

Since Divock Origi's header Liverpool have been simmering towards the boil, whereas Manchester City have been cooling. A late goal conceded at Watford, and then Liverpool won at Bournemouth, and nothing has been the same since. Liverpool doubled down at Wolverhampton and City have so far been unable to respond. So far.

They are an excellent side with fabulous players. Tottenham Hotspur the same. So far. But Liverpool kicked 50 metres ago, have heard the bell and glanced behind them to see they have some space.

This Liverpool side will presumably at some point wobble, but it won't be through nerves. They have shown magnificent bottle to this stage of proceedings and they have a sudden strength, as well as a strength in depth.

People will say the challenge changes once you hit the front but people will be wrong. The challenge for Liverpool remains the same – keep winning. The glory of needing 100 points is that the challenge never changes. Win. Nothing but that. There is no room to manoeuvre.

That's the glory of the 800m race. It hurts, and it exhausts, and it goes so quickly, but there is little room for doubt. You run 400m as fast as you can. A bell rings. You run the next 400m as fast as you can.

No one this season has run as fast as Liverpool. Serious Liverpool. Loving their work Liverpool. Seizing the day Liverpool. Carpe diem.

Nineteen down. Sixteen won. Three drawn. Nineteen down and we know whatever happens against Arsenal we go to the Etihad ahead.

Nineteen down. Nineteen to go. Carpe diem? Carpe jugulum. These are our boys and they are showing their teeth.

Liverpool v Arsenal

Saturday December 29, 2019

ROB GUTMANN'S PREVIEW

HERE we are again.

Face to face with the future we crave. All we've ever wanted. What we've ached for. It's carved in angry biro into every fibre of our long-suffering, Liverpool-loving beings.

We get up in the morning to win the league. We put up with the working week, to win the league. We kiss our kids goodnight, silently praying that one day they will see us win the league. We send our loved ones to their graves pledging that we will win the league for them.

We might win the league. In a way, that's enough. I've loved all the years when we 'might win the league'. Yes, we always get our comeuppance like the eternal tragic heroes we feel pre-destined to be, but the journeys to those points. Oh those journeys. I think I could just about live out my years 'nearly winning the league'.

In some respects, we've never nearly won the league like we've nearly won it this season. We're on the cusp of being the greatest 'nearly won the league' Liverpool team of all time. Whatever happens next, no one can take this nearly achievement from us.

I don't recall Liverpool achieving daylight in a title race since, I don't know, 1987? A gap at the top. Liverpool 'running away with it'. What a thing that is. What a concept. Never in wild dreams did I think I'd see Liverpool take such a decisive grip on this competition.

Of course, by 7.30pm on Saturday night things could look a bit more grounded. Arsenal are good enough to check our flow. But if we can just summon ourselves again, bring our fury once more, and just dispatch them, then we go to Manchester City as a bonus game of sorts. I'd take us coming up for air on January 4, with a four-point lead on City. Three points on Spurs would be fine too. The programme post City favours us.

Two weeks ago I made a deal with God that said: 'Just let us be within two points of Man City on Friday January 4'. From that base, with the easier 17-game run in, and a bit of fortune, I felt we could win this league. Never did we imagine that our worst case scenario would be a one-point lead over the champions.

Beating Arsenal would be enormous. It's no given but it's well within our gift to give to ourselves. They aren't in form and we're much better than them anyway. The leveller, the potential pitfall, is in fatigue. This Saturday's Anfield game is just 72 hours after the Newcastle victory.

Jürgen Klopp knows that there are five recovery days between this weekend's encounter and that looming six-pointer with City at the Etihad. It will tempt him to ask his A-team to go again, safe in the knowledge of that five-day buffer.

The Liverpool manager can partially refresh by giving starts to Fabinho and Naby Keita without diminishing the threat to Arsenal. Others like Trent Alexander-Arnold and Dejan Lovren, and even Jordan Henderson, have not played so much football that they can't be asked to step it up again.

The gamble, the recurring-theme gamble, is the temptation to put Mo Salah, Roberto Firmino and Sadio Mane into the fray yet again. Klopp could be calculated and pull Salah and Firmino out, knowing that he can still use them as a break glass option from the bench. If that happens it will be because he trusts Daniel Sturridge and Xherdan Shaqiri to more than adequately compensate for their absences.

The manager will allow himself one more sleepless night wrestling with this quandary before finally settling on the 'fuck it and be damned' solution of simply picking his best team.

Make no mistake, though – weary limbs or not – it's a very, very good team.

Liverpool 5 Arsenal 1
BEN JOHNSON'S RATINGS

I MEAN, what are we meant to do in between games?

Live our normal fucking lives? Are you for real? The greatest Liverpool side seen in our lifetimes, lad.

They had a go, there. Pressed high, set traps, risk reward. Got rewarded for the first. The Reds were meant to swallow their undies and panic, yer? Not easy being out on top, is it? Let's just play into their traps, aye. Bang, bang, 2-1. Bang, 3-1. Bang, 4-1. Honk, 5-1. Fucking easy, this shit. Come at the kings you best not miss, shit birds.

Alisson: 8

Nothing to do, made a point blanker when they were offside, then lashed the ball unnecessarily high, and half volleyed one through the eye of a little tiny needle to Firmino to set up the pen. Unbelievable.

Trent: 7

Looked knackered first half, up against their best player, in fairness. Kept at it though, got better as the game went on.

Degsi: 8

Caught in a trap, he couldn't get out. But then, pretty much the rest of the game is a piece of piss. That's how that song goes, isn't it? Or whatever.

Virgil: 9

It is getting a bit silly now. It's almost like he gets a bit embarrassed by having to do something, so spends the game so far ahead of the matrix that at any point in time he can just drop back in and bodycheck some fucker and stroll off with the ball. Glitch in the system, lad. A black cat. Too good.

Robbo: 8

Looked a bit tired so spent the game having a breather every now and again. Booked after a minute or some shit, and didn't get enticed into even half a tackle for the rest of the game. Intelligent as fuck. Like Hawkins, lad, but a taste more mobile.

Gini: 9

Seriously, that first half performance was up there with the best you will see. Sublime. No backwards steps, no foot wrong.

Fabinho: 7

His first 20 minutes made Gini's performance all the more important. Gave it away every time he got it, and that was it. That said, grew into the game as The Reds did and did nothing wrong, and a fair few things right, after that. Nothing to worry about.

Shaq: 9

Like Hacksaw Jim Duggan dressed up for Crimbo playing centre mid for The Reds.

Would not have looked out of place with a fucking big two-by-four in his undies. First touch was perfect every time. Head up every time. Front foot every time. Imagine him suplexing you.

Bono Firmino: 9

> *Si senor.*
> *Dos canas Por favor.*

Dragged The Reds off the deck, slotted the first with a little no-look fella. I spent the celebration getting a piggyback off Adam Melia while simultaneously telling him it had been disallowed until it had calmed down and then I told him it had gone in, apologised, and sat down. I panicked.

Tremendous for the second. Throws the whole ground a Micky Finn with the Mane non pass and then slots against their cold-armed goalie.

Sadio Mane: 8

Aware for the goal, weren't he? Lad next to me called it from before Robbo getting the ball. 'Salah get on your toes, lad.' Well in. Does that rope-a-dope thing where he pretends to be on his heels before legging people for a laugh these days.

Mo Salah: 8

So dangerous. Fair fucks to Big Ols for giving the pen, there. Easiest decision all day to give no pen, there. Makes so much space for everyone else to play in it is ridiculous.

SUBS...

Henderson:

Come on and won about 50 tackles in about 10 minutes.

Lallana:

Crutches turns all day. Spellcheck autocorrect of the day.

NEIL ATKINSON'S REVIEW

IT'S the 93rd minute at Anfield and the madness has taken hold.

The only disappointment is that Liverpool beat Arsenal 5-1, instead of putting six past Unai Emery's dishevelled, ageing cockneys.

That is the madness at Anfield just now. We score five against the fifth best team in the country. We'd love six. We are 6-1, 7-1, 9-1 better. We are head and shoulders. We are taking it easy. We are conserving. Show them the way to go home. Only half a football team.

It's the 11th minute of Liverpool playing Arsenal at our home ground and Arsenal's Ainsley Maitland-Niles receives a cross and slots it in past Liverpool's Alisson Becker. What the fuck. What the fuck. What the actual fuck? Thought the crowd and The Redmen simultaneously.

It's the 14th minute of Liverpool playing Arsenal less than an hour after second-placed Tottenham Hotspur have gone down 3-1 at Wembley to Wolverhampton Wanderers, the gradient suddenly too steep. The sudden dark horses wrapped in a blanket. And Roberto Firmino scores and it is bedlam.

The 16th minute. Roberto Firmino scores again. He scores like Barnes. He dances and shimmies and sways in the green light madness. In the stands, people fall over mad with the chutzpah. Driven mad with the passion and desire. Roberto Firmino is in charge of this game and he has decided Liverpool are going to win. How dare Arsenal come to fortress Anfield and score.

And there was the tone set for the rest of the game. They had the temerity. They had the gall. They even had the ball. But the game belonged to the mighty boys in red, to the best team in the land. Perhaps the best on our fractured continent.

It has been a while since Liverpool were awarded two penalties in a game, but neither Salah nor Firmino worked that hard for it and in truth the referee had little choice but to allow both spot kicks at 47 and 65 minutes respectively. In truth you had to feel sorry for the Arsenal defenders who could do little else but to slash and burn once the dangerous forces of Liverpool's front three were staring them down in front of goal.

Yet this wasn't a Liverpool performance that was all about the men upfront. Gini Wijnaldum battled and won those battles to create a central frame through which the ball could pass from wing to wing. When the manager brings on the club captain we got the rare spectacle of Jordan Henderson enjoying himself, the grown-up job done, dominance secured.

It is hard to put into words how much better than any opposite number Wijnaldum was. This could be the best central-midfield performance anyone has put in at Anfield for three years. He was incredible.

Fabinho demonstrates why Reds weren't crazy to mark his signing as compensation for a European Cup lost cheaply after being adored throughout last season. In a game like this, when Liverpool's passing looked like the best in a generation, Fabinho earned his place not by constantly being accurate but by being happy to lose it in the right way. Always smart and smart matters more.

Virgil van Dijk was, as always, Godlike. Like an actual deity. The whole football match happens on his terms. He possibly didn't play as well as the Big Dog but manages omnipotence and omnipresence every time he gets on the pitch.

In recent games, opponents have taken to putting two of theirs on our one Mo Salah. Their only hope to double up. Against better defences, it's still not enough to control him, but in this game he escapes almost every single defensive move. He looks like the most proper number nine. He looks like a force of nature. He dominated the game while barely getting on the ball.

For the penalty he wins, the ball from Alisson should dominate this article. But Gini Wijnaldum, Roberto Firmino and the whole top of the league thing end up prominent.

People will ask, do you dare to dream? I say no. There is better than dreams, there is something better than dreaming. We don't need to dream.

Living. Living is better than dreaming and this is our reality to live right now. Make us dream, Reds? No. This is living, all right.

Twenty down. Eighteen to go. Liverpool just crushed the fifth best in the country. They had the absolute nerve. We had the goals. See you in town.

Don't dream. Just live. Another Liverpool Saturday night.

Ability To Switch Styles Shows Liverpool Are Proper Challengers

Sunday December 30, 2018

CLIVE TYLDESLEY

THE tipping point came at Molineux. Or the Molineux car park to be more precise.

It was there that Gary Neville conceded that The Anfield Wrap had a pundit better than him. Pep, Poch and the rest knew they were in trouble then.

Neil Atkinson's elevation to Carra status may not prove to be the single defining moment of the season, but something the Breck Road Bard wrote in his TAW match review that night came back to me during the heady victory over Arsenal…

'… Our rivals for the big one are better than us at perfection, better at purity. Occasionally we crave purity, but our boys are brilliant at imperfection. Brilliant at the chaos…'

Liverpool led 4-1 at half time on Saturday, and yet it still felt like a far from perfect performance. It was a marvellous mashup.

Fabinho played a suicidal cross-field ball one moment, then quashed a dangerous break the next.

Sadio Mane turned into trouble and lost the ball on the halfway line, then turned effortlessly away from Lucas Torreira and ran at Arsenal's quivering heart.

Dejan Lovren tossed a nothing ball down the right flank that led to the opening goal and was putting put his body on the line to cut out a searching cross minutes later.

Georginio Wijnaldum… No, Gini didn't put a single foot wrong. But he was probably the only one.

This was a performance from last season. This was not the smoothly controlled lockdown display that Liverpool have been perfecting during the early winter weeks. The Grohl guitar was out again. Moshpit football. Heavy duty, full on, in your face, under your skin combat football. Come and have a go if you think you're intense enough.

Liverpool can do both now.

It is bordering on treachery to suggest that they are still not playing as well as they can, and yet Jürgen Klopp himself never misses an opportunity to say that there remains room for improvement. I don't think that's diplomatic flannel.

What has returned during December is the goal threat, the nagging doubt in the minds of even the most stubborn opponents that they can possibly keep Liverpool out.

Pundits (lesser than Neil) still talk about 'that front three' as if they haven't been paying attention to the now regular tactical tweak. When the full backs bomb on, it can feel like a front 10.

It can also feel a little chaotic and crazy. Fever pitch football. It's like grandpa has sat on the SkyPlus zapper and it's all running at x6. You find yourself shouting 'slow it down', 'just keep it', 'take your time' at 42 inches of plasma, but they don't hear you. Not when they are in that manic mood, not when they smell blood. They just keep on coming until the resistance breaks.

No wonder there are deflected goals, borderline offsides, disputed penalties. This is not luck, this is the product of pressure.

When even Kalidou Koulibaly gets caught out, when even Jose Mourinho can't find excuses, when even Lovren smacks a sweet half volley into the roof of the Kop End net, it's because of the build up of pressure.

It's a form of torture, an interrogation. All that arm twisting, all that thumb screwing forces the submission. It is not purity, it is not Silva to Silva to Silva, it is not Manchester City. It's just irresistible at the moment, that's all.

I don't know, you don't know, Klopp doesn't know how Liverpool will handle Premier League leadership. This is largely uncharted territory, but progress always comes with advances into new ground.

This is not a race like an Olympic 10,000-metre final, where the stalking pack are holding something back for the sound of the bell. This is a race where you run every yard flat out. The guys over your shoulder are breathing heavily too.

Saturday's flat-out football will no doubt be tempered at the Etihad on Thursday. Amid all the poppers and streamers that burst out of Liverpool's Christmas crackers, it should be noted that Jordan Henderson has turned in a couple of his best displays of the season. Klopp will want that mature management of games to return for a while now.

The curious thing about the utterings of Messrs Atkinson, Senior and Gutmann in the Wolverhampton rain was how bloody 'on message' they were. Three wise men fresh out of the boozer bearing gifts of caution, courtesy and conservatism (small c). As Rob, the self-proclaimed elder, said: 'I've seen proper Liverpool teams, they haven't.'

Anyone that truly cares about the potential of this season will toe the party line. Those 'proper' teams that Rob and I watched in another century were kings of 'take every game as it comes'. It's the only way, the Liverpool Way. No triumphalism here, please. Not yet.

Make no mistake about it, this team are 'proper' challengers. And in their own image. In two rather different images, actually.

The great and the good of the media were publicly purring about Liverpool's sparkling, splendiferous attacking football on Saturday. They must have missed the Huddersfield and Fulham games. This Liverpool can bump 'n' grind as well as they can rock 'n' roll.

As Neil wrote 10 remarkable nights ago, they are not perfect... But they are brilliant at that.

CHAPTER FIVE – THE CLIFF EDGE

WE all felt it at this point, didn't we?

I say 'we' as Liverpool supporters but I also say 'we' who have seen how these league seasons pan out.

At this point everything feels great, like you could conquer the world, send anybody our way and we'll demolish them beyond recognition. But you know it's early days.

'Don't get carried away.'

One of the worst phrases in football, that. Why not get carried away? For fear that it might not go your way? What a load of bollocks that is.

Absolutely get carried away. Celebrate every single victory like it's the last one you'll see. Dance long into the night fuelled by the fist pumps of Jürgen Klopp in front of The Kop. Live every single step of it.

Everything was still make or break for Liverpool after beating Arsenal 5-1 at Anfield but everything was amazing and it was an absolute joy to be alive. A joy to support this fantastic football team. To be a part of this magnificent journey they were taking us on.

Leave whatever happens in the future to fate. Enjoy the here and now. And we were doing just that. Our best Christmas as supporters of this club. A wonderful christmastime – as we sung from The Kop.

The games will keep coming, thicker and faster as they go, and we'll take nothing for granted. We'll appreciate every moment. The late strikes, the big scorelines, the Trent freekicks, the Divock winners, the Shaqiri magic, the Big Virg goals, the Firmino dances.

Above everything else, we'll remember what it felt like. Magic.

Josh Sexton

Manchester City v Liverpool

Thursday January 3, 2019

ROB GUTMANN'S PREVIEW

THE Reds standing on the edge of a cliff.

They daren't look down. Only look across, to the horizon, to the biggest prize. It's time for all to show faith. The faith that Liverpool will win the Premier fucking League.

That's how I'd feel if I was a Liverpool player. About to face Manchester City in their lair, now, on the cusp of all this. The wind is at their backs, pushing them ever forward. If it were me I would find it difficult to stay cool. I'd be too giddy. I'd get angry, happy, frustrated, bereft with anticipation. But these Liverpool lads are the best in the business. The very best. They're about to prove it beyond doubt.

A month ago we'd never have dreamed how things would play out. We were on Manchester City's coattails and grateful just to be in the same room. We were sighing that in any other season or era that it would be us at the top table. Not cast in the role of plucky seconds, but the real deal. Then crazy things happened. We got better. Much better. And they got worse. Much worse.

And here we are. Liverpool seven points ahead of the 100-point champions. Liverpool, 91 points in their last 38 games. Liverpool scoring, scoring, but barely letting a goal in. Liverpool, Liverpool, top of the league.

And on Thursday night it could well be City's night and they could make us look like shit for that night. But when we wake up on Friday morning and wipe the sleep from our eyes, the worst, the worst of it, is that we will lead this league by four big points. Do your worst Manchester City. Do your fucking worst.

This must bring an end to the sense that it's now or never for Liverpool. Every title challenge we've mustered since 1990 has felt like a smash and grab affair. Like, if we don't seize our chance now, we never would. That realisation tainted all of those ventures. I'm not in it just for the pot, of itself, I want us to be the best. The best team in the land.

We were once, and it made me feel proud. It made us all feel so very proud. We knew it was the lads on the pitch, with their talent, their style and their goals, but they knew too that it was all impossible without us. It's always been this way. And you, me, we know, that if and when this current crop of Reds bring it home, that it will be because of all of us.

Jürgen Klopp has navigated the Christmas fixture programme by keeping players focused only on the immediate challenge in front of them. He's preached 'one game at a time' in every press conference, but all the while he's been readying his side for the Manchester City game.

Legs will be weary, some changes are possible, but key men will be asked to go round once again. That front three and big Virgil are playing every game. They'll get best part of 10 days off after City, surely rested in the FA Cup, but they will need to summon every sinew for one last big push.

I think we'll win at the Etihad. Champions, at some point, definitively win their biggest game and leave no room left for doubt.

We've arrived at that defining moment.

Manchester City 2 Liverpool 1
BEN JOHNSON'S RATINGS

DAYS like today are mad days, aren't they?

I spent the day lurching from a position of admirable calm, serene confidence and general soundness, to one of sheer panic-induced mania.

Like my head is on a metronome and as it ticks left it is the head of a dog riding in the passenger seat of a lovely car with his massive tongue out having an absolute ball, might even have shades on, somewhere like Santa Monica, getting driven by The Rock.

But, uh oh, what's that? The metronome is launching right, I'm now one of them unfortunate souls who feels sick on a train and sticks their head out the window for some fresh air, only to be met by one of them Japanese bullet fellas going full pelt the other way.

Heavy.

Alisson: 8

Fuck all to do except play a bit of footy and then pick one out. Not a great deal he can do with that one. He fucking lashes it in. Makes two great saves second half. Passed to Degsi too much, which done no one any favours.

Trent: 7

Like all The Reds, played well first half and didn't deserve to be one down. Use of the ball was great bar one sloppy one first half. I'm not sure you will ever see a better ball with his wrong foot for the goal, mate. Absolutely means that, greatest ball you have ever seen.

Degsi: 5

Yellow card to mark his greatest contribution as a Liverpool player. Gets legged a few times but in fairness, their tricky lads are boss. You could say he was on his heels for their goal first half, but fucking hell that would be a bit on the harsh side. He's no Virgil. Not a great deal you can do sometimes aside from doff the auld cap.

Unfortunately, second half, they exploited his weaknesses. Mainly his mind. He was wild there, capped off with that ball to Virgil last minute. Hopefully Virgil is hitting him repeatedly in the grid with his boot as we speak.

Only messing, Big Dog.

Virgil: 7

Great block at 0-0. Didn't deserve to be getting beat. Pretty similar second half. Reckon he is in his trying to make a potion of Virgil's marvellous medicine for big Joey Gomez's leg. Missing him like fuck.

Robbo: 8

For a fella whose bird has been in the longest labour ever, he was spot on first half. I was a shambles when my bird was in labour. Ran out the house with no jumper or coat, and me bird had the fucking window open all night, the selfish fucker. Was frozen fucking stiff, lad. Great run and cracking ball for the goal. Didn't deserve to be on the losing team.

Hendo: 7

Played well. Front foot, broke it up. Fine lines, lads.

Milner: 6

Played well while he was on, as they all did. But looked knackered, there. The right change, really.

Gini: 7

Shows some balls to keep the ball in the positions he ends up in, with three fellas legging him.

Sadio: 7

Absolute hard lines with that effort first half. Does everything right. I don't know how that isn't a goal. I don't think anyone does. How the fucking hell does that go through Salah's legs. Seriously. Every now and again, you get one of them. We could have played for a year there and wouldn't have got the rub of the green.

Mo Salah: 6

Really unlucky for the one across the keeper. Great save. Didn't get much out of them, but then they had about six fellas marking him.

Firmino: 7

Thought he was really good all the way through. Linked it well, held his shape, worked hard, a threat, gets the goal.

SUBS…

Fabinho:

Did well when he come in. Great change by the manager. Don't agree with the inevitable cryarsing that says he should have started. Think our shape, tactics and selection were pretty much spot on. That was a coin toss, mate.

Shaq and Sturridge:

Tried to have a go.

NEIL ATKINSON'S REVIEW

GETTING beat hurts. It is rubbish. Hold that close, Reds. Remember that pain.

Four clear. Seventeen games to go. Arsenal and City completed. You'd have taken it at the moment when Virgil van Dijk slices the ball towards Jordan Pickford's goal, by God you'd have taken it. But.

But.

This was the only worry for tonight. The only worry was feeling a tiny bit 'what if'. Feeling regretful. What if we could have forced the issue a tiny bit more? What if Sadio Mane's goal hits the inside of the post and goes in? What if Leroy Sane's comes back out?

There is a reality dawning in these games that they are very 2005-2010. Fine margins, mistakes, pass the parcel football. You have five minutes, we have five minutes. No one playing frightening football, but all the football is frightening.

All the football was neutral. There were classically good performances in these games, Vincent Kompany and Fernandinho arguably both shading it over Virgil van Dijk and Jordan Henderson, each pair the two who most stood up to be counted for each side.

Neither James Milner nor David Silva could get to grips with the game, both were removed. Attackers were hunting for scraps, for moments. The referee bottled big decisions, but they loved a bit of that in 2008 as well.

Basically this: the two best teams in the country knocked lumps out of each other at the end of Christmas. One won. It happens. But.

But.

The game ebbed either way soundtracked at times by their frankly just plain weird bastardisation of the Allez, Allez, Allez song which is oddly about us beating them. Never has a crowd deserved a football team less.

Throughout it all Trent Alexander-Arnold battled with Sane, Sane probably getting the points decision without even counting the knockout blow of his finish. Arnold and Dejan Lovren came under real pressure and just wilted, were just found wanting today. It happens.

For the latter it may perhaps have happened a little too much, but we get nowhere forgetting these are the lads who brought us to the moment they could have gone 10 points clear. Nowhere forgetting the brilliance of their collective start. Nowhere forgetting they terrified Manchester City and made City play, if not the game of their lives, certainly as though their lives depended on it.

Fabinho made a difference and can be thought unlucky not to start. He and Henderson look to perhaps be a pair to bring it home.

The grass was long. The goalmouths scruffy, the game both brilliant and scruffy. Manchester City kept the grass long for Liverpool. They played a back four, a proper back four for Liverpool, they made it scruffy against Liverpool, they fought for everything against Liverpool and they got their win. Their win to be four behind Liverpool. But.

But.

It is not Liverpool's job this season to contextualise how good Manchester City actually are. It was their job tonight to find a way and they didn't quite find it, for all their effort, belief and momentary brilliance from many. It was their job to put five-minute spells together into more, their job to capitalise on a City side swaying before their eyes.

Liverpool's job is clear: 17 more hurdles to be taken and a lead to build back up. We know they can do it; they've done it already. We know how good they can be. They have been that good. Tonight hurts, Manchester City could take 51 from the remaining 51, Manchester City will take some beating. But.

But.

Forget 'what ifs'. Stuff your regrets. Put them in the bin. Forget the frustrations. Remember the pain, but remember the table. Look to the table, look to fact that today is New Year's Eve, tomorrow New Year's Day in a footballing sense and we are top, and top with a cushion.

They are our lads, our lads for record-breaking starts and frustrating defeats, for better or worse. These are the boys who will do this for us, who have done it for us.

Forget the 'what ifs', go with what is.

Liverpool top of the league. Twenty-one down. Seventeen to go. No one better than us.

They'll do for me. *Je ne regrette rien*. Because we are alive.

Brighton & Hove Albion v Liverpool

Saturday January 12, 2019

ROB GUTMANN'S PREVIEW

LIVERPOOL's 5-1 win at Brighton last winter was one of my favourite games of the Jürgen Klopp era.

The Reds were unbelievable that day. It rained goals. So many, that I missed two going for pisses. I didn't care though. It was a joyous afternoon and an indicator that this Liverpool team were readying themselves to become the force they currently are.

The stakes are much higher as Liverpool travel to the deep south this term. We're massive favourites to dispatch Chris Hughton's team but nothing can be taken for granted.

Any kind of Liverpool win should be savoured. It's not important that we're as fluid or destructive as the Liverpool team that tore Brighton apart so comprehensively a year ago. We need only focus on the points.

The long unbeaten run and winning sequence was broken at Manchester City's Etihad Stadium about 10 days ago. The ends of runs are dangerous phases. Many sides don't take becoming mortal again well. Look at City themselves.

A blue streak at the top of the league till December before defeat at Chelsea saw them go on to lose a total of three in five Premier League outings. Liverpool sit proudly four points clear at the league's summit because they were able to exploit City's mental fragility.

Piece by piece, Guardiola has set about rebuilding the confidence in his team that had previously made them so formidable. He has led them to seven and nine-goal wins in their two games since beating Liverpool.

Although the opposition they destroyed was lower league, it was telling that City took both games so seriously. Guardiola was prioritising momentum. He realises that momentum was the key to their 100-point title triumph last season.

I suspect Klopp would like to have followed suit and picked his best team at Wolves on Monday night, but he doesn't have the squad depth City enjoy. The FA Cup was sacrificed to prevent the burnout of key individuals. The price paid was a second consecutive defeat. Losing can become a habit. Just ask Guardiola and City.

Therein lies the scale of the challenge Liverpool face this weekend. It is not simply Brighton who await in our path but our own demons. The monsters that disseminate doubt and gnarl away at confidence. Klopp knows his men must slay the dragons first to defeat Brighton and move on.

It helps to be able to put out a side brimming with freshness after a testing and congested fixture programme. Let's predict that we'll see around nine or 10 changes from the side beaten in the FA Cup.

Although criticised – perhaps harshly – for his performance at Wolves, I can see Naby Keita keeping his place and being one of two to do so, alongside fellow summer signing Fabinho.

Fabinho will be relieved in the knowledge that his likely second start as a centre back for Liverpool will be to the side of the imperious Virgil van Djjk. Joel Matip is back in training but unlikely to be risked so soon.

Also welcomed back will be the keeper Alisson, and first choice full backs Trent Alexander-Arnold and Andy Robertson.

Chris Hughton set Brighton up to frustrate Liverpool last year and to use the attributes of their big men to counter threaten at set pieces. Expect the same again.

I think Klopp will line up with an attacking 4-2-3-1 formation, asking Keita to effectively be the fourth forward in tandem with Mane, Firmino and Salah. Behind them Henderson and Wijnaldum, rested in the cup, should anchor.

On paper, on grass, the 11 Klopp presents on the south coast should be far too strong for the home side. A manager who has mastered minds throughout his career will be tested this weekend.

If he gets his boys right, they win, and the path to the league title suddenly looks clearer again.

Brighton & Hove Albion 0 Liverpool 1
BEN JOHNSON'S RATINGS

I CAN'T take much more of this.

I watched the game kneeling down and started crying at full time. That isn't fucking normal. That's the last game I watch this season when I'm not off me barnet. In fact, I might just bat on like I live in the 1600s; no clean tap water, have to drink lager till The Reds win the league.

Alisson: 7

Not even sure he had to pass the ball first half, never mind anything else. Could have played in a cream pair of slacks and a pair of school shoes, there.

Trent: 8

Rumours he was hurt. Looked alright when he cut that one back that Shaq headed wide, mind you. Thought he was excellent throughout, proper man of the match stuff. Won his battles, kept the ball.

Fabinho: 7

They were trying to get after him and Trent with the big man cheating left wing for them, but did alright. Got sucked under the ball and absolutely forgot about his man for the quarter of a chance Glenn Murray had. Great block second half.

Virgil: 8

Tried to get The Reds playing from the back. Would quite like him just to twat one in there second half, if possible. Absolutely love his arm movements when he is trying to get someone to do something. Did like a helicopter thing for about five minutes to get Trent to move six inches.

Robbo: 8

Played well first half when there wasn't much doing at all. Does great for the Firmino chance that he maybe should have made more of and was great throughout. This defence mate, best in the business.

Henderson: 8

Not a great deal on offer for the midfield in general to pass forward to, first half. Played a couple of loose ones early on that let them break to the edge of our box before we took the ball off them again. Was great second half. Kept the ball, forced the play, broke it up.

Gini: 7

One of them games where he seemed to do nothing until he had to do something and then bossed the last 10 minutes. Extra prom points for going over when their big carthorse centre half was cryarsing about a handball pointing at his chest, to point at his arm.

Shaq: 5

Really unlucky with the header but, that aside, thought he was poor first half. Great little one around the corner to Mo for the pen but that was about it. Shite for the first time, but who gives a fuck?

Sadio: 6

Quiet today, Sadio.

Mo Salah: 8

Quiet first half. Got half a yard first thing second half and got his shot off. That seemed to spark him into life and then he just wragged their lad all over for the pen. Sneaky switch at half time to drop him deep worked a charm. Got The Reds playing today, the difference maker. When he missed that sitter I thought I was going to be sick, though.

Firmino: 7

Thought he was good, made space for himself, was pretty central to loads of stuff The Reds did right.

SUBS...

Naby:

Come on and give it to them for a laugh.

Milner:

Fella.

NEIL ATKINSON'S REVIEW

PRESSURE. Did you feel it?

I know I did. I was a quiet mess before the game and first half. I was a state, quietly bubbling, quietly seeing the worst at every opportunity. How's your bottle? Ask me on 23, there. Gone, mate. Gone.

The worst was only ever this: Nil. Nil. That was the worst I could see but that worst hurt a great deal. The worst was indeed the worst. Nil. Nil. Liverpool impotent. Liverpool stuttering. Liverpool knocking at the door. But. But. But.

And then Mo Salah happened to Brighton and then the game was different, the pressure (for me, at least) dissipated. Suddenly the birds were singing, the sky was blue and my shoulders unknotted. There, there it is and there we are. In *excelsis deo*.

Did you feel it, though? God, it was fabulous and terrible in equal measure to feel it. It reminded us we are alive. The most alive.

The thing is that the mighty boys in red played the whole game with unknotted shoulders. They were cooler than I was, perhaps than you were. They were never in their groove, but they were in their element and these are two different things.

Liverpool's spine had an excellent game without excelling. All of Alisson, van Dijk, Henderson and Salah were constant and certain. They don't always do what I would like but then their needs and mine could well be different. They have the game plan to implement. From my point of view I'd like us to score right now, if you don't mind.

Instead they pick their moments to force the issue and that forcing is as much about forcing Brighton back as it is creating a chance. It is to create space to then create a chance, and at times that is hard to watch but it is essential to see.

Between van Dijk and Henderson was Fabinho who produced, if not his best, his most important performance for Liverpool. He thought his way through the game with aplomb. He took the Glenn Murray elbow, shrugged and let him know 10 minutes later.

It was a performance of both character and nous, the performance of an excellent footballer who is now undoubtedly ensconced in this squad. He is one of the boys, one of the men.

It was a day that reminded you they are men. This column loves to remind you these are mostly lads in their 20s living our dreams, trying to match our ambition. We often think of them as far older, far wiser.

Today was that sort of day, that day where I am crumbling under the weight of it all, pressure pushing down on me, and they are standing up and being counted, they are shaming me with their certainty, their inevitability. How's your bottle? Mine is fine the other side of all that, but theirs was picture perfect before it.

The full backs constantly available and seconds away from being in. Brighton's blanket being compact and thick but struggling to stretch and Liverpool doing all the things that grown up teams do, make it so hard to break quickly, make everything feel arduous, make you yearn for the sweet relief of the final whistle whichever side you are on. Put us out of our misery, referee. We toil but we know. We know.

Brighton had a late semi flourish but there was not a shot on target. Alisson Becker saves something he should leave and in the end that was the dirtiest he got.

The achievement of this manager is that he has created and coalesced these most certain of footballers. They aren't getting carried away but theirs is a 22-game start which should carry us all away. They've been almost as close to spotless as is possible and they share that memory.

How's your bottle? Well mine is now absolutely glistening. Perfect. We're seven clear and we have the next two at home and we are back on track, back doing our thing. For the avoidance of doubt, our thing appears to be the avoidance of doubt.

Jürgen's boys are the steadiest, the most irresistible; their will is back to being what will be bent to, their certainty becomes the certainty of opponents and referees. And us. They lead us. They whisper things, the city sings them back to you. They live forever tonight.

You know the drill. Twenty-two down. Twenty-two. Liverpool top of the league. A state of affairs that will take some changing. Liverpool are certain. It will take a lot to make them uncertain. Sixteen to go.

See you next weekend, you magnificent lads. You magnificent men. It will feel an age since we have roared them on at Anfield. Imagine. What are we in it for if not that? No trepidation, no pressure, see you next Saturday when we live. The most alive, on the edge of the night.

See you next Saturday.

Liverpool v Crystal Palace

Saturday January 19, 2019

ROB GUTMANN'S PREVIEW

IT'S nip and fucking tuck time again.

We win. They win. But we have the edge. It's now very clear. Manchester City are very good, but Liverpool may just be the more complete football team.

In full attacking cry, Pep Guardiola's side can look a force of nature, as can Jürgen Klopp's Liverpool. But turn this City team around – not an easy thing to do granted – and they can be made to look ragged. This no longer applies to Liverpool.

I was privileged to watch the 1978-79 Liverpool side that conceded just 16 goals in a season. It was in no sense a defensive team, far from it (it scored 85 goals), but it just so completely controlled games that the opposition simply couldn't lay a glove on.

The 2019 model Liverpool has only seen 10 goals breach its defence with nearly two thirds of the season past. It is gaining points at a faster rate than the '79 side. Whisper it, but we may be witnessing a very special team emerging.

Bob Paisley's side amassed 68 points, then a top-flight record. Adjusted to today's 38-game season, with three points awarded for a win, that translates to a haul equivalent to about 88 points in 2019. This year's Liverpool need just 31 points from 16 remaining games to match the achievement of Liverpool's greatest ever league season.

Klopp's team could reach the 1979 total merely by winning eight or nine of their remaining fixtures. In many ways, what's unfolding before us beggars belief. We could be watching the greatest incarnation of a Liverpool team of all time.

So what does the greatest version of all time look like? It may very well look like Mo Salah, like Sadio Mane, like Alisson Becker, like Virgil van Dijk, like newly tied-down Andy Robbo. For Dalglish, Souness, Hansen, read Firmino, Wijnaldum and Gomez. This is how we may come to view today's crop.

And yet, the truly incredible possibility remains that the very best of the best could still be bettered by the current incarnation of Manchester City. For a 90-point finish by Liverpool in May – awesome achievement as that might be – would mean that they had still gone on to drop a further 15 points this season.

Even with a four-point lead over City, as it stands, it would be unlikely dropping 15 more points would be few enough to enable Liverpool to emerge with a first league title since 1990.

I don't know how Jürgen sleeps at night. I'm up till all hours. Kloppo knows to become the king of kings he can only face the front, and in his and our path stand Crystal Palace. Right now, they are the greatest threat to our ambitions.

Klopp will likely face up Hodgson's uber conservative 4-5-1 formation with his now preferred 4-2-3-1. Gini Wijnaldum and Trent Alexander-Arnold will join Joe Gomez in the treatment room and won't face Palace at the weekend. James Milner will surely take Trent's place, while Fabinho should return to his preferred midfield position in Wijnaldum's stead.

The biggest selection decision for the Liverpool manager will be whether or not to pick Shaqiri ahead of Naby Keita. I'd like to see Naby given the nod and the opportunity to play himself into form. Shaqiri is so potent as an impact substitute and could be best preserved as the not-so-secret late weapon.

It's just another game and just another day, Reds. A day nearer the greatest day.

Liverpool 4 Crystal Palace 3
BEN JOHNSON'S RATINGS

Alisson: 7

Couldn't do anything with the goal. Didn't see the second. Let's say it wasn't his fault. Probably should have saved the third, but I like to think he was saving his saves for when they matter.

Milner: 7

Great turn and through ball for the Joel for the chance. Played higher than Trent, pretty much. Got legged by Zaha but in fairness there aren't many full backs who wouldn't have been in that situation. Great run and ball onto Speroni's hand to set up the winner. Got sent off, we have now got no right backs. No one in their right mind is arsed.

Big Joel: 6

Mad one there when he got played in with his big Porcelanosa boots and he was the last fella on earth you wanted in that position. Good save, in fairness. He is dead dangerous on corners but not dangerous at all in the same breath. Boss movement to create himself a chance, head like Kryten. Played the fucking world onside for their goal, didn't he?

Virg: 7

Don't know what he did or didn't do for their goal, but it feels like he's so good that if he wanted to keep it out he would have done. Genuinely haven't got a clue how he played, but given we conceded three I'm saying he wasn't amazing.

Andy Robbo: 7

Good defending to save a corner when they broke midway through the first, but then absolutely emptied his position chasing a shadow and they looked dangerous for a weird little five minutes. Why didn't he hit that one first half when he played it back? Our only full back available now, but no one in their right mind is arsed.

Henderson: 7

First 10 minutes they broke twice and Henderson legged them and won it back. Loved the sort of middle defensive four we set up with. Twat of a ball to Milner for his second yellow. I was going to give him an eight but thought it was a step too far.

Fabinho: 8

Looked like they decided to let him have the ball first 15 and he pinged it all over the gaff. What a ball for the third goal to Milner. Went off hurt, hopefully something and nothing.

Naby: 6

He is nearly, almost, half a yard away from brilliant first half but instead tends to be ineffective at best, and maybe a little bit shite at worst.

Mo Salah: 8

Touch let him down three or four times in the first half when a possible half chance looked on. When I say let him down, I mean it wasn't fucking perfect. Lashed himself for a pen there in an absolute don't touch the red button brainstorm. Great finish off a big, horrible, spawny deflection. The best of goals.

Hahahahaha, his second, la. Their keeper with an assist. Fucking Red Shite bastards.

Firmino: 7

Fucking horrible, horrible, bobbly, spawny Red Nose twat of a goal that, weren't it? Get in. Get in. Get in. Get in. Hahahaha.

Sadio Mane: 7

From what I seen – granted, it wasn't a lot – he looked to be making some pretty fucking selfish choices. Slaughtering him to myself, but then he popped up with a goal that may well have been celebrated four times. I don't know who I am anymore. Are we going to win the league? Can someone just put me out of my misery?

SUBS...

I don't really know who come on, but was Shaqiri playing right back for a bit, there?

NEIL ATKINSON'S REVIEW

YOU know you are alive. My lord, you know you are alive.

Isn't that the point? It is, but you felt that maybe a bit too much.

It shouldn't have been this way. Eight minutes in, James Milner goes on a charging run from back to front, and you think Liverpool Football Club are going to command this game. For the first 14 minutes, we have total possession of the football game, edging inch by inch towards the goal. Side by side, piece by piece, we keep the pressure on.

Liverpool look cool. Liverpool are top.

And then. And then.

A freekick at the half-hour mark breaks the ice. Shortly after, Wilfried Zaha – a special player, by any measure – breaks Milner's wall and Townsend slices one past Liverpool's goalkeeper.

And from a team that was all in control and all on top of the pressure, chaos breaks out. A fixture that could always be straightforward but somehow never ever, ever is turns out to be pure madness once again. This could well have been the sixth most difficult game of our remaining 16. It became that before our very eyes.

Right at the point they score, we look strong at the front and OK at the back, and you would absolutely be forgiven for thinking that this game is going to end 2-1. If someone had said to me at half time, hey, this is going to end 4-3 with a sending off, I would have told them to do one. We don't do that sort of thing anymore. This is Jürgen's machine.

Crystal Palace are a well-drilled team. They look like plastic figurines on a table football set, such is the constant shape they hold especially that back four. The centre halves are terrific; van Aanholt tidy, Wan-Bissaka the business.

Palace look like a team that can control themselves against sides much, much better than them. They know what they are about. The Reds this season have been pure efficiency. At half time, this doesn't look like a game that is going to go wild with goals and misshapen defences.

But here is how it happens.

Half time comes at the right time and resets the agenda. Bang. 46th minute, Liverpool take their chance at last and last year's golden boot winner shows that any thought that he is only going to win that for one season can be dispensed with. He should be box seat given Kane's absence.

Bang. At 53, Bobby Firmino does likewise and it is 2-1. Liverpool supreme, roared on. Anfield ablaze. It helps Speroni suddenly looks his age.

These two goalscorers look great. They look like a pair today. They are everywhere, everywhere on the pitch. They are our everything. The greatest thing you have ever seen.

This is maybe how things should end. Maybe if Joe Gomez was on the pitch, events might have stopped there. Maybe if Dejan Lovren was on the pitch. Maybe Trent.

But they weren't, and my God, it didn't end there. Here's the scene.

Palace go berserk. Their lads put Liverpool on the rack for five, punctuated with the exclamation mark of the Tomkins header. Wilf Zaha is a torrent. He's almost unplayable.

After Salah puts Liverpool ahead again at the 75th, you think that must surely be that and the thing should finish 3-2.

The goals have come thick and fast, with the ball hitting the back of the net every 10 minutes or so. But what is really mad is how the strength of Liverpool's possession and the firmness of Palace's shape collapses into a game where Bobby Firmino ends up covering at the back, Mo Salah hacking clear and the unflappable Virgil van Dijk is running into the goalmouth.

Milner flies in at an acute angle and, understandably given a previous yellow, gets himself sent off. Roberto Firmino goes right back, because why not? The best way for Liverpool to see the game out is to kill it and Sadio Mane does just that. All over.

But even then. Jesus, Reds. Jesus. It was never meant to be this way. The entire crowd is punch drunk at this point.

Ninety plus five. Palace get one back.

But in Anfield, The Reds, both playing and non-playing, don't care, we've done it. Literally couldn't give a shit then. What we give a shit about is three points. Not one point or no points, but three points. Our points.

When you really want something, and that thing is really worth having, you have to constantly want it, and be constantly working out how to get it. Sometimes it comes easy, and sometimes it's hard, and sometimes, like today, the road is just crazy, a bit messed up, and all over the place. But the most important thing is to just work out a way, find a way through.

Liverpool won the chaos today. Our heads may be swiss cheese, but they did it. They did it at 0-1. They did it at 2-2. They did it at 3-2 down to 10.

They did it. They got it done. The final whistle sounds and while there are cheers there is this stillness, this peace absolute. That another challenge has been overcome, that we are three more closer to the promised land. A stillness that won't end till they take to the pitch again, frozen.

I'm glad of the 10 days. Part of me feels like I played. But part of me wants to scream, shout and jump. Contrary to the song that plays in my head when I go to sleep and starts again when I wake, we may well eventually be moved. Anything is possible. But, by everything that is holy, we will take some moving. We will take some shifting. We are here until the bitter end.

We've made that crystal clear today. We've made you feel alive, the most alive, face red, arms wrapped around strangers, teeth gritted and grinding because if you want to stop us you will need to consist of nothing but that want. We need this more than want this. And we want it for all time.

Fifteen more. Grit your teeth, Reds. Fifteen more for the greatest thing you have ever seen.

Until then we are alive. The most.

What Oxlade-Chamberlain's Return Means For Keita

Wednesday January 23, 2019

JOHN GIBBONS

QUIET, isn't it?

Liverpool have gone to Dubai and we are hearing very little out of the camp. The players are off social media, it seems – as if they have been asked to hand their phones in at the start like one of those shit stag dos with loads of rules.

The club website is very quiet. Just full of stories of youth team victories and those weird transfer rumour roundups they do that make the stories look real. We haven't even got the *Liverpool Echo* taking photos of players riding round on bikes. They've gone very under the radar.

All of us owe a huge amount of debt to the NAS Sports Complex, where the Liverpool team are this week, who just casually filmed Liverpool training on a mobile phone and whacked it on their Instagram for the world to see.

They've took it down now, obviously – probably after Jürgen Klopp battered someone – but you can still find it if you look hard enough. Or just on Trinity Mirror websites.

If you find it you will see Alex Oxlade-Chamberlain, not just running but actually playing football. Admittedly, he's only playing against yellow dummies but still. He's kicking, turning, heading, the lot. He looks like he could start for Everton next week.

He probably won't start that soon for Liverpool, but it does look much sooner that we all feared when the severity of the injury broke. It's always wise to be cautious on these things, so maybe they always privately felt some action this season was a possibility.

However, the speed in which he went from gym work to ball work seems to have caught everyone by surprise. The talk now is that he could be back in full training as early as next week, with an eye on Bayern Munich away in March as a potential return.

To see him back in a Champions League game, a tournament in which he picked up the injury in a typically fully committed challenge, would be lovely to see. But, sentiment aside, he will also be a fantastic addition to this squad. Maybe one of the only things we are currently missing. That driving force from the middle, linking midfield and attack, and supporting the forwards in the box.

That player was supposed to be Naby Keita, but Chamberlain's return isn't necessarily bad news for Naby. Chamberlain is a really good example for Keita in the need to persevere if you want a central midfield role for Liverpool.

Chamberlain also found himself popping up in wide positions for Liverpool in the first half of his first season, with many fans wondering what type of player he was and why we had invested in him.

Central midfield seems to be an area where Klopp seems willing to take least risks, but Chamberlain broke through eventually, through a mix of willpower and taking the opportunity when it arose.

Naby is no rookie, he's played central midfield in a top league already, but in terms of what Klopp expects from an attacking midfielder for Liverpool, he could do a lot worse than watch Chamberlain for Liverpool when he returns.

How he holds his position when he needs to, but breaks when the opportunity is there. How he presses and wins his battles. How he flourishes as part of a unit, not outside of it.

According to Noor Patterson, who met the Liverpool team in a Dubai shopping centre I once bought some socks in, the team are flying back to Liverpool tonight, so we should have some smiling Melwood pictures again very soon.

That they are flying back with a fit and, almost, raring to go Alex Oxlade-Chamberlain is a massive boost at a crucial stage of the season.

Squad depth not looking too bad, after all.

West Ham United 1 Liverpool 1

Monday February 4, 2019

NEIL ATKINSON'S REVIEW

THINGS that are blows:
- The lack of chances created.
- The equaliser.
- The last minute missed opportunity.

Things that aren't blows:
- The league table.

The league table still shows Liverpool top of the pile with a healthy cushion at this stage of proceedings, the league table is very much in our favour. You expected it to be easy? Surely you know – as I do – that league championships are battles, are grinds, are no barrel of laughs. League championships are about blood and bone and bottle. How's your bottle?

Mine is more solid than you may think. There was something I liked in the second half. Liverpool should have gone in having conceded two but they changed that. They were firm and certain second half. But they weren't good.

They will need to be good soon – they will need to turn this, to switch this soon – but they can look around the dressing room and know they were solid. Solid is a thing. Other things can come.

There was something cheery about Naby Keita's second half, a performance that nearly invited all of us to have a big bowl of soup. He sashayed, and shone, and needed a bit of luck, and to turn away from trouble rather than into it. He finds going backwards tough still, he needs to find his angles, but he is finding his essence.

We could do with it. Jordan Henderson, Gini Wijnaldum and Trent Alexander-Arnold all come through tonight with reputations enhanced.

The fact is that there were people missing tonight. Both on the pitch and off the pitch. You could see the gaps everywhere. The gaping hole where Trent should have been. The chasm that only Henderson can fill.

And then there is the gap in performance. Andy Robertson, who has consistently played out of his skin, looked edgy in his own skin tonight, for whatever reason. He skipped and passed like always but the pace was lacking and the passing less accurate than we have grown accustomed to.

Mo Salah lacked edge. There is no other way to call it. He was great, but that sharpness, that edge, that killer sense just wasn't there.

The midfield was full of holes and upfront we were a blunted instrument, Sadio Mane's fits and starts aside. Roberto Firmino is a concern but then he always will be when it doesn't click.

Meanwhile, West Ham were not at all bad. They are a top half of the table team and it showed.

They contained Liverpool effectively, even if it meant playing so deep they were practically in the stands. At times they broke with purpose, and while their attack never really threatened second half, they made us pay at set pieces. They'd done their homework; they reaped their rewards.

The fact is that the biggest challenge we face now is momentum. We have carried it with us and it has carried us. How you respond to a switch in momentum inevitably defines you. Can you dig deeper? Can you find strength where others are driven mad by the pressure? These are the questions that face Liverpool Football Club now. Jürgen Klopp, more than anyone has to answer them.

But here's the thing. We are not powerless either. We can get behind them. We can do our bit. We have an opportunity on Saturday to do so, and we can keep our nerve.

Where's your head at? Don't let the walls cave in on you.

Nobody said it would be easy. And we all fucking knew it would be this hard. These are our lads for the job. As ever they will do for me. Let them do for you.

Twenty-five down. Thirteen to go.

Liverpool v Bournemouth

Saturday February 9, 2019

ROB GUTMANN'S PREVIEW

THESE are testing times.

I feel I've typed that sentence before and will again before the year is out. We aren't sure if we're on the cusp of something truly historic or being drawn back into a recurring nightmare. The experiences of the past two weeks have been a new and yet all too familiar for us as a supporter base. In the week of Groundhog Day, our version has seemingly come back to remind us of the repetitive nature of the fan's experience.

I was part of a panel recording The Weekender podcast for The Anfield Wrap previewing this weekend's game against Bournemouth. The theme of the show was supporters and their feelings towards Liverpool's title challenge. Was our excitement at the prospect of the ultimate achievement creating an anxiety within us that might transmit onto the playing field and, in turn, damage the team's prospect of actually becoming champions?

The discussion considered remedies and recipes for the collective so that we might enhance the atmosphere within our home stadium, and in doing so lift our team. Virgil van Dijk's comments in the media about anxiety on the terraces filtering to the players was a reminder to all that we bear responsibility beyond merely paying our ticket money on the gate.

I was also minded of the iconic 1980s US comedy *Cheers*. It ran for virtually the whole decade and was set virtually entirely within the fictional 'Cheers' bar in Boston and chronicled the travails and insecurities of owner and head barman Sam, and the coterie of bar flies that frequented his joint and gave him a living.

As much as anything it was about class in American society. The everyday folk that frequented Cheers bar were from all walks of life but one thing bound them, gave them common cause. Sport.

The 'ball game' background commentaries emanating from the TV over the bar were a ubiquitous presence. We were frequently reminded that owner Sam had himself, back in the day, been quite a baseball player. This fact gave Sam authority. When Sam pontificated on sport, folks listened.

It came to pass that in one episode, I'm sketchily remembering, that a representative of a local TV news channel happened to be in Cheers bar and so became privy to some of Sam's sporting wisdoms. So much so that Sam gets invited to host a slot on the local TV channel giving his earnest and informed opinions on the burning sporting issue of any given day.

All the regulars are excited for Sam and eagerly await his live TV debut. The evening comes, and Sam is present in the bar room tableau but only as a talking head on the TV screen.

The news anchor cuts to Sam: 'Here's Sam with his thoughts on the Red Sox's worrying recent form...'

Sam passionately delivers a polemic that could've been proffered in support of any sporting institution at some point in time. He urges supporters to remember that they have responsibilities towards their team. He stresses that their heroes can't do it all on their own. That it isn't sufficient to be a passive bystander, a folded-armed critic.

True, committed, participatory support will take the whole enterprise up a level and, ultimately, be its own reward. Sam is nearly angry, Sam is forthright, Sam is clearly correct.

After three breathless minutes, Sam pauses, and the shot cuts back to the anchorman. 'Thanks to Sam there,' says the anchor guy cheerily. 'I think what Sam's trying to say is that we all need to ROOT, ROOT, ROOT for the home team!'

Quick cut back to shot of Sam looking bemused and a bit crestfallen.

It was the perfect reductive aside to Sam's archetypal sports fan's call to arms. It was funny because it put things in perspective. We can rage, we rail at each other, we can urge for more fire but when it comes down to it, we remain largely powerless.

And there's the rub. Our 'act of resistance', however much we seek to glamourise or aggrandise our importance, is futile if the boys simply can't get their shit together. I'd swap every one of our '12th men' for one calm lad who will just stick it in the goal when the chance comes.

I'm aware of the irony of my own position, here. I'm saying maybe we need to calm down, mainly. Very little more. I think we can say that while also acknowledging that it can only be good if we do more to raise the roof in the ground.

Beating Bournemouth can be the panacea we're all desperately seeking. Just a cheeky little win. I'd take the proverbial last-minute 1-0. I'd take a win so ugly that it made us wince. Winning properly would seem a right royal treat, but let's not be greedy.

Jürgen Klopp faced a similar kind of test of his abilities to lift a flattened Liverpool earlier in this campaign. Fulham came to Anfield in the wake of a worrying Champions League defeat in Belgrade. They'd ordinarily have been lambs to the slaughter but The Reds' form would've given them encouragement.

A no-nonsense 2-0 Liverpool win followed, that no one celebrated long into the night, but provided a platform for the resumption of normal service.

The Liverpool manager's burden should be lifted a touch by the return to availability of Trent Alexander-Arnold, Jordan Henderson and Gini Wijnaldum. Trent, particularly at Anfield, can make the pitch 'bigger' with his pace and expansive passing. Wijnaldum and Henderson can, in turn, provide the greater security in the middle of the park to license Trent for more offensive forays.

Klopp's selections aren't easy to second guess these days, but I think James Milner may be held back for bench duty alongside Xherdan Shaqiri and Adam Lallana. All featured extensively in the draw in London in the week, but could see significantly less game minutes on Saturday. Divock Origi's liveliness as a substitute has gone under radars a touch. Don't be surprised to see him as Klopp's first go-to change if things get sticky.

It may be a good thing for Liverpool that we will get to go about our business away from the glare of prime-time TV coverage this Saturday afternoon. Micro dissections of 'failings' during 1-1 draws feel like almost gratuitous attempts to belittle a team that have suffered just one league defeat all season.

The pendulum may have swung against us in the past 7-10 days, but it can just as swiftly return in our favour.

Remember, kids: 'ROOT, ROOT, ROOT for the home team!' It's better than getting cross, after all.

Liverpool 3 Bournemouth 0
BEN JOHNSON'S RATINGS

GO 'ed, the boys. That was perfect, that.

Alisson: 7

Made saves when he needed to. The first-minute fella was good. His starting position is perfect, all of the time.

Milner: 8

Busy as a pip. They are busy, them little pricks. Did he cross it for the first or have I made that up? Yer, he did. Is right, lad.

Big Joel: 7

Scruffy fucker, isn't he? I mean, everything he does is by the skin of his teeth. Reckon he is a hoarder. House is fucking jam packed. Got abar £600 nicker worth of newspapers as a table in the kitchen. Bath is full of boots. Big fucking massive white fucking boots.

Virgil: 8

Legged it on the break there to try and score, and Bobby just jibbed him instead. What more do you want, though? Perfect at the other end pretty much.

Robbo: 8

Back to his best pretty much after a couple of weeks off, there. Looks like he might have shipped the baby to his mother in laws last night, got a chippy, lashed on *Billions* and got his head down for a solid eight-hour fella. Back at it.

Gini: 9

The opposite of big Joelly there, isn't he? The neatest and tidiest of them all. Fucking hoovers up on the way out the house. Kim and Aggie, lad. Send him round to Joel's with a bucket of Domestos and a brush. Sparkling in about 10 minutes. What a finish for the goal. It was in from the minute he thought about it.

Fabinho: 8

He's boss, isn't he? Absolutely fucking booted that little fucker who made a show of us off the bench in the 4-3 first minute and set the tempo thereafter.

Keita: 8

The ball to Firmino for Salah's goal is sublime. To the extent that Bobby should hit it. For all the world he should hit it. Kept it, moved it, was pretty much everything you want from a midfielder, there. Needs a little bit of luck for a goal to go in.

Mo: 9

Untouchable today. Everywhere. What a finish. Unlucky for the one against the bar, the volley in the first, the fucking state of the referee. One of the best to play for The Reds.

Firmino: 8

Back to his proper role upfront and I'm saying that layoff for the third might be the best thing I have ever seen. I mean, he had no fucking right to do that. The ball from Naby needs hitting. How can you have the state of mind to know your goal hungry mate is on your shoulder there ready to slot? Scandalous.

Mane: 9

The go-to fella at the minute, isn't he? You need something here, lad? I'm your man. The fixer. Absolute balls on him. He's in the war room for this league, isn't he?

SUBS...

Trent:

Needs a song. I reckon the Maxi one works with a massive Trent to kick it off. Might need to fuck one of his names off to get a proper song.

The Rest:

Go 'ed.

NEIL ATKINSON'S REVIEW

NORMAL service resumed?

In a sense, yes. Liverpool cruise to victory against reasonable mid-table opposition, keeping a clean sheet, the question more about how many rather than how.

In that normal service sense, Mo Salah hits the bar, elicits a great save and scores. In that sense, Sadio Mane yet again opens the scoring and yet again leads from the front. In that sense, Virgil van Dijk barely breaks sweat and Jürgen Klopp gives it the big one in front of The Kop. In that sense, Liverpool are top, three clear.

Much hasn't been the norm, though. Naby Keita has promised but not served. Today he was sublime, deserved a goal, but his weight of pass was tremendous, his movement perfect. He clicked right into the shape and style of The Reds and raised them. This can become the norm quickly, could become a norm which powers the next 12. It's a suddenly exciting prospect. Big bowls of soup all round.

Gini Wijnaldum has 10 minutes which were abnormal from 22 or so. His entire performance is what we have almost become complacent about, gluing the side together, bringing everyone along. It is an ongoing act of quiet brilliance, generosity and determination. He will not accept anything less than his teammates' best but he will provide them the platform. That's the norm. What a norm.

But what he does from 22 hasn't been. He is ahead of the play, only Mo Salah near him. He is bursting forward. Liverpool have had too little of this but then something else happens. Twice he is generous, but the third time he is sublime, Boruc clawing at the air.

This Liverpool side with its clean sheets and its front three and its platform from midfield has missed one thing: goals from the centre of the park. Gini Wijnaldum delivering that, as we know he can, is also an exciting prospect.

It wasn't just him: Keita, as mentioned, has a great chance, Trent Alexander-Arnold has a great chance, Milner and Robertson are around the box. I love the front three. Great lads one and all, but they cannot carry that burden alone, they have for too long. Let that change.

What hasn't been normal this season but was last season was the makeup of that three. Today, the starting positions were back to last season's normal. Firmino mostly through the middle. But what matters isn't where you start, it is where you end up. And it is how involved you are.

In the last few games, the ball hasn't been with the front three often enough or early enough. Today, it was with all three quickly and where they wanted it. Mo Salah has just had more of the ball in 90 minutes from the right than he did in the last 180 centrally. This doesn't need to be a permanent change but should be remembered as a serious option.

What's also a serious option is getting right behind The Reds and enjoying it wholeheartedly and demanding more enjoyment. The first half was terrific, a tour de force from Anfield, Anfield roaring and raging in the right way. Anfield asking to be taken to the promised land, Anfield calling for Hallelujah in the highest, rather than blaspheming at the lowest.

Anfield showed love and respect and joy for the lads. This hasn't been normal. Don't get me wrong, this ground for 12 months has rarely been bad. I remember the end of Houllier, I remember the civil war. I remember the Rodgers equalisers, the Dalglish silences, the Hodgson disgraces. Leicester the other week was a Wacky Warehouse by comparison.

But the context mattered. It may have been a minor squall but one minor squall in the context of normalising brilliance, one minor squall for a side who have done so much for us was one too many. Even today, even when they are brilliant, they need us more than want us. And they want us for all time.

Imagine being a football player without a cauldron to play in. Imagine your crowd working against you. Imagine your childhood imaginings, your dreams of being a footballer and remember what happens when your daydreams turn brilliant. You turn to a crowd arms aloft. They respond.

You can do this for the fame, and the money, and the sheer brio of it, but in that moment you do it for around 55,000 people who have lived and dreamed and breathed. You do it to show off. Naby Keita today showed off and fucking fair play to him for it.

Up the Reds. Up the Reds who sang and roared and demanded. Up the Reds who danced and chipped and passed. The only way any of this makes sense is if we are together through it, better or worse.

It came to my attention that it is five years yesterday since this mad indulgence of a column started happening, five years since Liverpool put five past Arsenal, four in 20 minutes, five years since we roared those Reds into the improbable and they responded with the impossible and I started to write down all that is seen and unseen.

Right now, I prepare to pass this phone to Steve Graves to sense check as I did five years ago.

Through those five years there has been a hell of a lot – and thank you for being patient and indulgent – but through those five years one thing has been crystal clear: this thing of ours is so much better when we display togetherness, kindness and love. This thing is an exchange, a transaction.

They give us reason to go spare, we go spare. They give us everything, we give it all back.

We get to do it from now to May with this current incarnation. We get to live this with them, for them and as them. We get to have these weekends and midweeks with each other.

Let it become the new normal:

Naby Keita's brilliance and big bowls of soup.

Goals from around the pitch.

Salah, Mane and Firmino flitting about.

Us being marvellous.

Let it all become the new normal along with the rest of it.

What's always been there is needing more than wanting, wanting for all time. Love you, handsome. Love you, Queen. God has given us these days of leisure.

Twenty-six done. Twelve to go.

165

How Joel Matip Can Ensure He's On The Right Side Of History

Friday February 15, 2019

DAN MORGAN

WHAT'S the first image that comes into your head when you think of May 25, 2005?

Liverpool Football Club's finest recent triumph, the hazy Ataturk night which witnessed a footballing miracle so spectacular none of us can barely comprehend its reality to this day.

Do you think of Steven Gerrard or Jamie Carragher lifting the European Cup aloft?

What about Rafael Benitez? Ever so modest in the cradling of his finest achievement, while still maintaining an essence of modest discomfort due to the limelight bestowed on him.

A glorious night, full of memorable images and iconic figures.

Do you want to know what, or more specifically who I think of?

Josemi. Fucking Josemi.

One of Benitez's first, and quite frankly most underwhelming signings, the Spanish right back had the turning circle of the 68 bus performing a five-point reverse in Queen Square.

Yet when Gerrard, after the longest night of his short life, got his hands on The Reds' fifth European Cup, there was Josemi, front and centre draped in a Spanish flag, peripheral but overwhelming in his presence.

Of course, he deserved to celebrate the triumph. Anybody associated to Liverpool Football Club that night was ecstatic and joyous, and for very good reason.

It's just whenever I think of Josemi, I often wonder what he sees when he looks at that photograph? Does he see someone who unequivocally gave their all to be a part of a team who went all the way?

Or does he harbour some form of regret that he could maybe have had some more of a say on what turned out to be a season written into the core fabric of success within the club.

Sometimes, the opportunity to be a part of the action doesn't always present itself. In this current Liverpool team now pushing towards the summit of their own destiny, Joel Matip arguably has such an opportunity.

Injuries to Joe Gomez and Dejan Lovren have bestowed a responsibility on Matip to fill the right centre-back void, and to not let the collective defensive standards set this season drop.

However, this is Joel Matip, and this alone has proved problematic.

Guilty of his own injury and form inconsistencies, the Cameroon international continues to be dogged by questions of temperament, as well as technical and physical capability.

Matip was once described as the ever-cliched 'Rolls Royce' defender. Displaying an air of calm and tranquility drew comparisons to the likes of Sami Hyypia, while his grace was still good during the early stages of his Liverpool career.

Yet time has proved that Matip can look dithering when once described as considered, tame when once viewed as sensible, and inconsistent when once thought of as unlucky.

In his defence, Matip can point out he has spent the majority of his Liverpool career surrounded by other uncertain footballers in the form of the two previous goalkeepers he has guarded, as well as two teenage right backs who, despite an unbounded amount of potential, could both be described as raw.

Matip now has the blanket trio of Virgil van Dijk, Alisson Becker and James Milner around him to use as his base for competence when going about his work as a Liverpool defender.

During a cameo pre-Christmas, Matip earned some credible appreciation for his performances up until he was injured in the dying moments against Napoli at Anfield.

A return to the side has coincided with Liverpool falling back onto the ropes with draws in both the Leicester City and West Ham United fixtures.

Even the most hardened of critics could not lay any of the blame at Matip's door for those results, and both the individual and team were markedly better in the performance against Bournemouth last weekend.

With news that Lovren is yet to return to training and Gomez still recovering from surgery, the prospect of Matip's run in the team extending has increased significantly, and work in both training and in game is needed if he is to transition into the type of consistent performer the club now crave.

Another option mooted has been to revert Fabinho to centre back, as he did so seamlessly against Brighton in January.

This could be detrimental, as the Brazilian has come to the fore as the ball-carrying and possession-turning force that was hoped he could be when signed in the summer.

Fabinho was described in an interview with Goal.com's Neil Jones as a 'lighthouse' by assistant manager Pepijn Lijnders.

That type of midfield beacon will be pivotal in the run of fixtures coming up, and another midfielder sacrificed to the back four may just prove to be too much of an imbalance to the formula created by the manager and his team.

The simple truth remains that, in this moment, Liverpool needs Joel Matip just as much as he needs Liverpool.

For most of these lads it won't get any better than this. The party is still in our house, bring a mate, show him that picture on the wall that crowns the moment when life truly couldn't get any better for any of us.

Hopefully, in the case of Matip, he can look at his own portrait safe in the knowledge that he deserved to be there, and that he truly was a part of it.

Fabinho: The Beacon Of Calm Among The Klopp Chaos

Wednesday February 20, 2019

JOHN GIBBONS

EVEN the sight of one of Liverpool's most famous flags wasn't quite enough to inspire Liverpool to victory last night.

Joey might have eaten the frogs legs and made the Swiss roll, but it turns out Bayern might take a bit more Munchen than Gladbach did in '77.

But positives still arose from the game, particularly defensively where a makeshift backline managed to repel Lewandowski and co with relative ease. Much was made before the game of Liverpool having to field their fourth and fifth-choice centre backs in such a big game, but both Matip and Fabinho more than held their own.

Fabinho in particular is fast becoming Mr Reliable for Liverpool wherever he plays, to the extent that there was plenty of discussion last night over whether he actually should be considered fifth-choice centre half for Liverpool or much higher.

After the game, my dad said he would start Fabinho with van Djik at Old Trafford on Sunday, regardless of the fitness of others, and the only problem with that I could think of was that I want him in midfield as well.

It's quite the turnaround for Fabinho considering he couldn't even make the bench for Liverpool earlier in the season and was being linked with loan moves back to France by journalists who seemed a bit too keen to make it happen.

Now, for many Liverpool fans, he is one of the first names on the teamsheet – the only question being where best to deploy his considerable talents.

At times his game seems almost too dynamic to play anywhere else but midfield. His passing range and athleticism are perfect for a deeper midfield role. In style, he is the closest thing I have seen to Vieira since he left Arsenal. And they've had about seven 'new Vieiras' since.

But his performance at centre half certainly makes you think, well, maybe. It's not just his one-on-one defending – which you would expect to be excellent, as demonstrated by a great block on Lewandowski inside the penalty area – the biggest surprise is his positional play.

Things that young centre halves who have played that position throughout the academy system struggle with, Fabinho seems to have a natural knowledge of. Quite often it seemed to be him last night, rather than Joel Matip, who was deciding when the defensive line should push up and when it should drop.

Above all else, this shows his natural football intelligence. How he can read the game seemingly no matter where he is on the pitch. Jürgen Klopp has talked extensively of Gini Wijnaldum's outstanding versatility and his ability to 'switch from one mindset to another'. I am sure he is starting to add Fabinho to his growing list of players who can perform for him seemingly no matter where they play.

It is to everyone's credit, not least Fabinho's, that everyone stayed calm when he was struggling to adapt to Liverpool and the Premier League.

One of the most fascinating parts of the recent Pep Lijnders interviews was his discussion of the work they did with Fabinho. Lijnders admiration for Fabinho is clear. Calling him 'the lighthouse' within the 'organised chaos' of this Liverpool side. The cool head among the beautiful madness.

Now he's settled, you fancy Fabinho could be guiding this team for years to come. A big boss lighthouse in the middle of the park.

The Anfield Wrap's Craig Hannan said he was going to get 'Fabinho 3' on the back of his favourite hoody. I'm going to make a giant flag of New Brighton Lighthouse with Fabinho's head on the top.

Coming to an away end near you soon.

Manchester United v Liverpool
Sunday February 24, 2019
ROB GUTMANN'S PREVIEW

THIS is the end game.

Not literally the end game but the beginning of the end game. We could really do with starting the beginning of the end game by winning.

It's fun to bill games as metaphorical cup finals. Often it's just a dramatic device. On extremely rare occasions, the cap fits. Man United v Liverpool at Old Trafford this Sunday afternoon is as bona fide a 'it's like a cup final' game as it gets.

After this weekend there will be just 11 Premier Leagues to be fought out before the 2018-19 season is done. Liverpool have kind of let slip a clear initiative that they enjoyed for several weeks.

Defeat in Manchester this weekend will confirm a building feeling that champions City are not just back in the title race in a big way but comfortably in its driver's seat. A draw keeps the enquiry open but would please City's Pep Guardiola more than Liverpool's Jürgen Klopp.

The win though. A Liverpool win. That would be a tectonic shift. A Liverpool win would not just move The Reds three points ahead of City, it would position Liverpool to lead the run in from the front. City would know that Liverpool had opened up a clear length on them with the easier set of fixtures to play too.

Either team could recover from whatever plays out at Old Trafford, but there is an abiding sense that spirits will be broken if there is a clear winner on Sunday afternoon.

Sidebar: I continue to discount Spurs and, although it wouldn't surprise to see them finish ahead of either Liverpool or City, they will not finish ahead of both. Of that I'm near certain regardless of the fate tempted.

In this column, back in September, just before Liverpool travelled to London to play Spurs, I felt that to truly challenge for the league title this season, at some early juncture in the campaign, that Liverpool were going to need to put in a performance redolent of champions. Spurs were fancied themselves so to see them off in their own backyard would be a milestone of sorts.

Liverpool did indeed see them off and I don't think it's wrong to view that as a foundation result for all that has followed.

Liverpool performed like champions elect during an eight-match winning sequence that stretched across November and December. The landmark showing in that phase was perhaps the demolition of Man United at Anfield.

United were rendered so utterly ragged by a blood-sensing red pack that their manager Jose Mourinho was dismissed in the immediate wake of Liverpool's 3-1 win.

To be champions, Liverpool must now put in a champions performance. The time for accepting defeat as an isolated act, or a draw as a contextual 'decent result', is truly over. Klopp's team must dig the deepest. They simply must find a way to win.

That Solskjaer's United are motivated to beat Liverpool this Sunday is not worth dwelling on. That Paul Pogba, formerly the world's most expensive player, is in the form of his life, is a distraction. United's recent long winning sequence is not our business. I'm beyond being arsed whether or not their form lads Lingard and Martial will be fit enough to face us or not.

Our truth is bigger than Manchester United's. It would mean so much to them to beat Liverpool. It would mean more to Liverpool. It would mean the world to Liverpool. The whole world. All of it.

If Jürgen Klopp can harness the longing, the aching, the hunger within his team, within the club, with the fans, then only miracles will save United. Liverpool must find their power. It has been missing since the turn of the year.

Results have been manageable, moments have been impressive at times, but Liverpool have not shown as champions since demolishing Arsenal 5-1 at the end of December.

In his press conference, Klopp spoke of having decisions to make again as injury lists and illness based absenteeisms are diminishing. The manager longs to reinstate Fabinho at the heart of his team, in the number six holding midfield role.

He may well give the Brazilian the chance to run Liverpool's game from his favoured berth this Sunday but there is an alternative scenario. Fabinho, whisper it, could be the next best defender at Liverpool behind Virgil van Dijk. Make no mistake, there will be a temptation to pair the two in defence against United.

In midfield, I expect Klopp to persist with Naby Keita. Keita is improving with every appearance and if Liverpool are to seize their moment it may well be because Naby has decided to seize his. He will be partnered by Gini Wijnaldum in all probability and the pair accompanied in a three-man midfield by either Fabinho or Jordan Henderson.

Offensively, it will be fascinating to see if Klopp again adjusts his setup, as he did for United in December. Then Sadio Mane shifted from his left wing home to the right hand side of the pitch and was able to assist Mo Salah and Nathaniel Clyne in overloading in an area where United were more fragile.

Now, perhaps more than then, all of United's attacking gifts play down their left. If Klopp matches them up against Trent Alexander-Arnold, Salah and Mane then we may be in for one lopsided game of football. It may well be decided by who blinks first, because these players can't all attack at the same time.

It's a game I both can't wait for and yet dread. I will be inside Old Trafford watching the game through my fingers.

No horror shows please, Reds. There's too much at stake now.

Manchester United 0 Liverpool 0
NEIL ATKINSON'S REVIEW

WHAT did it feel like?

What was it?

How did it feel? It felt like two dropped. It felt increasingly frustrating. It felt like bad subs. It felt like Ferguson at Anfield. Where we are United and they are us.

What it was? The point that puts us top. Four points from United over the season. A solid rearguard performance at a tough place to go.

What it feels like is what it is. What it is will become what it feels like. All draws are defined by what happens next. What happens next?

Liverpool went to Old Trafford and stood up and were counted. The back eight, anyway. Alisson makes a phenomenal stop after a Lukaku through ball. Milner battles. Andy Robertson lives through a broken finger and produces.

Liverpool's centre backs impress. Joel Matip breaks forward well and while he is poor in the passage of play that leads to Lukaku's cunning he still performs well across the 90. It must be odd being Virgil van Dijk, entire game plans based around the idea of avoiding allowing you near the game. Play away from him rather than around him. Don't go near him.

The front three, whatever constituted them, showed a lack of quality, thought and touch. This needs arresting and it needs arresting fast. They would have a fair point if they wanted the ball faster, perhaps. But they had that at times and still struggled to be as impressive as you would hope.

The point of being Ferguson is hanging in for that moment of quality or luck. They lacked both.

The game was a maelstrom, United's supporters up for the scale of the task, and for what would be produced, and the nature of the game added to that. The injuries added to it – how much we felt we needed something and how much they felt they had a side to get behind. They wanted to believe and United encouraged that; a good side but one that needed to be clung to and encouraged.

There is something around wondering over every change. Sturridge ahead of Shaqiri, Origi or Keita. Then Henderson off at the moment he began to run the game. Then Salah for Origi. But this is the luxury of it not being your job.

He has to sort his out as he goes and he backs Daniel Sturridge. He has the experience of Shaqiri and also Wijnaldum's season. He lastly backs Origi after Salah being poor. He gets all that.

United defended well throughout, showed that they are good lads, Victor Lindelof deserves his full name. They showed. They get to. They are the fourth best side in the country.

Prior to the game I had hoped and thought Liverpool would go three clear. Anything for three clear. Give a kidney for three clear. I didn't care for the statement, I wanted the points. In 2001-02, in 2008-09, in 2013-14, I saw Liverpool make statement wins, put points on the board, produce. I saw no league titles.

Massive statements are bullshit; points on the board are reality. The only reality that matters right now is one point clear; 11 to go. I wanted more today but then I would have taken this in August, in November, on January 3. Liverpool can see this whole thing out from here. This is liberating. But there are a million miles to go.

Twenty-seven down. Eleven to go. We are in the box seat.

Attacking better isn't asking the world. Liverpool need to be better. If they are, they will be the best.

Liverpool v Watford

Wednesday February 27, 2019

ROB GUTMANN'S PREVIEW

IT'S not easy to make sense of the last week at Liverpool Football Club. In about seven days' time I think we'll know more.

Liverpool have faced significant tests, against Bayern Munich and Manchester United, but reaching firm conclusions on the state of The Reds' health depends on which end of the telescope you are peering through.

Liverpool thoroughly dominated both encounters against sides who had won virtually all of their most recent dozen games. At Old Trafford, many of the home fans expected United to put down a marker that it was they who would be where Liverpool are this time next year.

Liverpool came in for criticism post match on Sunday because, with just one shot on target all afternoon, they had appeared strangely toothless. But when the dust settled, and hands and heads had been shaken, Liverpool traipsed back to their dressing room refuge atop the Premier League once again. Not by quirk of the order of fixtures, but clearly first, with marginal but very real daylight between themselves and Manchester City.

Many of us had talked ourselves into Sunday being something of a shit or bust occasion. In the days coming into the game, I felt we must cut a swathe across Old Trafford and take a victory there like true champions would.

As kick off neared at the weekend, I corrected and calmed myself somewhat. The realisation that seven points from this week's three Premier League games would see Liverpool at least a point clear with just nine to play and the softer run in.

A draw at Old Trafford is a thoroughly decent result, one worthy of champions, if it's followed by two wins between now and Sunday.

Sounds easy. Man City besting West Ham at home and then Bournemouth away sounds easy too, when we say it quickly. The truth is, at this stage of the season and the contest to be top dog, nothing is precisely as it seems.

The bookies odds are on Liverpool and City both taking maximum points this week. However, the odds will be against on all four results going with the favourites. So, the likelihood is that something will give over the next few days.

Jürgen Klopp has moved to calm nerves. He has focused on the half-full nature of Liverpool's glass. The title challenge is 'pure opportunity' according to the manager. He is correct, of course. It bears constant repeating – we all would have torn our very souls to lead the league with just 11 games left.

Given that matches are now coming that bit thicker and faster, the Liverpool manager may have begun selecting his side for Watford's visit by picking his teams for both this week's challenges simultaneously. The derby against The Blues at Goodison is imminent too.

According to Klopp, Bobby Firmino's ankle is making the greatest comeback since Lazarus, but I wouldn't risk him for Wednesday night and I don't think the manager will either.

We can put out a side which has Mane, Shaqiri and Salah up top, abetted by a midfield of Fabinho, Keita and Wijnaldum. That has to be more than good enough or we might as well give up and go home now.

Bringing Shaqiri and Keita in freshens things up just a tad and also leaves scope for Klopp to, again, make solid changes for the derby, for which the likes of Firmino, Milner and Jordan Henderson might expect recalls.

Watford, for their part, are buzzing and basking in the glory of a 5-1 trouncing of Cardiff. Their form is solid and they continue to look capable of finishing as best of the rest. Klopp told the press that he expected Watford to sit deep and let us have the ball. I hope he was goading them with some passive aggressive mindgamery.

The visitors will arrive at Anfield without pressure and, if encouraged, are in the mood to earn the result of their season. Klopp's Reds cannot afford to play ball. We've come this far, and dropping any more points would start to look like a habit we were no longer capable of breaking.

Anfield must not show nerves and instead transmit the resoluteness it showed for Bournemouth's visit. Together we are always stronger.

Liverpool 5 Watford 0
BEN JOHNSON'S RATINGS

THAT was fucking sound that, wasn't it?

Alisson: 8

Nothing to do apart from looking all sound and that until he has to make a point-blank bad boy. Not being funny but they are almost impossible to defend, you know. Your lads play a belter backline, some cunt beats it with a late run but can't score from where he is so heads it across to all the fellas who were offside to nod one in. Got to be offside that, morally. Don't care what you say.

Trent: 10

Oh my God. Not being funny but they are some of the best balls in you will ever see in your life. A big blend of Johnny Barnes, David Beckham and Gegsi, but probably better than the three of them.

Virgil: 9

Me mate had Mane for a hat trick. Fucking made up when he went off. Virgil scores his first, he leans in, whispers I've still got a live one here. Got a Virgil brace. Queue mayhem. Glorious there, Virgil. Flawless. He is probably better than any one centre half to play the game.

Joel Matip: 8

Part of a backline that had to put up with Troy Deeney being pissed off with not getting a carrot out of Virgil and trying to bully everyone else. Gave no quarter. Belter block first half with his big schooner webs.

Robbo: 8

Mad the way he set up two from full back there, and wasn't the best full back on the pitch.

Fabinho: 9

I was in the Upper Main there, and for the first time I got to see him from a high spec in the ground. His movement with and without the ball is a joy to behold. Probably the best defensive midfielder knocking about. Glorious. A thing of beauty.

Gini: 8

Filled in where needed, ticked it over, kept it, moved it, all at the right time. Takes some doing that.

Milner: 8

I seen that side and, I'll be honest, I was worried about the midfield. I was worried it couldn't create. I was worried we were set up to contain. And then Milner plays like 2014 Milner playing for City as one of the best attacking midfielders in the league.

Salah: 8

Honest to God his attitude is unbelievable. One of the best in the world, things haven't been going for him, worked harder than anyone on the pitch. Ragged their full back, back to that 'I'll beat you inside and out, ball bag' mode. Unlucky not to get a couple of goals. Saving himself for the Blueshite there.

Big Div: 8

Fella behind me spent the whole game calling him big cock. I mean, first time, it was slightly unfunny. Second time, it was slightly unfunny. Unless it wasn't a joke, and it was a factual statement. I mean, he might have bumped into him in Crosby baths changies there, communal fuckers them, people bouncing around all over the gaff in all kinds of states of undress.

Belter finish. Did the old, 'I'm cutting inside. I'm shite, I'm shite, I'm shite, it's in.' Worked his plums off, offered a threat, horrible to try and mark as a full back.

Sadio: 9

First 30 minutes, probably one of the best centre-forward performances for The Reds all season. The header is a belter, the backheel a piss take. Is he messing? Turned a front three which, in theory, with Div with his back to goal and Sadio left and Mo right, looked uninspired, to a dynamic front three.

SUBS...

Lallana: 7

Come on upfront. Mad that. Did alright.

Henderson: 7

Won some tackles and that.

Keita:

Hello.

NEIL ATKINSON'S REVIEW

IT could well be Liverpool's best performance of the season.

Off the back of one of the most disappointing, that is quite something. Off the concern rattling around the diaspora it is everything.

It is what happens when a unit is genuinely resilient, what happens when a team is absolutely brilliant. Liverpool top of the league.

I wish you could have been there.

Nothing is quite like a 5-0, nothing feels more like a weight off. Five-nil is the score of dominance, and the thing is Liverpool dominated a good side. Watford were actually quite good. They were tidy in moments and had a clear shape and plan. They had thought about Liverpool.

But they had no answer to Liverpool in the flesh, nothing they could do to cope with every single outfield player. Liverpool were irresistible. That was the point of them today.

Almost everything is based on the start from Sadio Mane, James Milner and Fabinho. The three of them dictated the early tempo. Mane absolutely ran the show from centre forward, a Bobby Firmino karaoke performance that took light, became better than the original, became everything. The header is tremendous, the backheel is the best thing I have ever seen in my whole life.

I wish you could have been there.

James Milner bombed about the pitch, it was like playing with 12, like playing with 13. Watford will sleep tonight with Milner on their retinas – closing, and moving, and shifting.

Fabinho loved it. Loved the pitch and the contest. He is a joy to watch, reading the game better than any other on the park. He plays his position with joy and he made clearly, early and often, that the game was a Liverpool game.

But Trent Alexander-Arnold has just thrown in the type of performance which would make David Beckham in his pomp blush. He has done it from right back.

There is a crazy conversation around Trent that is desperate to move him into midfield. The game shifts and changes, and right now it is easier to create explosively from full back rather than from central midfield. Trent shows that time and time again tonight alone.

Why be one of the best centre mids when you can be the very best right back? It will be a debate reheated for the whole of his time at right back.

Yet it doesn't happen with Robertson. We saw his brilliance tonight too. He came alive.

Mohamed Salah made Adam Masina's life awful. I felt for him when two down, legged time and time again. The gulf between them was astonishing. Salah kept asking him questions, at times holding his position with chalk on his boots.

Imagine the courage it would take to hold shape knowing Mo Salah has 30 yards of space. Imagine the stress levels. I watched Masina not know whether or not to stick or twist, knowing that the doubt in his mind will be in the mind of his teammates, knowing that everywhere they are left uncertain.

Liverpool don't just outplay you on nights like tonight, they leave you spun, unsure, a wheel of fortune that cannot stop ticking. They tap one shoulder and walk past you. They put a pea in a cup and ask you to guess where it lands. And wink at you.

Divock Origi warmed up brilliantly for Goodison; always willing, always strong. He charged around, shuttles and then scored a goal that was never on until it was obviously in the back of the net.

Virgil van Dijk got his brace and left me willing a penalty, shades of Gary Gillespie in the run in of 1985-86. Liverpool battering sides while Everton squeak wins. Until they can squeak no more.

I wish you could have been there.

Let's see, let's see where we end up. For now, Liverpool are top and suddenly Liverpool are having a ball. Calm as you like. Anfield unwound tonight, Anfield enjoyed itself and Anfield stood agog watching the league leaders be outstanding.

Too many bottles have gone, you know. Too many of our lot have spent weeks secretly wishing they were having Manchester United's season. It isn't stressful, it is hopeful, playing for fourth, hanging on for a cup. Easy that. Being Liverpool has been weighty because of the number of points required, the sheer scale of the task. Fucking cowards, the lot of them.

The scale of the task is nothing to the scale of the potential achievement. The scale of the night out, the scale of the sheer fuck-off dance we can have together. There is no scale greater than spending the summer sitting in trees smiling at passers by.

There is nothing better than Liverpool top of the league, everything else pales into comparison.

Opportunity knocks. The manager knows it and his lads know it. They knew it tonight.

One point clear.

Twenty-eight games gone. Ten hurdles to go. They were our lads Sunday, our lads tonight. They will do for me. They are not cowards.

Neither are you, handsome. Neither are you, queen.

I wish you could have been there.

Everton v Liverpool

Sunday March 3, 2019

ROB GUTMANN'S PREVIEW

AS Anfield let out into a mild early spring night on Wednesday at about 10pm, there was a lovely feel about the familiar scene.

There was no raucousness, defiance, or backslapping as is often the case after a big win. The throng simply oozed contentment.

Liverpool had demolished Watford with such composed ease that, after several weeks of uncertainty, the future began to look clearer once again. As people made their way back towards cars, trains, buses, town, thoughts were turning to a weekend filled with renewed promise.

This is no time for Liverpool to be getting caught up in Everton's narrative. The derby is always about them. Will they break their long winless drought? Can they do Manchester City a massive favour in the title race? Will they reenergise their season and set themselves up for an improved finish?

I think when we beat Everton, what we enjoy first is the spoiling of their narrative. 'This is our year, Blues!'... 'Was it fuck'... All that kind of thing.

Even in defeat they don't so much as retreat back into the shadows – like Homer in that Simpson's gif you've all seen a billion times – as get dragged off the stage kicking and wailing. There's never an acceptance that Liverpool might just be a much better football team than Everton. I suppose that level of vain pride has to be admired, to a degree.

In my lifetime, there was a spell when Everton were as good as Liverpool, and the prides of Merseyside shared four league titles in four seasons – 1985-1988. The Blues never got over those four years in the spotlight. In a sense, maybe Liverpool didn't either.

Our period of dominance – that had lasted best part of 25 years – was to fade shortly after theirs. Everton haven't won the league since 1987, but Liverpool haven't since 1990. There's not much in that, in terms of how long the respective title-winning droughts have lasted.

There is one massive difference between the sides since, though. Liverpool – in the 29 intervening years – have not unreasonably dreamt of titles at the beginning of seasons on about 10 occasions. Liverpool have actually mounted sustained challenges for titles five times (including this campaign).

Since 1990, I don't think there's been a single Evertonian who, if asked on August 1 of any given year, has honestly thought Everton could end the forthcoming season as champions.

The truth is, Everton's truth is, that the gap between the titleless Reds and The Blues, since 1990, has more often than not been a chasm.

Our title rivals Manchester City go to Bournemouth this weekend. Bournemouth are just two points worse off than Everton this season and have a better home record, yet the bookies can only see a City win, whereas their odds suggest the derby will be a fairly tight affair – albeit that Liverpool remain firm favourites.

Bournemouth are 12-1 to beat City, whereas Everton are 5-1 to defeat Liverpool. These odds varying across the two fixtures despite the underdogs being of an incredibly similar standard, as with the favourites.

So are the bookies mad, the punters mad, or is the derby still a unique 'the form book goes out of the window' phenomenon?

Jürgen Klopp is answering that question for his players. He's saying: 'Lads, forget the bullshit, forget the blue narrative, forget the hoary old cliches, fuck the derby, the day will be yours to own. If you really want it badly enough.'

Everton corrected their slide to a degree with a calming 3-0 win at Cardiff in the week. It should bolster confidence. Marco Silva would love to beat Liverpool and get his Everton career back on track, but he'd celebrate a draw like a trophy win just right now.

Although he was bold tactically at Anfield earlier in the season and will feel his side deserved more from that game, I think he'll be far more cautious for Sunday. Despite being at home.

Klopp will tell Liverpool to go for the throat. Liverpool are much better than Everton and there will be hunger to demonstrate that fact.

The manager will be mindful that, for many of his players, this will be their third fixture in eight days, though. He will want to put some freshness back in the team. Having said that, Klopp will equally be aware that after Sunday, Liverpool have a full week to rest up and prepare ahead of Burnley's visit to Anfield.

Expect the defence to remain unchanged but for there to be new faces in midfield. Keita and Henderson could well return, with Milner, and the possibly over-played Wijnaldum back on the bench.

That's if Klopp stays with the 4-3-3 that served well against Watford and in other recent games. There is a reasonable possibility of a return to the 4-2-3-1 formation favoured for much of the season. Xherdan Shaqiri will certainly hope so, as it represents his best chance of a recall.

The clever money remains on the 4-3-3 and the manager sticking with a front three that scored three goals between them, and dovetailed exceedingly well in midweek.

Salah was goalless but back to his imperious best, while Mane revelled in the number-nine role. Surprise starter and scorer, Divock Origi, was something of a revelation and the manager should reward him with another first-team chance.

We've conquered all of Europe, we must treat blue imposters as we would Bournemouth.

Control the narrative, write the story. Live only our dream, not theirs.

Life's what you make it.

Everton 0 Liverpool 0

NEIL ATKINSON'S REVIEW

WELL that wasn't a barrel of laughs. Very, very far from it.

When Jürgen Klopp arrived at Anfield he said that, when coming up against stronger opponents, his aim would be to drag them down to our level and kill them.

Today Marco Silva can reflect on managing half of that for Everton but the other half was very much lacking. Morgan Schneiderlin excellent and limited. He embodied the idea that the effort and focus of the first part makes the second part so difficult.

Klopp can reflect on being dragged down and whether or not his side did enough to pull away from opponents who were spending much of the encounter simply trying to manage time, get through parts of the game before growing a tiny bit in confidence or opportunity. That Virgil van Dijk is comfortably the best player on the pitch suggests there was the need for him to be.

His performance was great, he read the game wonderfully, covered for his teammates from a mile away and even turned on the afterburners at times; he should walk away with both an assist and a clean sheet.

Liverpool don't play at all well but should score. It's good covering play from Michael Keane and Lucas Digne on two occasions and a smart save from England's number one on the other. We know England's number one is England's number one by virtue of the fact that a graphic comes up on Everton's screen when he makes a save.

How were we not prepared for this? How had intelligence not escaped that this was happening at Goodison Park? You could describe me as agog.

The biggest issue with the second half is that Liverpool's performance has a half life. Every five minutes it deteriorated by 50 per cent. Every sub made us worse.

James Milner, fabulous footballer, great professional, threw in a 10-minute spell which is among the worst I have ever seen. Roberto Firmino seemed to be surprised there was a game on. It would have been funny had the game not been so serious.

In fact, it was funny. As soon as we lose the ability to laugh at the enterprise we lose its essence. James Milner will score a big goal for Liverpool between now and the end of May. Roberto Firmino will dazzle us.

Sometimes the reminder there isn't always a million miles between them on television and you on your worst Sunday happens at the most serious time. They are our boys regardless and I hope they can laugh at themselves.

They may struggle, at least for a while. The talismanic forward fails to open the scoring, Sadio Mane fails to dazzle, Jordan Henderson fails to set a tempo, Joel Matip loves sauntering forward before giving it away cheaply. The keeper did well. They may struggle because of what it all means. But it should be a barrel of laughs.

It meant a lot for Liverpool to get three points. It meant an awful lot for Everton to play a part in stopping us. The roar that greeted the final whistle from the Old Lady was the second time I was left agog. It was visceral.

We will see if Everton will stop us. We can win all nine remaining but we cannot be dragged down again, we cannot be frustrated again, we cannot deny ourselves. Liverpool haven't conceded in five but they haven't scored enough. It is deflating.

But nor should we be defeated. Deflated yes, but 70 points are on the board and Liverpool still have their platform. Bottle the Goodison roar. Remember it.

Twenty-nine gone. Nine hurdles left. I can't wait to run them, I can't encourage Liverpool enough to run them.

Run them as hard as you can, Reds. Don't let anyone else drag you down.

CHAPTER SIX – THE NON MOVERS

THERE are times where you stare into the abyss.

Where ecstasy and frustration become the two emotions furthest from your mind. Like the devil and angel on your shoulder. And you're in the middle, staring into space. Because that's how it feels.

How? You're probably still not entirely sure.

Liverpool had given us the most joy we'd felt in our lives. It had to end, you might have said. And yet it still hadn't done that. There were still twists and turns to come.

You knew the joy would come back – a case of 'when' and not 'if'. But would 'when' be soon enough? Soon enough to keep you alive? Only time would tell, at this point.

All we knew was that we were on the knife edge; the toughest place to be and yet the place you want to be all at the same time. You want to play for the biggest prizes with no stress? You're in the wrong game, I'm afraid.

We knew it wouldn't be easy, no matter how much Jürgen Klopp and his side had tried to make it look so early on. All we could do was stay alive. Except it felt out of our control, even if positive forces tried to tell us it was.

At this stage, the league was no longer led by Liverpool. But all hope was not lost.

And that's the thing about hope. Whether you decide it thrills or kills you, it can often be found in the place you weren't necessarily looking the whole time.

Josh Sexton

Liverpool v Burnley

Sunday March 10, 2019

ROB GUTMANN'S PREVIEW

TRUDGING out of Goodison, away from the lights, onto wet pavements, street lights reflecting in puddles, Blues singing songs of shameful joy. We walked on with less hope in our hearts.

I felt powerless. It was a strangely comforting feeling and I'm not entirely sure why. To this recent point there has been a sense of control. That this Liverpool team want to win the Premier League title as much as we are willing them to do it. That combined we are an unstoppable force.

For the first time since November, Liverpool no longer truly top the league. We've been cut adrift by a solitary but significant point.

So what happens next? It's in the lap of the gods. It truly will be what it will be, and I'm at the point where I think I might actually be able to let myself enjoy the whole process from here. The league title is no longers ours to lose. It's ours to win. And we can still very much win it.

Much of what I've always loved about football, about the game, is how it maps out the near future for you in terms of treats, things to be excitedly anticipated. I could get way existential on y'all here but having lived this life for half a century now I think the only truth I'm certain of is that there is no such thing as pure happiness, there are only things to look forward to.

Maybe I'm a dumb optimist but I've always been able to take solace – however dark shit gets – that there'll come a day which represents doing something fun. I've broken life down into a series of activities to be relished.

Football, its seasons, its competitions, provides a relentless rhythm of such occurrences. It doesn't matter if your team is good, bad, or indifferent, there's always an immediate objective. I look back on the crowd I was part of at Villa Park in 2015 which celebrated a Rickie Lambert goal like it was our last day on earth, for example.

What were we actually so jubilant about? I couldn't tell you now. Yes, it sealed the three points that day, but those points took us no nearer to any high pinnacle. At that time we must've built ourselves up to believe that a Liverpool win at Aston Villa could represent something truly momentous.

If Liverpool win something this season I think at the precise point of realisation of the achievement I could be no more ecstatic than I was that day at Villa, or than I was in chucking myself about in the wake of a 94th minute Ragnar Klavan winner at Burnley about a year ago.

I'm going to milk the ride from here on in. I'll be messaging mates coming into the weekend about a meet up to watch City play Watford. It's the day before our game with Burnley. It'll be something to look forward to. I'll loosely plan the day around it. It's a game of football I have a stake in.

Few things are more precious to me than this contrived construct. City can ruin the day with an inevitable early goal and a near-certain win, but until they actually kick off they can't touch me. They can't stop me looking forward to the event – in highly unlikely circumstance – that should it go our way will make me deliriously happy.

A routine Saturday made up of a number of mundane rituals would suddenly become one of the most memorable Saturdays in memory. I'm prepared to get excited and look forward to this prospect.

Jürgen Klopp will have told his lads in sessions at Melwood all week to think only of Burnley. Klopp knows that Burnley are a more complex challenge now than they might have seemed when looking at the fixture list a few weeks ago.

For one thing, they've stopped being crap. Although they were beaten at home by Crystal Palace last weekend and at Newcastle the week before, they were unbeaten in eight matches prior to then. In that run they beat Tottenham and were close to an incredible win over Man United at Old Trafford.

Still, we should take heart in the fact that Newcastle and Palace have halted their resurgence and hopefully tenderised them for our purposes.

The Liverpool manager has a fairly fit squad to choose from and he will be at a point where he may want to settle on a side that he'll feel can take the performances up a gear and get the team over some big lines.

At the back, Dejan Lovren could feature after weeks out with injury, but Joel Matip has done enough to keep his place for now.

With the default front three picking themselves, all Klopp's musing will again be on how to set up his midfield. Fabinho perhaps the only certain starter. The imperious Brazilian has stepped up to the very challenge set him in recent months and the midfield anchor role is now firmly his.

I hope and expect that Klopp will recall Naby Keita. I think that after Fabinho, he has potentially the highest ceiling of our stock of middle men. He had been played into form before a bout of illness knocked him out of the team. He must be reintroduced soon.

The third midfield slot could go to Jordan Henderson – he is the captain, after all – or to Xherdan Shaqiri, who must be wondering what he has done wrong to have not started a game for so long. The smart money, though, will be on Gini Wijnaldum making the cut, and so he should too. When we're talking about 'men of the season' at the end of May, his name will be in most people's top three.

Midday Anfield kicks offs aren't ideal. They're not the best way to set up your day either. Getting out of bed and going straight to the game feels a bit rushed to most. Where's the opportunity to savour the build up? It's breakfast and then boom! No time for thinking.

Maybe it's best in a way. Thinking about this title race is getting us nowhere. Better to enjoy the travelling because it's in God's hands as to where we'll arrive.

Liverpool 4 Burnley 2

BEN JOHNSON'S RATINGS

I'M saying that is The Reds' best win of the season.

It's not an understatement to say that the weather all but tipped the balance in favour of them. Balls in the air were a coin toss, the wind was howling in some bits of the pitch, but not others. If Burnley could have picked a set of circumstances to play us at home, a 12 bells kick off and the weather from *The Day After Tomorrow*, would have been first on the list.

The Reds were absolutely fantastic. Seriously. This was a battle of wills, and The Reds' will is stronger than most, hopefully all.

Alisson: 8

Not sure from where I was what happened for the first goal, but given his reaction I'm saying the ref is a cunt who changed his name from Andrew to Andre, after the giant. Wears a set of his wrestling undies under his shorts.

He did give Joel a shout of man on in the lead up to him swallowing his kecks and heading it out for a corner but I can't be having that as something to criticise. Immense in the last minute. Seriously, immense.

Trent: 8

Sublime. A world-class footballer. Only thing I couldn't work out was why he kept trying to float it first half in that tornado corner by the Annie Road instead of twatting it and letting the wind do the rest. Hope he is ok.

Joel: 7

I'm giving him a seven on the basis that that is as hard a task as you can get that, playing against a gang of giants who haven't eaten for a week and fancy a nice big bowl of Joel soup for tea.

That said, he was shite for the corner for the first goal. Running along got it boxed, Alisson shouts man on to him as he was deciding what to do, and he reacted like The fucking Gruffalo has jumped out of a portal and whispered in his ear that his favourite food was Joel ice cream. Shit his kecks and lashed it out for a corner.

Virgil: 10

That's as good a performance as I have ever seen. He is just so good. He is bigger, harder, faster and has better positional sense than every other defender I have ever seen. One of the best of all time.

Robbo: 8

Unlucky not to score on a couple of occasions. Defended well, attacked well, what more do you want?

Fab: 8

His ability to play under pressure is great. Extra point for pulling out of that one that was such a nailed-on second yellow that Andrew the giant got a little bellend twitch in excitement and had already started rubbing his hand furiously back and too all over his yellow card.

Gino De Campo (typo that): 8

First sub off, I'm saying that means he's our most important midfielder for Wednesday. Remember saying superb Gini a lot first half but can't remember what for. Took one off Sadio's head.

Lallana: 9

On the way to the game, the news he's starting breaks, and everyone I seen, to a man – myself included – was calling him and the manager for all kinds. Which, you know, is mental really. He was excellent from the first whistle, his work rate and touch got The Reds back in it. Great pressure for the first, a constant pain in their arse.

Mo Salah: 8

Thought he was excellent today, just not having much luck in front of goal. When he's in and about to slot, their lad wellies him and Firmino scores.

It was good of the ref to implement the rules version two, which is their team can kick shite out of us and we can't touch them. Always a pleasure to see that.

Set up most of our goals, which is sound isn't it?

Firmino: 8

Scored two which he probably should just give to Mo because it was like that Dirk hat trick when Suarez got given all the goals by the dubious goals panel after the fact. Would like a drum in the ground to slow his song down.

Sadio: 9

Hard as iron. Great finish for the first. Banging them in now, isn't he? Was so happy when he got that last one, I couldn't have coped with them having one more foray into our half.

SUBS...

Sturridge:

Boss ball for the last.

Naby:

Hasn't been playing because he can't run backwards. Come on and didn't do much running backwards.

Hendo:

Was boss when he come on.

NEIL ATKINSON'S REVIEW

LIVERPOOL go 0-1 down in the wind and the hail and you wonder if they are going to break.

It's cycling up a mountain, a Tour de France stage with yellow jerseys and polka dot tops, loons running alongside the bikes. Cycling up a mountain and teeth are gritted, and then three weeks ago Tottenham faced Burnley and they broke. Left pedalling squares ever since. Not about bottle but about pace and not being able to handle it.

Liverpool go 0-1 down and you wonder if they will be pedalling squares for at least 85 minutes, headbanging in the face of Burnley and their elbows and the wind and the hail.

For the five minutes immediately prior to the equaliser I was staring into the abyss for the first time since October, let me tell you the abyss is deep. The weather pounded the Kemlyn, the stand itself moaned and groaned, grinding deep, the pathetic fallacy killing me, the prospect deep and hollow.

We are all allowed to wonder, to wobble, why wouldn't you wonder? But, unlike last weekend, Liverpool themselves had other ideas, a mountain to climb not an abyss to fall into. Other ideas are all I can ever ask when my own turn as gangster as the weather.

Jürgen Klopp had other ideas and God bless him. The selection of Adam Lallana would always be controversial under the circumstances, but the other ideas came through him – a vertical press forcing Burnley into chaos at times, forcing Liverpool onto the front foot, forcing the issue.

Lallana's slight frame and tender touch belies a smart aggression that, when fully fit, the Burnleys of this world struggle to live with. The equaliser and the second come from smart work leading to brilliant front-three quality. Mo Salah tortures a full back before throwing Tom Heaton into disarray. Sadio Mane's finish sharper, sweeter and fruitier than lemon meringue pie.

Roberto Firmino grew into the game to the point he began to run it. He ends up with a brace which rewarded the number nine side of his game, two tap ins, two triumphs for gambling; the other side of his game was pristine.

He loved the chaos – chaos of the conditions, chaos of Burnley, chaos of cycling the mountain. The game became one of his. That happening is among the best things in football.

The goal that opened the abyss, that made you wonder about breaking, was a foul on Liverpool's keeper but he responded brilliantly. He claims three or four very well indeed, commands and is certain with the ball at his feet. At some point the Anfield crowd will need to appreciate that he is going to play football.

What Liverpool do well through the game is keep playing, they manage it even at 3-2. They were a side confident in their football, backs never against the wall – as shown by Daniel Sturridge spraying it beautifully into space for Sadio Mane to keep his cool.

There is something so satisfying about that fourth, that 'fuck off' of a goal. Liverpool will not be pedalling squares today. For the challenge to come, scoring four is the way forward. No, Salah doesn't get his goal but apart from that it couldn't be better. Liverpool have shaken off adversity marvellously and walk on through the wind and the hail.

The pace remains remarkable. This is the first title race since 2013-14 to be going into April and the demands are to break 90 minimum. It's one hell of a mountain Liverpool are climbing but you listen to me, they are climbing it, they have gritted their teeth, they have other ideas. They will do for me.

Thirty gone. Eight to go. Liverpool bang on Manchester City's wheel.

Bayern Munich v Liverpool
Wednesday March 13, 2019
ROB GUTMANN'S PREVIEW

IN 1981, Liverpool went to Munich having drawn 0-0 in a first leg at Anfield in a European Cup semi-final.

Liverpool weren't fancied. Liverpool weren't playing well that season. The German side were confident.

I was 14 in 1981 and I was having a difficult time too. I didn't enjoy being 14. I suppose most people don't enjoy being 14, but at the time I thought I was the first to find it a testing age.

It's chaotic being 14. Nothing prepares you for the spiralling loss of control. You're lurching about grabbing for constants that are no longer there. Football anchored me at that time. I've needed football to keep things on a level on many occasions since.

Sometimes though, I need things to save me from football. But nothing quite measures up. Me and my best mate, who has been watching Liverpool with me since we were 13, always used to talk about having strategies for those times when The Reds let you down.

I remember sullenly walking down Walton Breck Road with him down the years after a bad result at Anfield. We'd start making plans. We'd talk about distractions. Anything but football. When we were younger, the prospect of going out on the town and the quest to find girls was a solid solution. Sometimes we'd settle for food. Going for a Chinese or an Indian. These were our options, our weapons of choice.

I liked that we shared those tough times. We all love the game, live for the game, but it tests us and we need to be as ready for its lows as we long for its highs.

When Liverpool are shit and not involved with anything serious then the edges aren't there. Defeats don't hurt as much and wins aren't as uplifting. When there's stuff to really play for is when it gets scary. Is when you feel 14 again. Anything and everything are possible and yet equally seem so unlikely to resolve themselves positively.

As Liverpool have hunted down a first league title in 29 years, its ever nearing prospect has yielded a season lived on the edge. It's what we want but it's not easy to handle.

A year ago the league wasn't a prospect but the European Cup was. I love the European Cup because it's a treat to be enjoyed in stages. Each phase perfectly compartmentalised. You build up, you anticipate each challenge, each round and, if you're successful, there's breathing space. A period in which to savour what's past and to relish the prospect of that which awaits.

The league? It's like a fucking pot that needs constant stirring. Like a film you can't look away from or you'll lose the entire thread. Go for a piss and you might as well not watch the rest. It's relentless pressure. A good pressure, like watching a complex conspiracy thriller like *All The President's Men* for example, but also a burden nonetheless.

I enjoyed the stressful 4-2 defeat of Burnley at the weekend. I celebrated our goals like they were the last goals I'll ever see Liverpool score. I've greeted every league goal this season in this way.

I'm not shouting when we score, I'm howling. I'm primal screaming. I wouldn't want to see any footage of my grid in these moments. All bulging mad eyes, gnashers barred like Jack Nicholson, forehead veins about to burst.

I'm quite looking forward to the respite of the European Cup. It isn't our everything this season. Not yet anyway. We can go out to Bayern on Wednesday night and it won't be the end of days. They'll be a swift dusting down and a realisation that Fulham away just four days later is a bigger game.

I'm ready to lose this one but very excited about the prospect of victory, to truly be taking this season to a level we'd daren't even dream could be possible.

I suspect Jürgen Klopp will also try and transmit to his players that the second leg in Bavaria is only to be enjoyed. He will be pumped up for this and so too naturally will be his team. This isn't the league, this is a one off, this is just a great party, so let's simply have the time of our lives.

Liverpool's prospects of success will depend on the players rediscovering and harnessing that energy that swept them past all comers during last season's European campaign. At times we were a force of nature. Everyone was scared of Liverpool. Bayern Munich were scared of Liverpool at Anfield. Their conservatism demonstrated this.

Bayern will tell themselves that they have seen what Liverpool had to offer and it didn't over daunt them. They will tell themselves, as did their forebears of 1981, that Liverpool aren't all that. But Liverpool are all that. This Liverpool are better than the Liverpool of 1981. This Liverpool will finish higher in the league than that side and with many more points.

Klopp will make few changes from Saturday's team. Again, only the midfield is in doubt (late injuries or illness notwithstanding). Again, it's Fabinho plus two. Jordan Henderson and Naby Keita were benched for Burnley. It could be that their legs were being saved for Munich.

Be bold, Reds. This one is something of a free hit. It would be nice to rattle Europe once again. It was clear last year that Liverpool were the continent's coming force. We are on the brink of a league title, we are getting better and better. Nothing to fear but fear itself.

I wish someone had told me that at 14.

Bayern Munich 1 Liverpool 3
BEN JOHNSON'S RATINGS

MAD the way they played The Vengaboys when they scored. Mad fuckers.

Alisson: 7

Stood up well when they were in at 1-1. Did he have anything to do apart from being the best passer of the ball on the pitch?

Trent: 7

They were trying to get after him all first half. They asked him questions all day and he answered them for a laugh.

Big Joel: 7

He's always very busy in games, isn't he? Like, busier than everyone else, heat map is fucking roasting. I think that's because he's, in the main, fucking shite so every team we play try to exploit him and also let him have it.

Did alright in fairness but then chose today to only have little boots on instead of his normal Ideal Standard fellas that would have stopped that ball dead and swallowed it down the plug hole rather than just prod it in. Played really well second half.

Virgil: 8

Oh Virgil. From the minute that ball comes into the box it's on his head. Just sucks it onto his head and then fucks it right off into the net. Glorious. Just before he scored I said to Robbo I'd pay £2,000 to be at home having a bath and a cup of tea. Hahaha. Get in.

Andy Robbo: 7

Up and down but gets caught out by a straight ball for their goal. Just knocked off for a second. Had hard lines for the yellow, but can have a little rest while we banjo City all over the gaff with Albie running the show.

Henderson: n/a

Think he's got gonorrhea of the heels again.

Gini: 8

Loads and loads and loads of filling space first half, loads and loads of breaking it up and linking Mo Salah down the wing on the break second half.

Milner: 7

Loads and loads and loads of filling spaces first and second half. Like a few of the boys the final pass was off for ages. And then it wasn't and we won.

Sadio: 9

What a goal. Best keeper in the world closing him down like a giant robot. Oh yer, yer, yer... I'll just go this way then. World-class dink. World-class fella. Boss movement for the third and a great header but in fairness that is probably the best ball you will see all year. Gave it the finish it deserved.

Mo: 8

Getting pushed, booted and basically blocked off all over the pitch. I'd like to think he is going to get a cob on again at some point and fucking wipe the floor with these pricks.

Had a go, should have done better with the one where it opened up and he had a free hit at their keeper but, if we are all honest, that ball for Mane is probably the best thing you will ever see. Absolutely perfect. I'll take him not scoring and just setting up goals all year till we win the double and that.

Bobby: 7

Not at his best, but worked and linked and once the reds were in front, come to life a bit.

SUBS...

Fab: 7

Come on does really well for 20 minutes and gets The Reds playing. Then when we need him to keep The Reds playing, he started giving it away and getting legged first half. Better second half, but oh my God he got sent for *The Echo* and a portion of chips more than anyone I've ever seen in the last 10, there. Looked fucked last 10.

Origi: 7

Was scared he would make us worse when he come on, but does great in the buildup to the third, slotted in and grafted.

NEIL ATKINSON'S REVIEW

ABSOLUTE scenes. The big one we have all been waiting for.

Liverpool's win means everything. It means they can be the best team in Europe. It means they can be the best team you have ever seen. The expectations should no longer be managed because this was the big one we were all waiting for.

Nothing should be minimised after this. Liverpool thought and played their way through 90 minutes in Munich with aplomb. They were stern for 15 and then dominant for 20 minutes or so. Dominant didn't mean owning possession but it meant owning space, pushing in quick moments, finding ways to expose and panic Bayern Munich.

A valid takeaway from the game is that Bayern Munich hated all of it. Bar the last 20 minutes at Anfield there is an argument that Bayern have had 180 minutes of sheer hell, of knowing they can never let themselves play, of accepting they were the junior partner in this marriage of European royalty.

To be Jürgen Klopp tonight and know you have decimated those who decimated you in the past must be so very satisfying. Munich are marvellous and are top of their pops. But they aren't Liverpool Football Club. They haven't got what we have at the minute.

We have this: Sadio Mane. Currently there is a fighting chance that the best attacker in Europe who isn't the greatest player ever to play the game plays for Liverpool. Tonight Mane has shown everything his game has, there isn't a third of the football pitch he isn't outstanding in.

His finest attribute isn't his speed or his touch, it is his brain. The pictures in his head and his ability to disrupt those pictures is second to absolutely no one. He gets the game in ways which stagger.

We rarely praise decision making in forwards, but Mane's has verged on pristine for some time now. He is a modern Liverpool great, adding silverware is all he needs to do to be a bona fide legend of one of the great clubs in world football.

Tonight is indeed that sort of night, a night which adds to the list of immortals. These are the lads who got to Kyiv on the whole, lads who send Liverpool deep in Europe again.

Mo Salah tortures another defence without scoring. As we tick towards the hour I lament Milner and Wijnaldum not adding more and hope for a change. By 70 both have made fools of me, both running the show.

The barrel of Milner, endlessly wiping his nose on his sleeve, endlessly showing five more yards, endlessly dying for his teammates stays on the retina. Wijnaldum all hips and makers, cunning and present and crucial. Atkinson left daft, not for the first time.

Munich fall back then. The heady days of equalisers where Liverpool's pristine left side proved poor long gone. Robert Lewandowski the loneliest man in Munich, the only living boy in Bavaria. Serge Gnabry plays well and hurts The Reds but can't sustain it.

Joel Matip takes his own goal as well as you can and does the business. Fabinho recovers from a very wobbly 10 to be the game's dominant midfielder. But Liverpool's attack. Good God. Smarter than you, faster than you, stronger than you, technically better than you. Good God. What are you meant to do?

What are we meant to do? Let me tell you. Start acting like they are worthy, worthy of tonight, worthy of being thought of as potential league and European Cup double winners, worthy of the greatest acclaim imaginable. Worthy of unconditional love.

This column has been saying it for weeks. These lads are our lads. That manager is our manager. And they will do for us. Winning 1-3 in the gaff of the side who has made six of the last seven semis should tell you that.

Belief is everything; belief they can win this competition. Belief they can win this league. Belief they should fucking bounce into Fulham. Belief that anyone else's crowd are from now till the bitter end only half a football team compared to the boys in red.

Our boys. Our belief. Our competition. Look at who is left. Look at who won in Munich.

Liverpool Football Club. European royalty. I whisper things, the continent sings them back to you.

Scenes.

Fulham v Liverpool
Sunday March 17, 2019
ROB GUTMANN'S PREVIEW

THERE'S nothing quite like a win.

There's nothing quite like a big win.

There's nothing like a big away win, against a massive side, in peak form, where you control the game so comprehensively that it makes anything and everything seem possible again. Liverpool are basking just right now, Liverpool are bathing in glory, Liverpool have the sun on their backs again.

Beating Bayern Munich in the Allianz was a result of epoch-defining importance. Well, it has the potential to be. If The Reds allow Fulham to find a way from stopping them winning this weekend then we all won't look so clever. But let's not even entertain that possibility because this is a time to be a Liverpool supporter and it is right that we milk and savour every moment.

I didn't get much done on Thursday. I was too embroiled in watching reruns of Sadio Mane's goal from every conceivable angle. I watched and rewatched every post-match interview. I gorged on the gushing punditry. Much as the story of this campaign has been about our very real tilt at the league title, it is performances in the European Cup which still appear to define us.

There has been much talk of it being better to gracefully exit the European stage and leave greater capacity for the push to win the league, and there is sound logic to that argument. Yet only in the glorious aftermath of nights like Wednesday night can we truly appreciate how ultimately flawed that assessment is.

Liverpool will go to Craven Cottage as one of the most confident Liverpool teams in modern history. You would have to go back 10 years, to the week Liverpool went to Manchester United brimming with a self belief empowered by a 4-0 demolition of Real Madrid, to find a near parallel.

Before then, I don't know when we're talking about the same phenomenon. It's not that Liverpool simply got a big result in Germany – we've had few of them down the years – it was the manner of victory.

In Munich they will talk about the Liverpool side that rocked up and taught them how to play football for years, maybe decades to come. We remember the great sides that blew our minds. Cruyff and Ajax in the 1970s, that Barca team and that Overmars goal, Rafa's Valencia, Ronaldo's Real Madrid at Anfield in 2014.

Those nights when we knew we were in the presence of greatness and that we had to take the pain and just admire the craftsmen demolishing our beloved team. Now we are beginning to look like those special once-in-a-generation teams. Now it's our turn.

Ordinarily we'd worry about the legs of lads who ran themselves into the ground in our cause. But, such was the nature of Wednesday's victory, that adrenalin and belief should be ample to power Liverpool through a final 90 minutes before the international break.

Jürgen Klopp has some injury concerns but they are in midfield where the squad is best stocked. Our captain Jordan Henderson limped out of the action early in Munich with an ankle problem. Naby Keita also apparently has a 'minor injury'.

Last weekend at home to Burnley, Adam Lallana earned a surprise start after impressing his manager the previous week in training. He will have accepted being dropped back to the bench in midweek but might expect a recall for the trip to West London. Fulham have lost their last six matches and are hurtling towards relegation. Klopp will treat this fixture as if it was a home game, and to that end will look to start with four attacking players.

Lallana's main rival for that fourth attacking berth will be Xherdan Shaqiri who was yet to start a game in 2019. His Liverpool career seemed to have really taken off when he bagged two goals against Manchester United in December and he would never have dreamed then just how significantly his progress would stagnate.

Shaqiri has always come across as a naturally confident player though, and Jürgen Klopp would trust him to produce a performance should he decide to unleash him after his relatively lengthy hiatus.

Liverpool's front three combined to stunning effect in Munich and the Liverpool manager will be inclined to let them go once more knowing that something of a rest awaits them during international fortnight (Mo Salah has already been exempted from duty by the Egyptian coach). Should Klopp look to freshen for the sake of it, Divock Origi might again deputise for Roberto Firmino.

At the back Liverpool are likely to remain unchanged although there will be a temptation to give Dejan Lovren some minutes to rehabilitate him in the team, post injury.

Fulham are on their third manager of a disastrous campaign and the latest incumbent, caretaker coach Scott Parker, will hope that he gets the proverbial 'bounce' that most new managers enjoy at some point. He's only been in charge for two games so far and presided over two defeats. No bounce, just business as usual at The Cottage.

Parker's challenge in facing up to Liverpool's visit will be whether or not to try and frustrate an awesome opponent or just go for broke and gamble. Draws and narrow defeats are of zero use to Fulham right now. They need wins and only wins.

Parker may, though, have his eye on preserving dignity rather than chasing rainbow wins. The new boss will know that the game is virtually up and that he is better served being seen to restore some pride. How he convinces his players to buy into such an abstract objective is a more complex ask.

For The Reds it's a case of let's get our heads out of the clouds and down to the task at hand. We would go top of the league by beating Fulham (albeit City would have a game in hand). It's an opportunity we cannot afford to squander.

It's the place we've deserved to be.

Fulham 1 Liverpool 2
BEN JOHNSON'S RATINGS

REMEMBER that article that these wrote the other week about Hodgson in their match programme?

That was weird, wasn't it?

Alisson: 5

His touch is immense. I mean, you know that already, but still, every time you sort of forget how good it is, he does something else mad and keeps the ball.

That said, he's shite there for the goal, along with Virgil and Milner. He basically comes out and throws himself up in the air. He's probably amazed that Virgil has made half a mistake instead of balancing the ball on his head and slotting it to Mo back stick to break his duck.

Trent: 6

Played a fine line first half between absolutely backing himself and looking like he thought it was too easy. Couple of sloppy balls, couple of times we got lucky with them being absolutely shite on the break. He wasn't the only one, mind you. Some belter balls in second half but gave it away for them to break for the disallowed one. Mixed bag today, la. Looked knackered.

Joel: 7

Got a scolding off Virgil for not giving him a shout. Imagine how that would make you feel. Good God. You have let your team down, you have let me down, but worst of all Joelly, you have let yourself down. Go to your room.

Gave the ball away. Might just set a template up and leave that in every week.

Virgil: 7

I mean, I'm sitting here trying to find every excuse in the world not to say he has made a mistake but if he heads it further it's boxed. That said, it doesn't look like he had a shout and that's some fucking backwards slice by Milner there, isn't it? Just watched his interview after the game and he is basically blaming everyone else so, so am I.

Robbo: 8

Does really well to get in after 10 minutes but should do well better with the final ball. Story of The Reds' first half, in fairness. Deffo going to score soon and was one of our better players all day long.

Gini: 8

I thought he was one of our best players. So unlucky with the effort that goes wide at 2-1. Kept The Reds playing when people around him were a) panicking b) strutting about.

Fabinho: 7

Does well not to get sent after the first yellow. He's good at that, isn't he? Did his job but looked like it might have been a game too far at times.

Adam Lallana: 7

Did a cracking job of blocking Mo Salah off when he was in first 20 and then followed it up by getting a chance to shoot and instead tackling it out for a goal kick and doing a nice fall over on the deck. Set the tempo at times when we didn't have the ball but by Christ he can slow a game down.

Mo Salah: 7

Absolutely got nothing going for him at the minute. Loads of half chances, loads of slightly off decision making. That said, when they broke with three against one, he does unbelievably to get back. That's why he's one of the best in the world. That work rate, that desire to help his side out. You can't teach character like that really.

Does well to keep grafting and getting shots off. Was fucking ecstatic when he wasn't on the pen because he was deffo missing with the luck he is having.

Sadio Mane: 8

Did a one two from the edge of the box and scored. Sounds simple, no? It was brilliant because it was so complex and yet so easy all at once. Pretty much what he is all about these days, isn't it? His movement is just so good. So unlucky with the header against the bar. The Reds' best forward again.

Bobby Firmino: 7

Started better than anyone. Popped up all over the place. His movement, touch and awareness for the first was sublime. Tired as the game went on.

SUBS...

Div: 7

Did well when he came on. Love this left wing Div with a sublime mix of loads of end product and absolutely no end product. Backing himself at the minute which is good to see.

Milner: 7

Absolutely the opposite of what the manager wanted when he first came on; giving it away, setting up goals for them and that. That said, settled us down last 10 and some balls to slot the pen like that.

Fucking get in.

NEIL ATKINSON'S REVIEW

YOUR heart pounding when James Milner steps up.

Your head hurts a little bit, that might be a sign of last night, your head hurts and your heart pounds, and you watch James Milner step up and you are pleased he is there but know what it all means. It means everything.

James Milner scores and your heart speeds up. James Milner scores and you throb with what it means. Everything. On the replay Sadio Mane falls to his knees. Remember this: Sadio Mane needs to win this league more than you do. And you want it for all time.

There was a lot of hot air about this Fulham game. A lot arguing that it was a chance for Liverpool to improve their goal difference. As with so many football arguments that manages to be both true and untrue, all that is seen and unseen.

The fact remains this was the end of a massive Liverpool week, a Liverpool week that ends with all of its objectives intact.

Fulham were poor, a team who spent more time in crisis at the back than many, but Liverpool could never be as crisp as we'd like. They should have done more, won by a distance, streaked away and proved the argument right.

In the end we are delighted with the one-goal win, the three points in the boot, flying up the North Circular our dreams held together with spit and string and a bloody-minded unwillingness to yield.

Liverpool were by a mile the better side, the game's dominant force. But across the pitch performances became sloppy, sharpness dwindled.

The only exception was Fabinho who had his sharpness taken from him by the yellow card and follow-up challenge. He had to be supremely disciplined second half, his manager keeping him on for his height and his quality but his brilliance going to ground diminished.

Elsewhere performances were bumpy, Arnold and Robertson epitomising the inconsistency, almost as if they had had a big night in Munich midweek.

The goal Liverpool concede is a howler, but they should have conceded prior to that, Fulham wasting a three on one. It became a three on two and a three on three as Salah and van Dijk ran back.

Salah will get a lot of chatter but in that moment you saw what this side and this opportunity means to him. His job was to harry there and then and harry he did. He needs a goal but nowhere near as much as we just need him. He is a treasure, a grafter, a true believer.

The performance from van Dijk and Alisson after the goal that they concede is simply marvellous. The level of assurance and certainty from the pair shows their character and their confidence. The goal itself is dreadful. Everyone needs a shout, but no one should need a shout. Ryan Babel's finish ends up being sheepish, he practically apologises as he kicks it over the line.

Yet again Sadio Mane is the best of Liverpool's front three, yet again he scores. He is irresistible currently. Part of Liverpool occupying the half spaces.

Out of possession Adam Lallana was again excellent until he tired. It's fascinating this small lad suddenly being Liverpool's enforcer but that he is. He is a barrel of aggression and nous. He knows when it is there for him, for us, and hunts accordingly.

Divock Origi came on and made all sorts of sense, switched on, sharp, doing bits, being part of the enterprise. James Milner the best of us, celebrating in front of the collected Reds. Nothing but sense as the clock ticks down.

When the whistle goes Trent on his haunches, Trent punching the air. When the whistle goes Liverpool are indeed released and relieved and realised. Top of the league.

Fulham away in spring, man. You remember it. You remember it for Yossi and you remember it for Steven. You remember it for sounding the siren – there is a title challenge happening here.

Steven Gerrard doesn't need to whirl the shirt. No one needs to sound the siren. Liverpool want to be champions. And while they put you through the wringer they are your boys, each and every one of them. You will hold them close. You will forgive them everything. You will adore them.

They are the kings of Europe, they have scraped through against 19th. Lord, lord, lord, let us adore them. You know they deserve it.

Thirty-one hurdles cleared. Seven to go.

Why Klopp's Comments Should Have Rivals On Red Alert

Tuesday March 19, 2019

DAVID SEGAR

JAMES Milner's fault? Virgil van Dijk's fault? Alisson's fault?

Whomever was to blame for Fulham's equaliser against Liverpool on Sunday, they owe me, and presumably all of you, for the years that goal took off us... For seven minutes at least.

Tongue out of cheek, all three played their part in calming The Reds down and eventually firing them back to the top of the Premier League. Manchester City have a game in hand, but it is Liverpool's name at the summit for the next two weeks, which could be an important mental advantage in this title race.

The importance of the three points at Craven Cottage cannot be underestimated. Some believe that City are unlikely to drop any more points this season, but to believe that they would drop points in two games, while a Liverpool side that failed to beat Fulham would win its remaining games, would seem a tad fanciful.

However, Jürgen Klopp's men didn't fail. They succeeded despite being far from their best and got the job done in a way that, dare I say, champions do.

It's funny how Liverpool's lack of perceived ruthlessness and electricity led some in the wider football world to suggest it was a fortunate win, or that it was a sign that they struggled to juggle Champions League and Premier League football in the same week.

Many of us had of course hoped that the confidence that would be coursing through the veins of the Redmen after their 3-1 win in the Allianz Arena against Bayern Munich last Wednesday would lead to a sound thrashing of Scott Parker's Cottagers.

That didn't turn out to be the case, although with some better finishing and Milner getting a better connection on his clearance, it could have been.

What made the underwhelmed reaction to the victory particularly funny was that it was far from the first time Liverpool have played supposedly poorly and won this season. Reasons for that have varied from Mo Salah being off form, to missing Phil Coutinho, or even that some teams have 'figured them out'.

After 31 league games, Klopp's men sit top on 76 points. More than they achieved in 38 games last season, as many as they achieved the season prior to that, and 16 points more than the season before that when Leicester won the league. In fact, Liverpool already have five points more than the final total of the team that finished second that year.

The many who are itching for Liverpool to fail have been grasping at the luck card again. Tim Cahill and Leon Osman appeared on Sky and the BBC respectively saying that the game-winning penalty shouldn't have been given. More realistic critics pointed to the fortune that Sergio Rico would make such a huge error to gift the opportunity in the first place.

As the old saying goes, you make your own luck... Unless you're Liverpool in which case you're jammy and get everything your own way and life's not fair and it's all a conspiracy and some day the devil is going to come for your soul and you'll be relegated to the Hell and District Counties League Division 2.

Sarcasm aside (the highest form of wit I'm led to believe), moments of fortune can play a part, but across a season you generally finish where you deserve to. No reasonable person can argue that Liverpool don't deserve to be in this title race with Manchester City, even if there have been some wins that have needed to be ground out along the way.

Simultaneous gulps of terror could therefore be heard when Klopp addressed what he felt was the real reason for the slight lack of cohesion in Sunday's performance, and some others throughout the campaign.

The bespectacled German told Sky Sports after the game: 'I am not in any doubt about my players' nerves. It is about intensity. We go for perfection but it is rare that you get it. People will say we need to be more convincing, but we are at the start of a development, not the end.

'They are cool enough. On our day we are a flying team, that's all there, but the consistency is rare.'

He believes that this Liverpool team is merely just getting started. He knows they can play better and to their highest level more often. At the same time, despite inconsistencies, this version of Liverpool is on course to achieve the second best points total in Premier League history (unless City finish above them, in which case it will be third).

Klopp believes further development is possible. Of course, he believed the same at Borussia Dortmund and was ultimately thwarted by the might of Bayern Munich's spending. The same could happen this time round with City, but this time he has had sufficient money of his own to strengthen his hand, and with all due respect to his Dortmund team, now has better tools to work with.

It may concern those who love a good transfer window to have heard Klopp's recent comments about not needing to splash the cash again this summer, but it is because he has such faith in the squad he has already put together and knows that this team developing together is what will make them stronger.

He will sign some new players, if only to replace the outgoing ones, but the heavy investment has already been done to get the spine in order. Anything else is likely to be finishing touches to what will hopefully be a masterpiece.

Every key player is signed up long term to the club, and youngsters with their whole careers ahead of them are given opportunities to become a part of it. Trent Alexander-Arnold and Joe Gomez have already take their chances, while Rhian Brewster is likely to get his next season.

This current Liverpool team is capable of so much. Who knows? It might even achieve a historic double in the next couple of months. And yet, as Klopp says, there is still plenty of room to grow. Rivals are likely to grow as well, but at the moment nobody is matching the rate of development that The Reds are showing.

The scope for achieving higher is getting smaller the more points Liverpool accrue (you can't lose many fewer than one league game). However, if in the future they can put in convincing performances more regularly, generally win games more comfortably and continue to develop a widespread fear and respect throughout football, then the building blocks could be in place for something sensational that could go on for years to come.

Alexander-Arnold also commented on the development of this team after Sunday, citing the three games won last week, and suggested that previous teams would have crumbled under some of the pressure.

'Maybe a few years ago we might have won one of those games. Especially against Fulham, maybe a few years ago we would not have got the three points, but we've showed how good a team we're becoming.

CHAPTER SIX – THE NON MOVERS

'We're a force to be reckoned with.'

There is plenty to be excited about with this current Liverpool side, but its evolution is even more tantalising as far as I'm concerned. Mostly because once they improve to the point of regularly winning games like Fulham 3-0 instead of 2-1, I can stop having mild coronary issues every time I watch these Reds do their thing.

Liverpool v Tottenham Hotspur

Sunday March 31, 2019

ROB GUTMANN'S PREVIEW

AND then there were seven.

Seven games, seven days, seven plots yet to be written. Seven beginnings, seven endings.

Our silent prayer must be that they all remain relevant. We've come this far that the minimum we're surely permitted is to be there to see how this all plays out, to be part of the story on the final day.

Liverpool can and should win this league. Liverpool have been more consistent than Manchester City. Liverpool have beaten Paris Saint-Germain, Napoli and Bayern Munich. Liverpool have been beaten only once, City four times.

Liverpool have had brief periods of mediocrity, in what has been an intense and complex season but never have we been on the ropes, not like City were in December and part of January. Christ, City weren't half bad. I'm talking like they're still fatally flawed. They remain the bookies favourites.

Both they and Liverpool should finish the campaign with over 90 points. That has never happened before in the history of top-flight football in this country. Liverpool and Manchester City are two incredible teams cursed to be in existence at the same time as each other. Put either in any other era and they would be peerless. Both without competition domestically.

City and Liverpool face a combined 15 matches to see the season out. I predict that there will be 10 wins, four draws and one defeat across those fixtures. There will be five games when one or the other of these sides fail to win. In these five matches the destiny of the title will be decided.

One of the games vulnerable to a be a 'failure to win' is Liverpool at home to Tottenham Hotspur this weekend. Liverpool know that this is one of the higher fences they must yet hurdle on this final lap.

Until a few weeks ago, Spurs were in contention for the title. Heads were being scratched as to how that was still possible given the unspectacular and often underwhelming nature of their season. A sequence of poor results confirmed what most had suspected – that Tottenham are good, but not quite good enough.

Now 15 points adrift of the league's summit, Spurs cannot win the league but they can still decide its destiny. Both ourselves and Manchester City host Mauricio Pochettino's team before the season's end. I'm not happy that we have to face them first, but it is an opportunity to put serious pressure on City.

It is a fixture where, in effect, more than three points are at stake. Not literally, obviously, but City will look at games like this and count them as two pointers. They'll calculate that it if Liverpool were to play Spurs four times that they'd probably win two and draw two. That they'd average two points per encounter. If Liverpool win, therefore, they gain an extra point on the par expectation.

Jürgen Klopp does not need me to tell him that he needs to find a way to win this game. Of course a draw would be no disgrace. Even a defeat is more than possible when the biggest sides match up. Yet neither scenario is contemplatable within Liverpool's current context. A win will be deliriously celebrated but anything else will feel like a mortal blow to our title aspirations.

I now can't imagine what Liverpool winning this league will feel like. I know exactly what losing it looks like, though. For nine minutes at Fulham a fortnight ago I stared into that abyss. I want us to win this title more than I think I've ever wanted anything ever. But I'm also ready to forfeit it, should fate so deem.

Liverpool cannot live forever in the world of 'now or never'. I've always wanted us to do more than just win the big one. I want us to win the league so that we can win it again, and again.

Leicester loved that they won it in 2016. We love that we won the European Cup in Istanbul. But we both love these things a little less with each passing year. Time makes them increasingly irrelevant to the here and now. I love our glorious past, but I want to be excited about our future more. And right now, I'm very excited about it.

That we are almost as likely to win the European Cup as the league is an incredible thing. It is a signifier that it is not 'now or never'.

Liverpool may finish this season potless but when the dust has settled and we look forward to next season, we will reflect upon the huge possibilities that will lie ahead for a team (at least) good enough to have been top two or thereabouts in two successive Champions league campaigns and in our domestic league. Our average 'placing' will have been as good as any side in Europe.

For now, we have eyes only for Spurs. No wins in four games Spurs. Season at a crossroads Spurs. Their boss Pochettino may have one eye on his own Champions league ambitions or he may have one eye on a bigger European job.

Spurs may yet have to decide if they are expending all of their energies attempting to finish top four in the league, or in pursuing unlikely European glory. In some ways, they are where we were a year ago.

Jürgen Klopp and his players know that they face the prospect of scaling the Everest of their sporting ambitions and that all dreams could be fulfilled within the space of a matter of weeks.

Klopp will look last year's footballer of the year and record scorer Mo Salah in the eyes and ask him to cast aside concerns about his goalscoring form and to subjugate himself for the cause. Mo don't need telling though. Nor will the on-fire Sadio Mane, or Bobby Firmino, or any of his men. They realise that together they are always stronger. Always greater than the sum of their parts.

This is what sets Liverpool aside from Manchester City's travelling football show. City roll up to towns the length and breadth of the land and put on demonstrations. They provide precisely what was paid for.

Every point, every pass, every tackle, every goal is there within a balance sheet. Somewhere. Some place. The men in the offices in tall buildings planned exactly what could be achieved with their epic spending. They budgeted for a team that could regularly deliver 90-point seasons.

Liverpool could deliver a 90-point season too. It may not be enough to win us the league. Let's see. But it will be enough to make those fellas who plotted for City's eternal domination scratch their heads.

This weekend may be the one we come to see as the defining one in this season's title race. To this extent, The Reds have it all in their hands. Not just to keep the dream alive, but to knock the ball firmly over the net and back into City's court. To back foot them and make them doubt.

Spurs may have all the other ideas in the world, but our time is now and we must seize our moment.

Liverpool 2 Tottenham Hotspur 1
BEN JOHNSON'S RATINGS

I MEAN, for the love of everything that is holy, how the frigging hell are we meant to live our normal lives?

Work tomorrow, yer? Yer, yer, sound. These civilians, just wandering around living their lovely, ordinary, no peaks no trough lives and The Reds are fucking bouncing round all over the gaff. The highest of highs, the lowest of lows. Oh the highest of scruffy, spawny, Red Shite highs.

It's hard not to think our name is written all over it when shit like that keeps happening every other week.

Alisson: 7

His passing was a bit shite and that and, I mean, I don't know, he made one save where he just palmed it straight to their lad in front of the goal, but so fucking what?

Trent: 8

Sounder than any fucker you have ever met. Reckon he is a disco Beat Hotel fella, giving it loads to yer man Greg Wilson.

What's The Joelly Doing Tom: 7

Thought he was really good you know, twatting into the back of Kane and giving the fucker away every now and again aside.

Virgil: 9

It really is ridiculous at this point. There has never been a better defender to play for The Reds. The block on Kane in the first half, the defending space on his own in the second.

What's that, lad? You're the best centre forward in the world, yer? Got an MBE for services to keeping your fucking mouth open and having a fucking big fucking dry old fucking tongue, yer? Fuck off, dickhead.

His influence, his ability to inspire, to make sure it happens, to get us over the line regardless is immense. Second to none.

Robbo: 8

What a ball for the first. Then is just about The Reds' best player for the rest of the game.

Henderson: 6

That midfield of doom mate, when the team plays well it purrs. As soon as we don't it is shite. Henderson has a lot to do there, but it was genuinely bananas that Fabinho didn't come on at least 10 minutes earlier. The one where he tried to knock it in the box and he cobbles it out for a goalkick was a low point.

Gini: 6

The six for the midfielders feels a tad harsh because they all grafted like fuck, and it should probably be reserved for the manager rather than them but fuck it. Aside from the first 20-30 minutes I'm not sure what he did. A byproduct of the three of them rather than anything else. Caught in between their line an awful lot.

Milner: 6

See above and that. I don't really even know. I mean, I spent the last five minutes, which felt like four months, flitting in between a crouched on my haunches pose and a standing on the seat in front. I have no sense of anything and you want intelligent, articulate analysis of something or some jokes? You fucking do it, bellend.

Mo: 7

Couldn't buy a goal for weeks and then gets given one which deffo weren't his by George. Well in, George. Best thing you have done aside from play that Arcade Fire/Bruce Springsteen double header that time. Probably score every game now.

Sadio: 7

Had a week off. Saving himself for Southampton away.

Firmino: 8

The Reds' best player first half. Took 10 minutes to get to the rhythm of the game and then brought the game to his rhythm. Belter goal. Drifted out of it second half.

SUBS...

Fabinho: 8

Crying out for him for 20 minutes before he come on to the extent that you start questioning yourself. Have I forgotten that he is shite or something? Come on and was the best midfielder on the pitch, broke it up and got The Reds on the front foot again.

Div: 7

Love left wing Div, you know.

NEIL ATKINSON'S REVIEW

TRANSCENDENT. Here's the scene.

Last season in this fixture late in the game, Mo Salah went around their whole side and finished beautifully.

It went off.

It meant nothing. Both there and then and in the bigger picture.

This season he just keeps it alive back across goal and it ends up there in instalments via all sorts of nonsense. It's one of the worst goals ever scored. It is one of the best I have ever seen.

It went off.

It meant everything. It means everything. Everything now. And in terms of the bigger picture? It would be easy to say, 'We'll see'. But that's not true. It means there actually is a bigger picture to look at. It may seem an exaggeration, especially when I say to you that Liverpool can both drop points and end up champions but they couldn't drop those points, not today, not after being ahead, not given everything.

It was transcendent. There is a lot of all football support which is a slog. Remember Huddersfield Town away? Nil-one Liverpool, dismal stuff but what 0-1 Liverpool does is set up this. Huddersfield away made this possible you know, in a way you forget.

The whole point of this enterprise is when it transcends reality, makes Monday morning seem something another person needs to deal with, injects absolute joy into your veins. Leaves you with nowhere to go but wallow in paradise.

It transcends everything. Transcends the game itself, analysis and so on. But we must try. The rules…

Liverpool go in half time the better side and their own worst enemy, a goal light and most likely to bring about an equaliser against them. They failed to put the hammer down at 1-0 and that is the greatest failing of that first half midfield.

It was a first half contest of two sides trying to make the pitch big, rare at Anfield these days. Tottenham tried to shape in a way which asked Liverpool questions but once the side started playing those questions were answered. But Liverpool failed to connect properly until the Andy Robertson cross and Roberto Firmino header led to it being 1-0 and very little thereafter.

That was the first half. The second saw Tottenham be the better side. By some distance. They changed their shape and dominated the half spaces. And the whole spaces. They owned Anfield. It was some performance until they scored, to be honest.

In the five minutes prior to their goal, Klopp and Henderson were trying to change the shape but it just didn't take. It needed the change which came too late. The goal probably shouldn't have stood but it was reward for the best period of play from any away side at Anfield this season. Spurs were excellent and showed why they are the third best side in the league this season. Fabinho came on, made a difference but it felt too little too late.

Moussa Sissoko's miss is among the best things ever to happen in association football. Virgil does brilliantly, don't get me wrong. What he does makes Sissoko make a decision he doesn't want to make.

Two-one was everything. It felt both deserved and stolen, both in equal measure.

I mean, it hurt prior to the goal. The abyss was everywhere. More abyss than you can shake a stick at. It looked like it was without end, but then there was nothing scarier than when it went 2-1. Remembering last season there was no relief just another form of torture. When Tottenham came back at us it gnawed inside. Imagine throwing it away twice. Imagine that.

It didn't happen. Liverpool transcended the table, the occasion and possibly our lives.

Few things have ever felt like this, you know. I sobbed through the last 10 against City in 2014 at 3-2 up, overwhelmed by everything. But this wasn't that. Nor was it Yossi at Fulham.

There is something both rawer and roarer about this sojourn. Something which isn't defiance or improbability but pride. Been this thing that these lads are our lads and there are 20 of them. Divock Origi and Xherdan Shaqiri. Joel Matip and Naby Keita. Along with the stars, along with the hits.

You saw it all tonight, the crescent and the whole of the moon.

Transcendent. We ended playing with or in the sky; Wall-E with the fire extinguisher in space on the one hand, or Formby beach when the wind blows and the sky is enormous on the other and everything makes sense, when you suddenly make sense, when this whole adventure clicks in, kaleidoscopic twisting, the beauty lost in a moment. All you hear is time stand still in travel and feel such peace and absolute.

I don't know if we can handle this again. But we might need to.

Thirty-two down. Six to go.

It was a joy to be alive this day, my friends. It was agony, too. Imagine that. Taste it. Six more heaves.

Virgil van Dijk: Klopp's Colossus
Tuesday April 2, 2019
DAVID SEGAR

'TAKE a walk around my centre half, gentlemen. He's a colossus.'

That was Bill Shankly's famously declaration when the media first clapped eyes on Ron Yeats in a Liverpool kit back in 1961.

Shanks was keen on an exaggeration, but Yeats went on to prove the colossus assertion to be accurate, winning two First Division titles and becoming the first player to captain The Reds to an FA Cup success.

Jürgen Klopp made no such statement about Virgil van Dijk when he made him the world's most expensive defender in December 2017, but if he did, the words would have had a new meaning.

'Take a walk around him gentlemen. You can't, can you? Try running around him. Nope, can't do that either eh? How about if you get him in a two-on-one situation in the last five minutes of a game?' Followed by roaring laughter and a fist pump.

Just seven years ago, things looked very different for van Dijk. As referenced in a recent interview with *FourFourTwo* magazine, on April Fool's Day in 2012, the big Dutchman was lying in a hospital bed having suffered a burst appendix and could have died from the resulting complications. He fought back to recover and move on with his football career.

Fast forward to 2019 and van Dijk was rightly receiving adulation from the football world after another top-level performance in Liverpool's dramatic 2-1 victory against Tottenham at Anfield, including an astonishing piece of defending with the game level, and Moussa Sissoko and Heung-min Son bearing down on him.

The vast majority of centre backs would have panicked and lunged at Sissoko, leaving Son open, or been too concerned about the South Korean and allowed Sissoko a simple finish, but van Dijk judged it perfectly, putting the emphasis on Sissoko, pushing him onto his weaker side and forcing him to rush the shot.

You could imagine Alan Hansen, Mark Lawrenson, Phil Thompson and Jamie Carragher getting on their centre-halves' WhatsApp group and sending countless fire, shocked face and aubergine emojis.

While the Sissoko incident was rightly lauded, perhaps the best thing van Dijk did all day was in the aftermath of the winning goal. As his teammates went off to celebrate in the corner, Van Dijk was only interested in retrieving the ball. He then ran over to the side of the pitch and despite playing on an injured ankle, volleyed it as hard as he could, comfortably clearing the gigantic Main Stand.

Of course, there was another ball in the stadium so it didn't exactly waste time, but it was a symbolic gesture. Game over. Last season, he and his teammates were cruelly denied by Tottenham despite taking a late lead. Lightning would not strike twice as far as he was concerned, and it didn't as van Dijk himself made sure by heading away a final freekick.

The performance was important not just for Liverpool and their Premier League title challenge, but for the widening belief that van Dijk might just be the best defender walking the planet right now.

His recent error against Fulham was so out of character that it was noted as a rare chink in the armour, and meant that his next high-profile showing would be scrutinised thoroughly for those trying to find evidence to allow them to take a contrarian – and therefore headline-worthy – viewpoint.

Netherlands faced Germany in Euro 2020 qualifying last week, and van Dijk comfortably dealt with everything that Leroy Sane and Serge Gnabry threw at him in the early stages. His young partner, the very highly rated Matthijs De Ligt, showed moments of inexperience as he was pulled out of position, but van Dijk covered and dealt with anything that got through.

That was until one moment of brilliance from Gnabry. The former Arsenal and West Brom man ran at Van Dijk, who was again forced to come over to the right to cover the space De Ligt had vacated. The Liverpool man jockeyed him, much like he did to Sissoko, but allowed Gnabry to cut onto his stronger right side.

You could argue that he should have shown Gnabry onto this weaker foot, as he had done earlier and did again later in the game, but it still required a finish of world-class quality to result in a goal. The commentary team weren't having it though, and started laying into Van Dijk, as if he had stood out of the way completely and let Gnabry have a tap in on the line.

They had enthusiastically praised his earlier work, particularly in dealing with Gnabry, but all of a sudden, every touch from the big man came with a comment of 'he's having a shaky game' or 'a rare wobbly performance this from van Dijk'. It took 'build them up to knock them down' to a completely new level.

It wasn't just the commentators. Articles were written on fairly reputable websites about a supposed weakness that had been exposed. The weakness apparently being that if you drag van Dijk to the right side of the defence, he struggles. Given he plays on the left side, it's not exactly a revelation that he shows some vulnerability when covering for an errant centre-back partner and/or right back.

These things will always happen of course, especially when contrary opinions are currency in today's world, but it was perhaps also another sign of why it is so hard for defenders to get wider recognition in the game. Why Fabio Cannavaro winning the *Ballon d'Or* in 2006 was such an event. Why, since 1994, only one PFA Player of the Year award has been handed to a defender (John Terry in 2005).

However, as things stand, van Dijk is the favourite to buck that trend. He's still odds on to be announced as the winner of the PFA award in around three weeks' time. It is testament to the impact he has had on a defence that was once derided as one of the shakiest among the top six, but since his arrival 15 months ago has become the best in England, and one of the tightest in Europe.

It is why Liverpool waited for him. When his original move to Anfield was blocked by Southampton in the summer of 2017 after accusations of tapping up, many Reds fans desperate for improvements in the backline begged the club to move on. Sign an alternative. Sign Mr Right Now rather than waiting for Mr Right.

Klopp waited for Mr Right, and ever since the 6ft4in Dutchman made his Reds debut that decision has been fully vindicated, not just with his qualities as a centre back, but the much-needed leadership he brought to the team.

In his interview with *FourFourTwo*, Van Dijk laid clear the way he sees leadership: 'Look at LeBron James in basketball or Tom Brady in the NFL. They are proper leaders, who are among the best in their sports of all time. They are under immense pressure every day, but they still show their teammates what can be achieved and inspire them to bigger heights.

CHAPTER SIX – THE NON MOVERS

'I want to get the best out of myself, but I also like helping the players around me to make the most of themselves, too.'

Six games to go for Liverpool in this title race. Their best player will be key in every one of them. He won't just stop goals. He'll lead by example, he'll calm the nerves, both on the pitch and in the stands. He'll kiss everyone on the forehead and make cups of hot chocolate for all.

Take a walk around him, gentlemen. He's a colossus.

Southampton v Liverpool
Friday April 5, 2019
ROB GUTMANN'S PREVIEW

IS there a noun for feeling simultaneously excited at the prospect of an event and yet dreading it in equal measure?

The Germans surely have such a word.

This is all Liverpool games for me now. This my life.

It is hard, without the benefit of hindsight, to appreciate the degree to which we as Liverpool fans are living on a knife's edge at present.

I was thinking about poor, old Tottenham earlier. Just a few weeks ago they'd moved within less than a handful of points of ourselves and Manchester City. They were very much in the title race. Now look at the schmucks; 18 points behind us. Far from sure they'll even qualify for Champions League football next term.

Whatever happens from here on in, Liverpool will emerge from this campaign with heads held high. Their haul of 79 points is 9.5 points off the equivalent highest total in the club's history. If Liverpool get just 10 points from their remaining six games it will be a total bettered by only seven teams in the history of the English top flight.

We are already four points better off than we were in the entirety of last season and we are thus far matching last campaign's run in the Champions League. These are heady times.

Neither The Reds nor rivals Manchester City are playing with particular panache at this stage. There have been moments of true excellence in recent weeks.

City will point to their 6-0 drubbing of Chelsea, Liverpool felt deep satisfaction in the displays that saw Watford beaten 5-0 and Bayern 3-1 on their own turf. The bread and butter though, has been the ground-out results.

Liverpool have now won five of their last six matches, and most of them have felt like very hard work indeed. None less so than the dramatic, last-gasp win over Spurs at the weekend.

Ignore the narrative that cries 'fluke' at that outcome. Liverpool took control of, lost control of for a period, and then reasserted mastery of a football match. That the denouement felt fortuitous – because of Hugo Lloris's error – obscures the reality.

Liverpool scored because, a couple of nerve-shredding Tottenham breakouts aside, they had gathered themselves in the game following the visitors' equaliser and had nigh on camped on the edge of Spurs' box.

Klopp noted in his press conference this week that the winning goal was born of a routine straight from the training ground. Few will have been listening, but when faced with an immovable deep defence, playing the percentages is sometimes the only way to break through.

A five-day gap between the final whistle at Anfield on Sunday and Friday night's kick off down at Southampton will provide enough respite for Liverpool manager Jürgen Klopp to have enjoyed the training time to prepare for their next challenge.

Klopp will ask his lads to cut out the background noise. Southampton are just another football team not us as good as us standing in our way. We must push them aside.

Ordinarily the Liverpool boss would have one eye on the imminent first leg Champions League game with Porto. But that's five days and a lifetime hence. Again, the scheduling has been kind and Klopp will not have to worry too much about freshness.

For Spurs last Sunday he opted to start his captain, Jordan Henderson, ahead of the emerging leading light, Fabinho. It was a move that didn't exactly pay off. Henderson did not have his best game and Liverpool's level markedly improved when Fabinho entered the fray as a substitute for the skipper. Fabinho surely starts at St Mary's.

Yet again, a Liverpool starting line up can be confidently predicted, save for the two in central midfield berths. Given Southampton's recent revival and confidence, Klopp will expect them to not be passive and don the mantle of the away side as so many lower-level sides do on their own grounds against this powerful Liverpool team. More of a war than a siege will be anticipated.

To that end, expect the Liverpool manager to go with a more warrior-like midfield. This means less chance of a recall for the likes of Adam Lallana, Xherdan Shaqiri, or even Naby Keita and likely starts for two from James Milner, Jordan Henderson and Gini Wijnaldum.

A few weeks ago we spied this fixture, sandwiched between testing games against Tottenham and Chelsea, and saw only an away banker. It now looks like something quite different.

But, although Southampton are feeling much better about themselves these days, Liverpool too have reason for confidence – with four league wins in five, including three on the bounce.

The Reds are building up a head of steam again and just in the nick of time.

Southampton 1 Liverpool 3
BEN JOHNSON'S RATINGS

FUCK me with a big shiny shovel.

Alisson: 7

Nothing to do first half but open his mouth in disgust at the shitshow happening in front of him. Nothing to do second half except admire the bollocks of this side in front of him.

Trent: 6

Jesus Christ he struggled there, first half. Flashes of brilliance, but gave it away for a laugh. Looked either injured or fucking goosed. Great decision to take him off.

Joel: 7

When big Joel is sliding into centre mid like Jockey Hanson on a Gary you know you are in a bit of trouble. He is like an absolute accountant who rubbed a lamp and wished to be a footballer. The maddest player any fucker has ever seen.

Virgil: 8

Captain Virgil. Can't do much about their goal. Mad the way he lashes in a performance like that and you are like 'yer, he didn't really do much'. But, it's probably up there with the top 100 centre half performances of all time.

Andy Robbo: 7

Loved it when he fell over at the end and tried to head the ball at their lad's feet.

Naby Keita: 7

Got pounced on every time he got it first 20, and looked weaker than your ma's kitten. Scores the goal off the back of one of their bellend's heads. Grows into the game, keeps the ball, shows for the ball, like every time. Like every time, which takes some doing. Deserved to stay on.

Fabinho: 7

People cry like fuck when the doomsday midfield is picked but fuck me the first-half effort was the opposite. Without the ball it was a shambles. Ragged, sloppy, their goal a direct consequence of no one doing what they should be fucking doing. Felt sorry for Fabinho in that he had fuck all support off the other two. Looked well better when he had some legs around him second half.

Gini: 6

Looked fucked. As in, I played fivos the other month. Said to me mate who asked me to play 'What's the standard like lad?' He said 'You will be sound, you know. It's decent but you will be better than most.' Great, turned up full of beans.

What the little fucker didn't tell me was every cunt was fitter than Mo Farah. I spent the hour doing shuttles and had to sit on the pan for an hour and a half when I got home.

My bird thought I was having a stroke. Gini that, there.

Mo Salah: 8

Not much space. Bits and bobs of hard lines. Put him in, Mo. Play him in, Mo. Mo? Mo? Bedlam. Took his top off, stood there, better than anyone I have ever seen. A God. Carved out of stone.

Bobby: 8

Grafted as per, fiddled with his hair for a bit, a daft amount of unreal defensive headers, busted his cock off to have every fucker screaming at Mo to lay him in. Great play for the Hendo goal. Hero.

Sadio: 8

Picture the scene. Alder Hey, 2012, 16 hours of labour. Mayhem, gowns everywhere, emergency surgery culminating in a genius NHS doctor, supported by 12 other amazing colleagues passes me my newborn son, fit as a fiddle. The greatest thing I have ever seen in my life.

Until Sadio lashes in that tackle on the edge of our box and The Reds break and The Reds break and The Reds score. Best there ever was. Sorry, family.

SUBS...

Henderson: 8

Funny, isn't it? The internet hates him. Maybe we should ignore the internet for a bit. Was tremendous when he came on. Bullied them. Set the tempo. Got The Reds adding layer on layer of pressure. Scores. Celebrated. Stick that up your arse.

Milner: 8

Come on, like his mate above and set a tempo and a half. Massive impact on The Reds winning.

Degsi: 8

Kicked one up in the air.

NEIL ATKINSON'S REVIEW

EVERYTHING is emotional. Everything hurts. Everything feels fabulous. Every song I write is about you.

After 30 minutes, I was glad you weren't there. Glad you weren't putting up with it. Glad you weren't watching Liverpool's first, second and third worst 10 minutes of the season. We all didn't deserve that. In a strange way, the lads on the pitch didn't wholly deserve it but it was happening to them. I was glad you weren't there.

When Mo Salah stares at the whole end with his top off and loves it, when Mo Salah milks every last bit of his own brilliance, when he comes back up after praying, after putting his top back on, when Mo Salah turns back one more time and urges the roar from the travelling Kop I wish we all could have been there to respond.

I wish you could have looked right at him, our slightly frayed superhero, I wish you could have acclaimed him.

Everything is emotional.

Liverpool's captain Jordan Henderson slots the winner and explodes when he has come on and changed the game for his side and I just wish you could have been there. We all should have been there.

It had been horrendous. It was watch through your fingers stuff, the worst things could possibly be.

Southampton got to the half hour only one up and Liverpool were flattered by that. There was no ball The Reds weren't second to, no danger they failed to anticipate, no easy pass spurned. It was, frankly, a shitshow.

Southampton deserved credit. They played entirely in the half spaces, turned Liverpool's powers against them, asked questions few sides outside of the top six have managed to ask. They pinned Liverpool against the wall and Liverpool looked helpless, weak as a kitten and twice as naive.

Everything hurts.

Liverpool drove us all to distraction, no decision right, unable to build pressure. And then they stretched Southampton back and forth across their own box and Naby Keita did brilliantly and time stopped and it was, after what felt like an age from 100 yards away, a Liverpool goal. A Liverpool equaliser.

To say it was scarcely deserved is a monumental understatement. Liverpool have never been genuinely lucky this season; they have rode their luck, they have fought to the end, they have shown fitness and sharpness and desire, but they have rarely not deserved what they have had during games.

The only thing Liverpool deserved at 1-0 was to go 2-0 down.

The midfield was atrocious, Trent was having a nightmare, Matip was uncertain at best and calamitous at worst and Mo Salah just couldn't get near the ball.

We end the game legitimately concerned about Gini Wijnaldum. There have been too many games now with not enough influence; a midfielder who gave everything, who was our best until February may well now have been our poorest through March and April.

We saw footballers flop physically today. They mostly wore the red and white stripes of Southampton, we can see how things can go wrong when legs go. But for Gini now it has been too much of a battle for too long.

Naby Keita scored and wanted the ball. Fabinho has credit in the bank. But the truth of the matter is that these three points are driven back to Liverpool in the boots of Jürgen Klopp, James Milner and Jordan Henderson.

Liverpool's grown ups got on the pitch and played like two men who have a league to win. They were immense performances. Game changing. Suddenly the pitch belonged to Liverpool. Milner made it huge, Henderson covered every blade of grass; pent up having watched things slip away before his eyes.

Everything feels fabulous.

God, the scorers of the second and third deserved that. Henderson's goal belongs to his manager and to Milner but also to his own bravura leadership, Salah's belongs to his own belief and perseverance. He has needed this for so long. We needed him there and then. He delivered.

They were and are our heroes. There was a patch when they were villains, when they were inexplicably throwing so much of their own good work away. And then the opposite happened.

They deserve all of our acclaim. I want this not to stop. I'll remember this end, I'll remember how much it wanted, craved Liverpool winning the game. We needed more than wanted. Henderson wants for all time.

Every song I write is about you.

Longing on a large scale is what makes history. The history Liverpool can make is not the history happening elsewhere in the country, but it is the history of a city, the history of a state of mind, the history of thousands of people in one place, the history of millions around the world, the history of our lives and our moments and our rhythms, our needs and wants.

Perhaps we shouldn't long for this as much as we do, but we do and these are the facts of the matter. The scale and scope overwhelms but liberates, there is something about them on the grass doing what they do that frees us from mundane concerns. They give us life. Heart thudding, hormonal life. This is what it is to be alive, in the blood and the bone.

Longing on a large scale is what makes history. The Reds have the hand of history on their shoulders. It still may not happen. But they give us this. Like they have given us similar so many times this season.

Thirty-three down. Five to go.

Everything is emotional. Everything hurts. Everything feels fabulous. Every song I write is about you.

Liverpool 2 FC Porto 0

Tuesday April 9, 2019

NEIL ATKINSON'S REVIEW

ALRIGHT. A bastard of a word.

But that was the most alright, wasn't it? Good alright, I mean.

It was, however, almost much better than alright. However, Liverpool have a big game at the weekend. However, Porto are a tidy side. However, sometimes it just doesn't take flight, not for 90. 'However' is a bastard of a word, too.

Liverpool looked at it from the first minute of the first half; the same couldn't be said of the second. But on the first, it wasn't as simple as winning every ball, more being first to every half space.

It was a side who were so often where they expected one another to be. They found one another without looking, anticipated runs, played first-time passes. They were too much for Porto to cope with in and out of possession, and it told for both goals.

In the first half the oft-discussed midfield appeared as balanced as it has all season. Naby Keita scored, albeit deflected. Jordan Henderson played the quintessential pass before the pass for the second. Later Henderson played a delightful half volley to Roberto Firmino but nothing came of it. Keita's through ball to Sadio Mane was unlucky not to elicit a chance.

What's fascinating given the nature of each of this pair's Liverpool career is how much each appeared to be enjoying their evening. Henderson alternated between barking at Trent Arnold and Fabinho and praising the pair. He seemed unleashed, dare we say it 10 years on: the shackles were off. His ball for Mane's disallowed goal a belter.

Keita revelled in the occasion after the goal. The yellow card cheap but pleasing, a man in the thick of battle. Neither was perfect: Keita too easily ran away from, Henderson at times has a brain too quick for his footwork, but both delighted in the opening period.

The second was different. Neither was anywhere near as influential but then neither were Liverpool, full stop. The two things will be linked to some degree, but it isn't the whole story. The game never really came alive in the second period but some credit for that has to go to Porto. They played better and neutralised Liverpool.

James Milner showed willingness and stability throughout. Given dogs of balls by both Divock Origi and Naby Keita in the second half, he found his way out with the latter and into the penalty area with the former, oddly running away from Porto players left prone but doing so slowly.

Milner offers certainty to his teammates, he offers one more all the time. One more option, one more heave. It's the least any player can do, it's the thing very few actually do.

From the replays post-match it appears Mo Salah may be lucky to have remained on the pitch. He was ever willing though and a nightmare to face, squirming around the box like live squid in a restaurant about to be cooked. Every angle is unlikely until he coils himself. He will be a massive threat to Porto in the second leg but he should score tonight and kill the tie.

That Porto carry a threat is undeniable. We saw it from set pieces and passages of play that led to set pieces. They couldn't open Liverpool up tonight, but it isn't impossible to imagine them opening the scoring at home.

Marega got little encouragement from the evening, no change from either van Dijk or Dejan Lovren. The Big Dog came back and reminded everyone of the best version of himself. He loves the front foot and Liverpool seemed higher than we have seen recently – a feeling more than a fact, perhaps. He will be an asset for this run in.

The point there is that this game is part of a piece. Not just a two-legged affair but one of what Liverpool hope will be 10 games for the rest of the season. Tonight has to have an eye on Sunday given how the game played out, Sunday an eye on Wednesday if at all possible.

Last season Liverpool's European adventure was able to be deemed the thing and the whole of the thing. This season it is one side of the same coin. We see that in the odd last half an hour and in the substitutions. While Lovren and Keita put themselves forward as options, the front three are necessities.

Liverpool have a foot in the last four. Think about that – today was our second Champions League quarter final this decade. Our second in two years. Our second with the first leg won to nil. While some games play out with you eventually only shrugging about results that you would have been made up with before a ball was kicked, well that sometimes is what mature football is made of.

The strangest thing about where this European season finds itself is that the side in the last eight for only the second time this decade are suddenly also the most mature – last season's finalists and top of the most hotly contested big league on the continent. How did that happen?

However, it can all go wrong from here. And the closer to the finish line the more profoundly wrong it can go. But yet again a match finishes and you can ask no more than where this Liverpool finds itself. Liverpool are fit and firing. They may be improving. They are in control of this tie.

Liverpool are that very best of things. On the march. And game by game it becomes clearer they can really, really shake it up.

They may be the greatest football team. And that's alright by me.

Liverpool v Chelsea
Sunday April 14, 2019
ROB GUTMANN'S PREVIEW

HERE we are again and here they are again.

It's 2014 all over again. Us on the edge of fulfilling our destiny and them cast in the role of spiteful dream wreckers. There was no need for them to take the title from us and hand it to Manchester City in 2014, and equally now, this is a contest that is all about us and simply not about them.

The parallels are unavoidable. Three games to go then, just five now. Anfield the stage, Man City waiting in the wings, willing us to fail.

Looking back, our greatest folly in 2014 was in treating a must-not-lose game as a must-win game. We were too greedy then. We were in a rush to get the job done, to be crowned champions.

Perhaps a more experienced team and manager (than Brendan Rodgers) would have done two things differently – firstly, the maths, and realised a draw was a perfectly excellent result and secondly, not underestimated the opponent. Chelsea had no skin in the game, but it didn't make them not a very dangerous challenge.

I sympathise with Rodgers. He chose to face only forwards and wanted to channel the momentum of an 11-match winning run. He felt that we should remain fearless, even to the extent of showing a significant opponent a degree of disrespect. Klopp may face a not dissimilar dilemma. Chelsea are strong but deeply flawed, their 6-0 trouncing at the Etihad still fresh in the memory.

We could be bold and wild. We could blow them away. But they could resist us too. They could stay calm, and as in 2014, wait for their moment.

A win would be a fantastic step towards our goal but still with much work to do. A defeat, though, would be catastrophic. We could survive the draw. Yes, we'd then need two slips rather than one from City, but a defeat would mean we'd require them to fail to win in half of their remaining games.

Yes, of course it's a must-win game, all our games remain so until there is daylight between us and City. But it is in equal measure a must-not-lose game.

I'm not sure Jürgen Klopp will see this my way. He may have done a few weeks ago. I felt in certain games, maybe Everton away, that he felt we shouldn't risk turning one grudgingly attained point into zero. There was a sense of a 'what we have we hold' mentality. It has helped keep Liverpool unbeaten in 12 and fearing no team because of it.

Against Tottenham at Anfield a fortnight or so ago, Klopp changed tack. He could've taken the point on offer. Spurs had equalised and it clearly gave them the belief that they could steal the win. The Liverpool manager had other ideas, though.

He threw Divock Origi into the fray and set four attackers bearing down on Spurs. It was a risky strategy that was ultimately rewarded but not before Spurs had broken on an undermanned Liverpool backline and threatened to score again themselves.

Although Liverpool's victory that day was scruffy and appeared fortuitous, secured by Alderweireld's last-minute own goal, it was a product of the attacking intent of a home side that wanted only to win, or die trying.

Enter Chelsea. Klopp will feel that this is the decisive moment and that all must be risked on taking the opportunity. If Liverpool win, they will have four left to play and the very realistic prospect of concluding this league campaign with nine straight victories.

From where we stand, ahead of Sunday's matches, Manchester City have only around a 20 per cent chance of winning all of their remains six matches. Think about that. In all probability, it can be classed as 'extremely likely' that City will drop points in at least one fixture.

Of course this can also be said of Liverpool, but the odds of The Reds winning their last four games currently sits at about 50 per cent, if Liverpool can see off Chelsea. On paper the league title is not in our hands, but in probability terms it most definitely is.

'City WILL drop points,' is not a hopeful statement. It is a very sensible prediction. To this end, the destiny of the prize is for us to decide. Simply win all of our remaining five games and we will be champions.

Sounds easy. It obviously isn't but it will become a significantly more realistic prospect should we defeat Chelsea.

Let's not obsess about what Chelsea will do to resist us. I was up nights in that week in May 2014 trying to second guess Jose Mourinho's team selection. We must look within ourselves and find out how badly we want this.

The team has had moments requiring profound soul searching during the past six fixtures. All of these have been won, but all after moments when it looked like the result might be escaping us.

We have been tested and tested again. On each and every occasion we have found the answers. Let's make the numbers add up one more time.

Liverpool 2 Chelsea 0
BEN JOHNSON'S RATINGS

I DON'T know about you but I need this fucking season to hurry up and end.

I'm like fourth season Bubs in *The Wire* at this point. A ghost of a man. Hollowed out. Somehow, this morning I agreed to buy my bird a caravan if The Reds win the league. A fucking caravan. Like a proper caravan that you pull round like a house. I mean, I didn't even know my bird wanted a caravan.

Alisson: 8

Another save at a key point. Added 15 points on his fucking own this year. Gone a bit Si Mig with his passing in the last few weeks but so the frigging hell what.

Trent: 8

Asked a load of questions by them but was great, with and without it. Full of balls, and battle, and guile, and quality, and everything else you could ever want in a player.

Big Joel: 8

Fantastic today. Front foot, lashing people that needed lashing. Looked like a proper player today. The best defender on the pitch. Mad that. Still passes it like a weirdo, mind you.

Virgil: 8

Second best defender on the pitch which has probably happened about three times in his life. Liked him a lot.

Robbo: 7

Was mad today. Defended really well first half but when The Reds went 2-0 up he went all Albie Moreno and thought he was a fucking Jack Russell on the beach, underlapping and overlapping like fuck.

Henderson Henderson Henderson: 8

Tremendous again. The amount of times he arrived in the box, la. For the Mo Salah chance first half, it's Henderson up for the challenge. Tremendous for the first. I'm screaming at him to lash it across the face but he's all 'I'm the best centre mid in Europe, I'll just hang it up for Sadio to score, aye'. Does the internet still think he is shite?

Fabinho: 8

I think I might love him. That natural instinct to kick people and win the ball, mate. Lovely. The tackle on Hazard first half, leaving a little bit on him, glorious. Frees the reds up to play, frees the lads up next to him to leg it.

Naby: 8

Great on the ball first half, wasn't he? It was like watching YouTube from two years ago. Front foot, won the ball time and again first half. Got a bit excited second half when Robbo was berserk. Needs to learn to do some horrible work without the ball, but looks a player.

Mo Salah: 9

I mean he fucking hit that, didn't he? He hit it, it stayed hit, would probably still be travelling now if it hadn't been stopped by the net. It's boss when racists have to cop for one right in the fucking eye, isn't it? Stick that up your horrible arses you Farage-loving, butter-faced twats. Looks like he has realised that he is boss again.

Firmino: 9

Tremendous. Properly tremendous. Like a Rabbit out of a hat keeping the ball surrounded by baddies. Frightened the life out of them whenever he got it. A glorious glinting-mouthed colossus.

Sadio: 8

Great goal. That one was stood up for an hour and a bit. Easy to miss. Had his lad marking him on toast all day long.

SUBS...

Gini and Milner:

Massive dose of sensible. Boss set of subs.
Well in, big men.

NEIL ATKINSON'S REVIEW

AT Anfield we only get to watch them three more times maximum. Only four more league games.

Acclaim them. Love them. Commune with them. Be prepared to bleed with them. But be part of their brilliance and have them be part of our need. Time has accelerated around us.

You don't need to be Einstein to understand that time is relative. You don't need to be Einstein to know that the first half of Liverpool's game against Chelsea this afternoon goes slow. There is a level of control from The Reds that is welcome, but tense.

Forty-five minutes with no goals goes slowly. We breathe in and out as Chelsea and Liverpool fight over possession, fight over where the line is, test each other's courage. While Liverpool are precise and effective, 45 minutes without a goal is a drag.

The shape of Chelsea is deeply impressive. They are like a sponge, stretching and flexing to soak up the fluid Liverpool attack. The breadth provided by Cesar Azpilicueta and N'Golo Kante is hard to manage.

Liverpool at times look a bit weak and too hollow in the midfield. We can't get enough build up, and while Naby Keita makes lightning runs and Mo Salah is everywhere (just everywhere), Chelsea are able to balance our pace with their distribution.

Fabinho is good in the middle but you sense how hard Liverpool are having to work to get the ball from front to back, when Chelsea are managing their shape so effectively.

Alisson is tested from time to time. Hazard is no mug and nor is Willian. These are lively players. Good players. Chelsea get to be good. It makes what happens to them all the more impressive.

Half time comes; 15 minutes passes quickly and we are all impatient. We know that this is it. We know that this is the final act in a league battle that at times has seemed to stretch impossibly long ahead of us, with countless hours, countless potential losses or mistakes, countless opportunities.

Here we are in the final moments of the season. Having fallen in love with this football team and wanting so calmly simply for them to win. Time to win the league. It's time. We've waited long enough.

The second half kicks off.

Out of nowhere time speeds up. The ball shifts around the box, Jordan Henderson hangs it up and it is a cross you can celebrate. The ball being where it is makes it a goal. Sadio Mane converts and everyone explodes, Henderson wheels away ecstatic, these are the biggest games of his life, this is his whole life, these are the days that define him.

A second passes. Barely a second. A blink of an eye. And then Mo Salah turns and picks up the ball lifting it with power and purpose, and sends it with fire into the top left corner.

Grown men who have watched The Reds for 60 years stand dumbfounded at the clarity of the thing. Little kids at the match for the first time have their hearts won forever by this beautiful smiling man who came from Egypt via Rome, Switzerland and Chelsea to win us the league.

He celebrates. We go bananas. But he celebrates and all the racists who dare shout obscenities at the man are silenced. All the racists can fuck off, frankly. This complicated

227

20-something man full of a jumble of identities is acclaimed as an idol. He is globalisation. He is a Muslim, and an Egyptian, and a footballer, and a dad, and a friend. And he is a fucking Liverpudlian.

Those that use his identity against him fail on every level to understand that, wilfully fail to understand the complexities of identity. People who reduce others to one thing are at root wrong, offensive and the problem.

Sadio Mane wants to win the league more than you. His pace helps this afternoon and though Chelsea are solid in the back, he tests them. He is uncontrollable bursting from left to right.

Firmino, relatively speaking is the quietest of the three, but he finds moments of fine form. Backheels and flicks not quite finding their way to the goal but nonetheless testing for those playing in blue, making their legs work, making their brains work harder.

I love the subs. Both the decisions but what they do. That mad five minutes after 2-0 where Chelsea get in 63 times needed something from the bench. Gini and James delivered. Immediately Wijnaldum holds it up marvellously in the middle of the pitch and everything feels better.

Chelsea were good. They were. Liverpool were better. They are. Twenty points better. Imagine that.

Until this season that has felt improbable; last season we went to Stamford Bridge with them breathing down our necks. This season we grabbed a late equaliser. But now there is a gulf between Chelsea's good and Liverpool's great. Time has changed an awful lot. It moves and shifts and now we are almost done.

They deserve to lift something up.

Make no mistake. This is a great side. Whatever happens from here we are talking and deal with greatness. It is distressing we only get to watch them at Anfield three more times at most. Not because I believe they will separate but because seasons are distinct things.

What they have done for us and with us is just splendid. We really are in this together. That's all of us, each of us. Each of you. Part of you pours out of me in these lines from time to time.

Thirty-four down. Four to go. What a thing. We get to watch them four more times in this season. We get to love them four more times. We get to see their box of paints. I could drink a case of them, a case of you and still be on my feet.

Time to lift something up, Reds.

April 15, 1989: 30 Years On

ROB GUTMANN

I WAS in Sheffield on April 15, 1989.

I was 22 years, four months and 10 days old. I try to think about that day as little as possible.

The years have passed to become the decades that are now drifting by at pace. My memory of that April day is razor sharp. I think the more you try to push something away the more indelibly inked into your psyche it becomes.

There are a number of things I can recall which, in the retelling, would still feel as if I were describing events that happened to someone else. It is as unreal today as it was then.

I've only ever seen death up close like that on that day. I was a child of older generations that had seen far more. I hope my kids will be luckier than we were. Seeing people die, lots of them, and in such a short space of time was beyond being merely shocking or upsetting. It made me despair and feel utterly helpless and bereft in a way I'd never felt before, and have never felt since.

I cried after Hillsborough. I cried, and cried, and cried. For two weeks. Everything made me cry. I had to pull over when I was driving to cry. I cried if I went out of the house for five minutes. I cried when I read the papers or turned on the TV.

I went to Anfield every day for two weeks. I looked at the floral tributes on The Kop and read the inscriptions. I cried every time. After that fortnight I stopped crying and I've never shed a tear over the disaster since.

So much haunts, but a feeling more than a memory has stayed with me the most. It must have been about an hour and a half after it happened that I exited the ground. All I could think to do was to get to where we parked the car and wait for my friends. My best friend Giulio had been the only one of us that had a ticket for the Leppings Lane end.

I turned up a hilly suburban street flanked by small 1950s style houses which had front gardens that gave them the feeling of being more rural-type dwellings than they actually were. Sheffield people who lived in those houses were standing by their front doors, obviously aware from their TVs and radios of the tragedy that had been unfolding just a few hundred yards from their homes.

Us fans were walking like zombies down the streets where these people lived. I recall being called out to by a middle-aged woman who asked me if I wanted to come into her home and use her phone. I hadn't realised that I needed to do that. There would be people who were worried about me.

When I got to our car, no one was there. My other friends John and Pete hadn't been in Leppings Lane, so their absences were no cause for anxiety. That briefly made Giulio being missing more bearable. If they had safe reason to be delayed so might he. I sat on the kerb by the car and waited for him. I waited for a long time.

I did honestly set out to write a preview of the Porto game today. I will be in Porto on Wednesday. I'm really excited about the game and about this Liverpool team and the wonderful experiences we are having with it. But, as I write this, it is exactly 30 years to that day.

I've never really written anything about Hillsborough. I've sort of never known where to begin. I feel I needed to say something today. I'm not entirely sure why now. Thirty years is a long time. It feels like the blinking of an eye.

Giulio finally appeared trudging up the hill of that street in Sheffield. God how I treasure that memory. His shuffling countenance. Broken but not bowed. Indefatigable.

Giulio and me have been to a few thousand games together since that day. We've lived through every incarnation of Liverpool. He still sits next to me at Anfield. He always has done. He gets to his seat very late. Last minute. He keeps me waiting. My heart still leaps when he finally arrives. I die inside just a little.

I've never told him this. I'll always be pleased to see him.

More than he will ever know.

Barcelona: A Big But Beatable Test
Thursday April 18, 2019
CLIVE TYLDESLEY

DID you witness the sheer, unadulterated brilliance of that Barcelona performance on Tuesday night?

Were you fortunate enough to see with your own eyes the unprecedented artistry of the genius called Lionel Messi?

Did the earth move for you too?

Not for me, Clive. Not for me.

Barcelona are the runaway leaders of the league that has produced the last five champions of Europe. The wealth of Champions League nous and know how within their ranks made them the team to beat even before the quarter-final draw was made.

Liverpool were nothing like as good as last night's scoreline in Porto suggests, were they? Come on, be honest, were they?

But I still think Liverpool can and will beat Barca.

Such was the paucity of talent in the United side that faced them in the last eight, it is difficult to judge The Reds' semi-final opponents on what we have seen of them in their quarter.

The bloodied nose that Messi got at Old Trafford was a symbol of a snotty, scrappy first leg. Barca started Tuesday's return as if they were scared of getting hurt again and then, all of a sudden, the tie was over 20 minutes in.

When your best player starts making kindergarten errors like David de Gea's, you've got problems. United have got plenty of those. Plenty.

Barcelona have not suffered a meaningful defeat since November. They have a nine-point title lead and have started resting players *en masse* in La Liga. In Europe, they were outstanding at Wembley against Spurs in October. They despatched a Lyon side full of promise in the last 16 every bit as convincingly as they accounted for United.

They're good. Ernesto Valverde's idea of a dilemma is a choice between Philippe Coutinho or Ousmane Dembele. Arthur is not Iniesta, but he does a reasonable impression for a first season in the job. Sergio Busquets is nearly as skilled as Fernandinho at avoiding yellow cards, while at the same time throwing muscular spanners into your works.

But even when you toss fine players such as Luis Suarez, Ivan Rakitic and Jordi Alba into the mix, there is only one thing that truly unsettles you about facing Barcelona.

If Eden Hazard had got lost en route to Anfield, beating Chelsea would have been a Sunday afternoon stroll. If Lionel Messi chooses the end of the month to take a short break from football ahead of this summer's Copa America, Liverpool can relax.

Sadly, I've not heard any rumours to suggest the little fella is considering it.

Messi is simply my favourite footballer. If Queen Daenerys decrees that I can now only commentate on one player for the rest of my career, then it's Leo. Tackle him by all means but try to leave him in one piece for us all to enjoy some more of.

The only thing I didn't enjoy about watching him in action on Tuesday was repeatedly being told that he was playing exceptionally well. He was playing like Messi, that's all.

His first goal was typical, his second was fortunate. Yes, there was a hand-brake turn and a DRS-zone getaway in the second-half but have I seen him play better than that? I'm afraid so.

Messi just happens to set the bar somewhere around the level he played on Tuesday. That's why he's the best. I think the whole Barca performance was a little overegged. Good – as good as it needed to be – but no more.

If Messi turns up and turns it on... Well, then Liverpool know that he will probably hurt them more than Chris Smalling managed to hurt him. At the very least, The Redmen will have moments to survive like Hazard gave them last Sunday. Probably even more moments than Hazard gave them.

Survive those and it's an even tie, or better.

Against Messi, you need a game plan, you need a concentration fix, you may need a block and a save or two, and you need some luck. None of those are beyond the powers of Robertson, van Dijk and Alisson.

If Liverpool's own magic men are giving Barca more of what Marcus Rashford gave them in the opening seconds of Tuesday's game, then Pique, Lenglet and co will have some moments to survive too.

Barca's fixtures either side of the semi final are against two clubs involved in the relegation scrap in La Liga. It will be interesting to see if they have the front to rest half their team for those games.

It is important to remember that the last time Liverpool played a Champions League match in the Nou Camp 12 years ago, they won.

The Return Of Suarez And Coutinho
Friday April 19, 2019
DAN MORGAN

OH, how far we've come.

As this season evolves, I find myself often referencing how far we've come in these pieces of writing.

Thinking back to Gerard Houllier's cup-conquering machine of 2000-01, and to last season's rollercoaster of a side.

It feels as though this team are maturing every second in front of our very eyes.

Wednesday's victory over Porto provided another reference point. A Champions League quarter-final tie negotiated with such ruthless efficiency that you could only stand and admire the certainty of the boys in red, who reduced the best team in Portugal to very much only half a football team with a staggering 11-1 scoreline over two seasons.

And I had the audacity to be disappointed with the one.

We all have our own pins in the map of how we have got from there to here.

One understated yet relevant marker in my own journey occurred on October 22, 2014, when Brendan Rodgers' Liverpool very much welcomed Real Madrid to Anfield in a Champions League group game that felt every bit the antithesis of The Reds in Europe.

On the pitch, Liverpool were comfortably dispatched by three goals to nil. Yet it was the atmosphere in the stands that night which to this day pains me.

Anfield was passive, disbelieving and generally contrite in the presence of the opposition.

Particularly sobering was the moment when ex-Manchester United man Cristiano Ronaldo, who orchestrated the visitors' victory in a flat-track manner, was clapped off the pitch by some Liverpool supporters.

All evening, Ronaldo was met with a cacophony of pantomime boos, but was gifted a rousing applause when he departed in the latter stages.

Anfield will always appreciate a great footballer as much as they will an opposing goalkeeper running toward The Kop. But that day they gave Ronaldo exactly what he wanted – a faux hostility he was more than comfortable with, followed by a fulfilling massage of his boundless ego after he had served up a massive dose of reality to all Liverpool fans present.

I felt confused and alone with everybody that night. That wasn't my Liverpool, especially in our competition. The European Cup at Anfield is our house, no matter how long we've been on holiday.

This all comes stirring back to me in a cafe in Porto as I write this, because I have one thing on my mind currently – FC Barcelona.

Events in the quarter-final stages have blown this year's competition wide open. What awaits Liverpool in the coming weeks is a mouthwatering prospect. The two sides possess a cohesive attacking style of play which should make for a feast of entertainment.

Yet off the pitch, there will be a whole other battle taking place.

It felt as though that battle had begun as early as Wednesday when, while dowsing themselves in Super Bock, Liverpool supporters were furrowing a brow at a nonsensical story emerging the Mohamed Salah had asked to leave the club.

The place of origin of such a ridiculous article: Spain.

This, in all likelihood, will not be coincidental. That a PR agenda to unsettle and gain even the most subconscious of conscious victories may have been started by Barcelona before Liverpool had even cemented the tie should serve as a stark warning for what may lie ahead.

Attempts to try and unsettle some of our most prized possessions will not be uncommon and is entirely unsurprising.

Another tactic from our opponents will undoubtedly be to encourage Luis Suarez and Philippe Coutinho to speak openly about how much they love Liverpool and their supporters, a clear attempt to soften the Anfield crowd in the buildup to what will be a cauldron come 7 May.

We should be mindful not to fall for any of it, should such a story transpire.

Coutinho's departure and the manner of it is still raw and will not form too much of a contrast of emotions.

Yet Suarez remains revered by most fans due to the sheer individual brilliance we were able to witness from him at times in a Liverpool shirt.

If we remember one thing about Luis Suarez it is that he will go to any lengths possible to win a game of football, whether that is in the confines of the rules or not. He does not deal in sentiment.

If he is presented with an opportunity to win the tie for his team, he will do so without a contemplation of consciousness.

That is not to say we as a crowd should either provoke or laud either player. There may be a time for acknowledgement and respect, but only if the correct opportunity presents itself.

The same goes for Lionel Messi, even if seeing him play in the flesh will be a tale to bore the grandchildren with in the distant future.

However, treating these players as part of the collective being, a being which wants to prevent us from reaching our second European Cup final in as many years, will be the only approach we should take.

This is the same being which, for the last 10 years, has tried and succeeded to assert a form of dominance in the transfer food chain over Liverpool when they have decided they would quite like what we have.

Such situations have led to protracted sagas around Suarez, Coutinho and Javier Mascherano, which all were undoubtedly damaging and unhealthy to the harmony and prosperity of our club.

How far we have come now means that Barcelona are absolutely full of trepidation about the prospect of facing Liverpool.

Jordi Alba is up nights thinking about Trent Alexander-Arnold. Ivan Rakitic is apprehensive about Jordan Henderson as a number eight.

All of them are quite rightly telling themselves Anfield is a myth while harbouring a deep unsettling feeling of what may face them when they arrive on Merseyside.

How far we have come is constantly displayed on the pitch in these hazy days under Jürgen Klopp's mighty red machine.

If we show Barcelona that we won't stand for anything that isn't Liverpool prevailing to another European Cup final, no matter what they try, then another reminder that we are back where we belong will only be reinforced off the pitch, too.

CHAPTER SEVEN – THE HOME STRAIGHT

SO this was it.

All that time and emotion you had invested into this thing had come down to a collection of weeks, days, hours, minutes, seconds which could make or break a season. More. An era. The reputation of a manager and a group of players.

Nobody could doubt that Liverpool had performed at the highest level up until this point. But would that really matter if there was nothing to show for it? No big shiny thing to be hoisted above heads?

It's hard to console yourself with records. They're there to be broken, after all. In that sense, they never quite feel tangible. Trophies and winners' medals you can touch. As tangible as it gets.

Some of us, myself included, had gone through the majority of the season with a one-track mind. Suddenly that one track had become a dual carriageway. The roads divided just before they ended, but that didn't mean you couldn't live every second of travelling those roads.

The journey is so crucial, in football as it is in life. It is what defines us, shapes who we are when we reach our eventual destination.

This particular journey had been long. There had been bumps, as with any journey, but you couldn't say you hadn't enjoyed it. That the twists and turns hadn't kept you gripped. Coming back for more.

And yet here we were. Eyes on two prizes. No long an 'either or' question to be answered. Liverpool had shown they could go the distance on two fronts. They had kept themselves and us alive. The rollercoaster still as exhilarating as at its starting point.

And yet the end's in sight. The ride's about to stop. You might just have to scream louder.

Josh Sexton

Cardiff City v Liverpool
Sunday April 21, 2019
ROB GUTMANN'S PREVIEW

THERE'S going to be a five-day stretch that spans from this Saturday morning until next Wednesday night in which the destiny of this season's league title will be decided.

In that space of time, Liverpool will play Cardiff City, and Manchester City will play Tottenham Hotspur and Manchester United. One side will emerge with the results having gone in their favour. In probability terms, that side will be 75-80 per cent likely to then lift the trophy. It's as binary as that.

Chasing down titles is stressful and fun. If you're getting the results, every fresh conquest reaffirms your belief that you can be the ultimate champion. The future can be yours. But there comes a point when the future flowers into a present. It may smell of shit or bust, or the sweet perfume of ultimate success.

I'm crapping myself over the prospect of the next few days. This is the phase where the cards are flipped over. All hands revealed.

It is this simple – if City beat Spurs and United, our goose is all but cooked. They would then have just three matches to play, with a strong likelihood of securing the trio of victories that would guarantee them the title, no matter we are able to do.

But, in a parallel universe, maybe not so far away, City draw… Just the once. Liverpool, in this reality, beat Cardiff City. By Thursday morning, both combatants have played equal games, have three more remaining against lightweight opponents, and Liverpool lead by a solitary point. That is a world we want to live in. We would be overwhelming favourites to be bringing the title back home.

It's not over yet, and it won't be by Thursday morning. But, make no mistake, this is the end game. I'm old enough and sage enough to know that the giddiness of Wednesday night in Europe, where we won handsomely and City lost despairingly, could all be chimera, a misdirection ahead of the main event which is the coming five days.

Jürgen Klopp will be rebuking me now for worrying about what may happen in games not involving Liverpool. 'We can only win our games', he will preach. He's right, he's right, of course he's right. But I can't win our games. Nor can you.

This is our lot as supporters. We can tell ourselves that we are part of the process. We can even viscerally feel that we are at times involved in the biggest games. In the final analysis though, we can never be more than, at best, rabid cheerleaders. We cannot pick teams, we cannot play passes or make tackles, we cannot score goals.

All that remains for us is prayer.

That's why we do not think only of what Liverpool do, Jürgen. We are helpless and yet feel delusionally powerful. We can pray/wish for Manchester City to fail. Klopp and his team can remain aloof, but we can't. We are witnesses and we can no more turn our gaze from City as we can from our own team.

Je suis Tottenham. Nous sommes tous Man U-fucking-nited.

Depending on when you're reading this, City may have already rolled over Spurs. It's likely that they will. It will then turn to us to beat Cardiff and in doing so, make Man

United versus Man City next Wednesday night a game that they should be showing in cinemas across Merseyside and on a giant screen on the Anfield pitch.

If you have any mixed feelings over this you are little less than a traitor to our cause. Liverpool's bond with the red half of Manchester this week is as dirty as the Molotov-Ribbentrop pact of 1938 (Google it), but more morally justifiable and definitely essential.

Cardiff, then. They need wins. Warnock's warriors just attained a massive one in their midweek 0-2 defeat of Brighton. They have a touch more than a ghost of a chance of avoiding relegation. It makes them dangerous opponents, of course it does, but it also makes them desperate ones. That's how we like them.

Klopp rested Jordan Henderson and Naby Keita for the Porto away trip and will surely start both in South Wales. Fabinho will probably be asked to go again, although the Liverpool boss may choose to put Henderson back in the number six position and start Wijnaldum ahead of the Brazilian.

It was interesting to observe Klopp's keenness to reintroduce Joe Gomez in Portugal. The manager knows that the best version of Gomez is a footballer we could really use at this crucial phase. Don't be shocked to see Joe reintroduced alongside Virgil at centre back in Cardiff.

It could well be that we see Liverpool's very best 11 on show at the Cardiff City Stadium. I hope so. This all feels emblematic of a team peaking at precisely the right time.

It is not yet entirely in our hands to win, but it's in our hearts to summon the power for one last push.

Cardiff City 0 Liverpool 2
BEN JOHNSON'S RATINGS

OH. My. God. I mean, you can't watch that fucking match and not think The Reds are not going to somehow win the league.

We are fucking spawny, la. How hasn't that lad scored? How hasn't he scored? How hasn't it at least hit his massive head and gone in instead of it somehow bouncing off his back?

It's a fucking Red Shite diddle.

Alisson: 8

Has nothing to do then makes a save and a half. Has nothing to do then comes and punches everything second half.

Made a save second half that looked like he just caught it. His footwork is incredible. Mignolet – at best – stands still, throws himself, makes a wonder save out for a corner and creates more pressure. Alisson just caught it.

He doesn't have to make belter saves loads of the time because he is just so clever and good and 10 yards ahead of play. A superstar.

Trent: 7

Mad the way he had to mark Carl Lewis first half. Fucking Grease Lightning him, lad. Hop skip and a jump about 400 feet. Better second half. Kept the ball well.

Matip: 8

Is like being marked by a massive big lizard. Komodo Dragon at the back, tonguing it away. Did well today but fucking hell he doesn't half love getting the wrong side of his man.

Virgil: 8

The greatest.

Andy Robbo: 7

Struggled today, I thought. Looked leggy, made some mad decisions with the ball, I was screaming for Milner to come on left back at half time. Grafted though, in fairness, and had a big impact last 20.

Gini: 8

Was good to see him sitting and not have to leg it around all over the gaff. Had a boss game of 'Where's Gini' second half. Popped up on 60 or whatever – there he is twatting that one right in the top bin. Love a corner routine, you know. Was then very impressive for 10 and bossed it.

Henderson: 7

Didn't quite live up to his billing as the best attacking midfielder in Europe, but then if he scores that one its 'numbers our us' and 'Ballon D'or, por favor'. Should do better with it. Can't be dealing with a side-foot finish, fucking lash it lad.

Naby: 8

Won the ball back all day long, there. Reckon 15 times. Confident on the ball, trying to get The Reds to play, some ball through for Mane first half as well. Sound that he's sound, isn't it?

Mo: 8

Probably should have been three penalties, really, as in he is fouled three times before the ref actually gives it. Does well to carry on twisting and turning, forcing the foul. Unlucky with the one on one.

I've been struck down with a cold, there – having to do that thing where you sleep with your mouth open, propped up like a dying auld fella.

Woke up yesterday and my mouth was drier than their pitch. Like a ravine. Never seen moisture. Had a few burnt-out cacti languishing on me tongue.

Firmino: 7

Unlucky with the big chance first half. Reckon he thinks he's offside, otherwise he's dancing round that prick and slotting. Kept picking the ball up and getting The Reds playing, didn't he? Tremendous.

Sadio: 8

The only fella who could slip over on a pitch that was drier than the sun. Just kept slipping. Was mad. Imagine marking him, though. Falls over, you go to get the ball, somehow gets up, holds you off and keeps it. Again and again. Stronger than an ox.

SUBS…

Fabinho: 8

Come on and pure butted their lad and then got off. Is right, lad.

Jimbo Milner: 9

Mad, isn't it? Wasn't even meant to be on, comes on cause Fabinho pure butted some lad and knocked himself spark out, then runs the game and slots a pen. You can't help but think this league is ours when shite like this keeps happening.

Joey: 8

Well better than Degsi.

Zeus: 10

Their lad, about to slot, free header back stick, head bigger than a bull, can't miss the ball, Zeus pulls some strings, moves the ball by about six inches, lashes up a forcefield, and The Reds don't concede. A latter day miracle.

NEIL ATKINSON'S REVIEW

EIGHTY-eight points. I whisper things the city sings them back to you.

I am my age. I can't argue with the facts on that one. I am my age. These lads have more points than anyone since 1988, at which point it was 90 points from 40 games.

The 1978-79 team were a great set of lads – 98 from 42 that year. They must have been incredible, you know. What a football team. They barely conceded a goal. Sixteen in 42 games. I mean, wow. The very law of averages would expect something different.

This one, though. This one you know. This one – 88 points now.

We can – and we will – talk about today in and of itself but today means they are better in the post-92 era than any of those who came before them. With three games to go.

I am my age. You are yours. You will know what you have seen and lived through. But if you are reading this now, what a time to be alive. Imagine that, Easter weekend, and this is the best football team of your Liverpudlian lives.

The City sings them back to you. Pep Guardiola yesterday said that Man City were up against the best ever Liverpool side. It would be right to be scared of that; would be right to understand the scope of that.

James Milner said this week that if Liverpool win the next seven they will win at least one trophy. They have now won one of those seven.

I love that Milner said that. I love that he has become one of ours. I met him once, interviewed him – liked him, if it matters. He had jokes and he had style and he had setup punchlines – which is different to jokes but a thing.

Today was, in one sense, horrendous. Adam and Ben had lost their heads at the break. They were struggling to compute and copy. It meant too much but Liverpool hadn't been especially good, Liverpool hadn't been at their best, and the whole thing felt sticky and hard to get to the good stuff like bad ribs.

Liverpool's lads had opened the door three times but for the first time in a while you worried the front three weren't going to oblige.

They didn't. But it was fine.

It was fine because Jordan Henderson, Gini Wijnaldum, and especially Naby Keita were the absolute business. It was fine because Liverpool had scouted their own corner routine. It was fine because Liverpool had too much for Cardiff in every area of the pitch.

When Wijnaldum scores it is simply the best, simply the achievement you have been waiting for. Simply our Sunday Candy.

There have been few as special but let's chat about Naby Keita. While on the pitch he was the absolute business in and out of possession; he was Liverpool's best and most pleasing midfielder, he was the liveliest of the lively. Imagine marking him. It would be awful. He is delivering right now in the most direct way.

Cardiff should have equalised. A forcefield keeps the ball away from the goal and it is exactly what Liverpool need.

From that point they are almost impeccable. The arrival of James Milner for an unfortunate Fabinho changes the game. Milner is the liveliest and the most certain. There is something about him and Henderson right now which is never going to stop. And Milner's penalty proves irresistible and Liverpool are home and everything feels like it can't get any better.

The reality is there is one thing we need; them to drop points. Manchester City to drop points. But in a sense I am with the manager. We can do our thing and our thing is its own thing; our thing is sacred. It is just gorgeous. I've been waiting for Liverpool for this whole week; praying for Liverpool, our Sunday candy.

What they do is their business. I am 38 years old. I am my age. And I am watching the best I have seen.

Acclaim them. Love them. There is nothing but this from this stage. These are our lads. I can't let go.

We get to watch them five more times minimum. Three more times in the league.

It's 35 down. Three to go. You got to move it slowly. Like it's holy. I've been waiting for these for years, you know. I've been waiting for them since 1990.

Three to go, Reds.

Guardiola's Right – Reds Are Among The Best Ever

Monday April 22, 2019

GARETH ROBERTS

ONE of the best teams Pep Guardiola has seen in his life.

A team that has bettered the Rafa Benítez side that clocked up 86 points and featured 24-goal Steven Gerrard, one of the best of our own.

A group that has won more points than the Brendan Rodgers team that included 31-goal Luis Suarez, a player many believe to be the most skilful to wear the red.

However you choose to look at it, Liverpool's record over 35 Premier League games this season is deserving of enormous credit. So let's give them it. All of it.

Eighty-eight points is a phenomenal tally. Clubs have won the league with fewer. Only 20 goals conceded. Only one defeat.

From August to April, it's been machine-like consistency. And what a life it's made for us. Week in, week out, watching a side perform magnificently. Left to talk about a side that could win the double. Left to dream about an incarnation of the club so much better than so many of those we have lived through in the past three decades.

The suggestion continues to circulate that all will be forgotten if the Premier League trophy is not wrapped in red ribbons come May 12.

Not only is that nonsense – we found joy in 2013-14 even if it didn't end how we wanted it to – that particular fate is not in Liverpool's control. And for every doom-mongering scenario painted inside and out of our bubble in this tightest of races, there is another sunshine-filled one if you think about it hard enough.

Liverpool win three times. City draw one of their four remaining games. That's enough. That's all it would take. So now is not the time for white towels or whinging or whining.

We go on. A title still within reach deep into April. Bars filled with smiling faces. Every match a pleasure to be at. The 'what ifs' and 'just imagines' are a joy to discuss.

There's a European Cup to play for. A title to play for. For so many others who love their club the world over there is just plodding routine. Players on the beach. Meaningless matches. Going through the motions. Thinking already of next August and what that may bring.

So many times that was us. Already by now we'd be deep into the season review – where it all went wrong, what needs to change on and off the pitch, how deep the problems run. Attitude, application, players, manager, owners. All of it.

Where Manchester United are, basically. And Everton. Just as a couple of examples among the many…

Instead, it's cheekily planning parties. It's booking multiple trips to Spain. It's celebrating one of the best teams in the world to watch right now and enjoying the moment of us being us and us not being them. The right here, right now is fantastic.

Let's drink it in.

Jürgen Klopp was right, like he so often is, when he described this squad as 'fucking mentality monsters' after the win at Southampton.

The pressure and tension of this title race is there by the bucketload if you allow it in. You've probably felt it. I know I have. If you haven't, you'll know someone who has.

Yet we see players still enjoying it. James Milner with his imaginary walking stick this week. Andy Robertson calmly taking in the golf on the telly while Manchester City played Palace pre-Chelsea last week. This is not a club fraught and frayed by what is playing out.

So much of sport psychology is finding the right place to perform, silencing the noise, being able to do what you've done thousands of times before at the most crucial of times. Liverpool are doing just that, over and over again. And it's left us with a chance. An opportunity. 'Possibilities, no?', as a great man once said.

This Liverpool isn't going away. Whatever happens, the 'mentality monsters' are sticking around. Transfer talk around Liverpool's top stars currently feels so fanciful that it barely raises a ripple when it happens. Why would they want to leave this?

The last time Liverpool won the league John Barnes was linked to Real Madrid during the run in. It was laughed off and the club cracked on.

This time Mo Salah has been linked to Juventus. The club is laughing and cracking on once again.

It wasn't always this way. Sometimes it felt like this place would never be reached. That players would always be picked off. That The Reds couldn't compete.

Last season, Liverpool finished 25 points behind City. Guardiola's side won it by 19. They had it all their own way. Not this time.

The Reds could have regressed after Kyiv. Boom then bust could have kicked in once more, like it has so many times before. Klopp willed it differently. And now look. Another week. More hope. More prayers. Just a draw, please. Then The Reds again on Friday.

Any spares? Not a chance.

It wasn't always this way. Enjoy it.

Why Hope Still Springs Eternal For Liverpool's Title Dream

Thursday April 25, 2019

PAUL COPE

WHAT'S your perspective on hope?

I think that's where we are now. What it all comes down to.

What do you choose? Do you believe it's the hope that kills you? Or that once you choose hope anything is possible?

Do you still believe? Do you dare to allow yourself to dream? Or are you too afraid of what the pain will feel like at the end if you choose hope and the holy grail doesn't arrive?

I've written on these pages before about life and love, dressed up in a beautiful red football kit. I've talked of dancing in the aisles and singing in the streets, of laughing with your friends and hugging complete strangers. I've encouraged you to give all of yourself even though it's a risk. Even though there can be no guarantee of winning.

The question for each of us is how many times are we prepared to keep dreaming. To keep taking the risk. To keep believing.

It was fascinating watching the build up to the Manchester United-Manchester City game. Liverpool fans all over the world telling ourselves that United are crap and don't really have a chance, while simultaneously believing that it was possible.

That even crap teams pull off shock results sometimes. That they only needed a draw, a world-class goal out of nowhere or a man of the match goalkeeping performance that we've witnessed so many times before from David de Gea playing against our lads.

We didn't get any of it. For all the talk of United fans wanting a City victory to stop us winning the league, I can't imagine any of them enjoyed watching the pitiful display we witnessed last night.

The gulf between the sides was so frightening that the blue half of Manchester was able to win a crucial derby at a canter, not even adding to the fatigue in its players' legs in the way we'd hoped.

For a league season in which the lead has changed more than ever before, Manchester City has reclaimed the summit with three games left. But we play next.

In what is arguably the greatest ever head to head for a title at the pinnacle of the English league football, the shouts of 'over to you' being tossed back and forth between these two great sides has been a weekly occurrence for longer than I can remember.

And it's our turn again on Friday night. As our charismatic leader often says, we can only look after our own business. We can only control what lies in front of us. And, right now, that's a Friday night home game against the team rooted to the bottom of the division. A beleaguered opponent wishing the months away so that it can regroup and put the past 12 months behind it.

Our job is to lay down a marker. To blow Huddersfield away on a night of drinks and joy and laughter. That's all we can do this week, before shouting 'over to you' to Pep Guardiola's men another time.

We play our next two games before them, which means we just need to do our job and put the pressure on them to do theirs. Make no mistake, if they beat Burnley, Leicester and Brighton to finish the season with 14 wins on the run and 18 out of 19 in the second half of the campaign, they deserve the title.

But it's by no means certain that they will.

I always felt that Burnley away would be a bigger test for City than United, which speaks volumes for our former great rival.

While the negativity searchers among us will point to the fact that The Clarets are now safe from relegation as a reason to lose hope, I have no doubts that Sean Dyche and his lads will want to show the world that they are capable of matching Manchester City as they have so many times against the big boys of the Premier League in the past.

Regardless of anything else, that game still represents the end of an energy-sapping and leg-destroying run of games for Raheem Sterling and his mates, and the threat that Burnley poses is a completely different animal to that of Manchester United or Tottenham Hotspur.

One thing we can guarantee is that Ederson and whichever centre backs are tasked with helping him to defend his goal will not have as little to do as they did at Old Trafford. The aerial bombardment will be intense, and that's before factoring in the possibility of our old friend Peter Crouch coming off the bench to snatch a late draw or win.

That would just add to the plethora of things that have gone our way in this epic quest that will be talked about long into the future (mainly by Evertonians) if we do go on to win our first league in three decades.

I still believe that too many things have gone our way for it not to be written in the stars. Sometimes football just does funny things, and often this very special football club does very special things that defy logic and have opposition players, managers and supporters shaking their heads in disbelief.

I've seen it too many times before to give up hope now.

I've seen the greatest striker in the world in 2005 miss an open goal from three yards out in a European Cup final then spend the rest of the match – up to and including missing a penalty in the crucial shootout – looking like a ghost and repeatedly looking like he'd come face to face with destiny and seen that it wasn't on his side.

I've watched shots fly past goals that still look as though they go in when watching replays 14 years later. I've heard managers talk of results not having any rational explanation after witnessing their side implode when confronted with the power of this mighty football club.

This is not over yet. Not by a long way. All we can do now is enjoy ourselves and do whatever we can to help our boys win three more league games. What happens after that is beyond our control.

But what is in our control is to keep believing. To never be afraid to continue to hope, even beyond the point at which everyone else has given up. That's where the real glory is. That's where the true supporters and the true believers can hold their heads high and say they never stopped.

Through the wind and the rain. Our dreams will always be tossed and blown, that's part of the journey. That's part of what it is to be a football supporter, to choose to have this weird thing as such a big part of our lives.

Without the hope what's the point? Without going into each of our remaining league games believing that the ultimate glory can still be ours, we are just wasting an opportunity to live our best lives.

Imagine if you spent the next three weeks moping around, only for City to drop points in dramatic fashion against Brighton on the last day, in the dying seconds. What a waste of three glorious weeks of your life that would be.

CHAPTER SEVEN – THE HOME STRAIGHT

My favourite thing about our defeat in Kyiv last season was the mood of everyone I knew and everyone I saw and heard after the game. People repeatedly saying how much fun it had been and how not winning one game of football wasn't going to take anything away from the glorious adventure we'd been on.

It's the same now. Of course, we all want to win. We want it more than ever before. But we can't let the fear of finishing runner up to one of the greatest sides in modern football take away from our enjoyment of the next three weeks. This is what we're in it for. These Reds, this football, these battles. This is what it's all about.

I choose hope. I choose to believe that no matter what happens in life, we should keep giving everything we've got. Better to have loved and lost than never to have loved at all.

I will keep hoping, keep believing and keep falling in love. I will dedicate everything I have to enjoying this life as much as I possibly can and to helping as many people around me to enjoy theirs.

To live our best lives. To sing and dance and laugh and cry. Regardless of the outcome. Regardless of whether someone gives us a shiny trophy at the end of it all or whether we just have to keep hoping into next season.

I will hope and believe and love to infinity. Because that's all I can do. What happens after that is out of my control.

I believe that once you choose hope, anything is possible.

Keep believing. These are the best days of our lives.

Barcelona v Liverpool

Wednesday May 1, 2019

ROB GUTMANN'S PREVIEW

WE'VE come a long way.

Just typing out the header – Barcelona away – made me shiver, made me twitch. To be a team facing them in the semi final of a European Cup is something to be.

We can know we should feel lucky to be where we are today yet simultaneously feel entitled. Our journey isn't nearing its end, it's only just beginning.

It's strange as we get ever closer to a summit that seemed a crazy dream a year ago just how suddenly frightening the fear of failure becomes.

My friend and Anfield Wrap contributor Adam Melia said the other day he couldn't simply enjoy the process, the wins along the way. I agree with him. He noted that every victory was a charge to our optimism and that could only ever be validated by ultimate success. You have to believe you will achieve your objective or the path towards it is tainted.

If we beat Barcelona we celebrate the prospect of what comes next. If I were to tell you we'd beat them but fail in the final of the Champions League you'd glean little satisfaction from knocking out the mighty Spaniards. It would all have been in a vain purpose.

It was right that we took time out to celebrate reaching the 91-point mark achieved in the week of victory over Huddersfield last week. It helps occasionally to be deliberately rational even if the heart doesn't want to hear it sometimes.

I watched my youngest son's face in the wake of Manchester City's win over Burnley last weekend. His features contorted, tortured and despairing. I wondered if it was correct that I had contributed to bringing him to this point. Was it worth all this? Wasn't this all meant to be fun?

My answer, my only truth, is that I know no other way than to be utterly obsessive about Liverpool and I think I have always been this way and always will be this way. That means that I don't see it as a pleasure but as a duty, a struggle, a quest, a cause.

I do not begin to understand the mentality that sees following The Reds as some endless party. I mean, fair play if you're having all those good times, I'm just not, and I really don't mind.

Folks have been talking for weeks about what they will be doing the day of the Wolves game or the day of the Newcastle game, or their travel plans for Madrid, or any day they can forecast that Liverpool might win the league or another trophy upon. They're talking about how they'll indulge like it's 1999.

I don't begin to understand that mentality. Apart from the obvious fate tempting involved, it's projecting that the celebration is the key event not the simple fact of the victory.

Do I sound like I might not be much company at parties? That's OK, I'm not having a bad time and although I'm not feeling happiness, contentedness even, I'm feeling great pride and that's carrying me through.

No more so than in knowing that I'm supporting a Liverpool team that is going to the Nou Camp for the first time in living memory not just to compete, but as equals to the legendary Barcelona.

I'm confident that Liverpool are good enough to knock out Barcelona and go on to lift the European Cup. The league, despite a likely final points haul in the mid 90s, looks surreally beyond our control. The Champions League is a different matter.

Obviously, Barcelona, Messi, Suarez et al stand in our path, but my sense is that they will face a Liverpool team that will harness the anger they must feel from the 'injustice' being done to them in the Premier League.

I cannot begin to imagine how frustrated the likes of Mo Salah and Virgil van Dijk must feel at the moment. They know they are the best, have proven that their best. They and their colleagues have scored all the goals for and prevented all the goals against required to win a league title and yet to still face the prospect of falling short.

Jürgen Klopp is a master at taking anger and frustration and channelling it for positive gain. It is not easy to second guess his selection for the trip to Spain, not least because of fitness concerns over Bobby Firmino and Fabinho.

Because Barcelona represents the zenith of challenges a team can face in football, it's hard not to pick teams for the manager that are over laden with defensive players.

Trent Alexander-Arnold has become such a key feature of Liverpool's attacking play but will he be trusted to thwart Barcelona's world-class forward line when turned around? Some are picking Joe Gomez ahead of him at right back. I'm not, and I don't think the manager will either.

Midfield will be interesting if Firmino is left out. Rather than just throw another forward in his stead I think the Liverpool boss could go with a four-man midfield, with Naby Keita the point of a diamond formation behind a twin strike force of Salah and Mane.

I'm frothing at the prospect of seeing how this brilliant Liverpool team matches up against the current world's best. They're the majestic reigning kings of world football and we're the plucky street fighter with no fear and insatiable ambition. We'll know so much more about both of these forces come Wednesday night.

There may be more pains and blows to be endured but we have our faith and our power.

They can't hold us back forever.

Barcelona 3 Liverpool 0
NEIL ATKINSON'S REVIEW

THE lonely painter.

Well, it hurts. Let me tell you, it hurts. Be prepared to bleed. I told you. I warned you. To bleed is to love.

The worst thing, the most painful thing about the enterprise is that at no moment did they feel two goals better than Liverpool let alone three. At no point were The Reds played off the park. Far from it.

At almost every stage Liverpool seemed the best team on the pitch. We've seen this trick this season from Liverpool; these rope-a-dope moments. But tonight Liverpool weren't truly victim to that, instead Liverpool were victim to their own lack of ruthlessness. Again and again Liverpool were an inch away from finding a way. Again and again it didn't quite happen.

Liverpool bled. Always turn up there and always get within yards from the goal and find it suddenly very difficult. Barcelona did nothing special. Nothing remarkable. It's why there should still be hope. Why there should be frustration.

To be done, right now, right in this moment, feels unfair. And Liverpool aren't done. It takes little imagination to see The Reds 2-0 up with 10 to go at Anfield. Even with Barcelona's brilliance, even with Leo Messi's brilliance. But there should be frustration.

Look where and when The Reds knocked off. We can expect better from our best at both ends of the pitch.

Virgil van Dijk has been marvellous but he can't look back on the first goal feeling faultless. Instead he falls short, knocked off and deep. Then at the very end of the affair Mo Salah hits the post when he should score, when he should give Liverpool some just desserts. The ball bounces out.

There was a strangeness to the enterprise; every early moment saw Barcelona accept Liverpool's superiority. I may be naïve, but this wasn't the plan. But they played like an away side in front of 100,000 Catalans.

They accepted that Liverpool were better and, therefore, it is no surprise that until a brilliant freekick, it was Luis Suarez who stood out for our opponents. More than anything he is a natural underdog, a man who loves that fight, a man who shows for a year and a day, a man looking for one more at all times.

He's marvellous but then again, who isn't? A takeaway from the first half is this: these are 22 of the very best footballers in the world. It's an uncomplicated point, but the sheer quality on show was phenomenal. Liverpool are one of the best teams in the world. This is their breathtaking domain. This is what they go to school for. They are better than Barca. But…

But there is the main fella. He is a joy, an astonishment in human form. Leo Messi is the best person ever to play this game of ours by a distance.

He is remarkable in brain and in feet. He is an outrage and a kaleidoscope, something to stop and something to adore. He is all twists and all marvellousness. He is the best of us all; he is your dreams. He is what you always wanted to be writ large. Leo Messi is the best person to play this daft game by a mile.

And Liverpool did well. Until he banged one in from 30 yards, because why not? Until he reminded us and hurt us. Until he was the thing and the whole of the thing.

Go to him. Stay with him if you can. Be prepared to bleed.

Be prepared to bleed. Liverpool were tonight. They expected to see some magic but they thought they would score. All of them, especially James Milner, didn't just live with opponents but outstrip them; Milner the best player on the pitch tonight. Apart from the very best players, apart from the magicians.

We shouldn't think Liverpool are beaten. It is earthy to think until they score at Anfield this tie is alive. Liverpool are capable of being 2-0 with 10 to go. That should be their aim. They can beat this side. Apart from the brilliance of the greatest to play the game, they have little to be scared of.

Er. Yes.

Be prepared to bleed. Liverpool tonight could have been better at 1-0. They could also have been luckier. But nothing will let me give up on this season. These are my lads; our lads, for better or worse.

To take us to Madrid they will need to be outrageous versions of themselves and we will need to do that too. Nothing is finished tonight but everything now is graft. But Jürgen's lads love that.

Liverpool should go out. But should is doing a lot of work in that sentence. But I still back them, the dope that I am. Stay with them if you can. Be prepared to bleed.

Barcelona come to Anfield to deal with the bloodied. This Liverpool are better than Barcelona; this Liverpool are capable of showing that. However, like everyone else, this Liverpool is capable of being Messied. You go up against the King, you better not miss. Liverpool missed tonight but they get one more go.

Thing is… So does he.

The Lessons From Barcelona
Thursday May 1, 2019
JOHN GIBBONS

GREETINGS from Barcelona. Where the sun is shining, and the weather is sweet, yeah.

Football aside, we've had a lovely time of tapas, sangria and cerveza. The city was hospitable and we were very open to hospitality. Between rooftop bars, beaches and tavernas, we've sampled it all. What a city it is. Everything you could want in one place. Perfect.

Some Liverpool supporters chose to enjoy themselves in a different way. Videos of locals being pushed into fountains are as frustrating as they are embarrassing. People are desperate to have a go at people from the city so I wish we didn't give any further ammunition.

We sing about 'conquering all of Europe' but this shouldn't be taken literally.

There seems to be an attitude in England, which Liverpool is part of whether we like it or not, of going abroad and 'conquering'. Find an area and take over. Maybe we are all guilty of fuelling that mentality. We travel like no other set of fans but occasionally the 'take over' mentality can spill over into hostility. And then police respond with their own.

It's not hard to get right. The vast majority manage it. For everything you might have seen on social media there are bars around the corner full of songs, laughter and ultimately respect. Liverpool enjoying Spain and Spain enjoying Liverpool. As I say, it's not hard. There is so much of both to enjoy.

On the pitch, unfortunately, Barcelona were anything but hospitable. Ruthless in front of goal and miserly at the back. Liverpool had plenty of the ball but none of the goals. We arrived with so much promise but leave with just regret and disappointment. What ifs and maybes.

For all the positives, it now feels more likely than not that this season will end without a trophy. We all hope for a miracle on Monday or Tuesday, and it is possible. But more likely not.

I'm not giving up. What's the point in that? But I'm not ignoring the probabilities either. That Barcelona and Manchester City prove to have too much, even for this great side. That we are beaten to the line.

Tonight we fly home and reintroduce ourselves to our partners and then text friends asking what time the bus leaves for Newcastle. A season which felt like it would never end at one point now feels it is ending too soon. A week or so and it could be over. Should be over. Just over a week and our fate will be clear. We'll have the summer to celebrate or regret.

But no point feeling sorry for ourselves yet. Tomorrow the hangover will be gone and the sun tan and memories of singing in bars and believing another famous night was ahead of us will remain.

This team has taken us on some amazing journeys. No point stopping just yet.

Make them work for it. All of them. The bastards.

Newcastle United 2 Liverpool 3
Saturday May 4, 2019
BEN JOHNSON'S RATINGS

BEEN listening to a lot of modern-day hymns today.

When I seen the team, Dan Sturridge is starting. He fucking loves God. I'm taking it as a sign. I mean, Allah has been doing most of the heavy lifting for The Reds so far this season, it's about time Auld Goddo fucking pulled his finger out, aye?

Alisson: 8

Made about 20 saves, all of them dead easy but should have been dead hard. What a fella.

Trent: 8

Hahaha boss handball, that. Just a strong arm that, referee. Love the way he should have been sent off and spewed it, and set up two for a laugh. Boss all night long.

Virgil: 8

Belter movement for his goal. Had to deal with playing next to a nonsense. Boxes the ball in for the last by telling Trent to swerve it. Defended really well. What a hero.

Lovren: 5

Was dogshite. Like one that you have stood in, not realised and bounced straight up the stairs to the bog, gone into your bedroom, closed the curtains in your son's room, gone the kitchen, checked you had turned the telly off in the living room, maybe checked the fridge and left a trail like fucking Hansel and Gretel of Degsi Lovren's dogshite all over the house.

Clean it? Nah fuck that, burn the fucker down and start again.

Starts the rot with a mental pass to Alisson, got legged by Rondon all day long, was worried that we had only one centre half on for the last 10 minutes and then realised that the alternative was two with Lovren being one of them.

Andy Robbo: 9

Was absolutely tremendous. Tremendous. Back to his absolute best. Everywhere. First to everything. He needed more like him all over the pitch but then we won so he didn't really.

Henderson: 6

Thought he struggled tonight. A bit sloppy on the ball, a bit leggy, a bit… You know. Kept fucking going though, didn't he?

Fabinho: 6

The one where he twatted it out when The Reds were crying out to keep it was desperate. Was good-ish first half, tired second, but still there knocking about and is a well better centre half than Lovren.

Gini: 7

Gini, la. Like a ghost on Mario Kart. Floated round the pitch, done bits, was goosed from legging it all over the Nou Camp.

Mo Salah: 8

The finish for the second is absolutely first class. Running backwards, wrong foot, absolute Robbie Fowler slot. Very nearly got killed trying to get onto the end of a Degsi Hail Mary. Apparently he isn't dead. Which is absolutely the second best news we have had tonight.

Sadio: 7

Should score the one in the first when Mo puts him in. Could do with him scoring from every shot he has again, which was boss while it lasted, in fairness.

Dan Sturridge: 7

It's like an experiment at this point. Let's play a fella who can't run in a side that does nothing but. A juxtaposition squared. Plays some great through balls first half, but for the love of God, he has got to score that one, doesn't he?

SUBS...

Milner: 8

Come on to calm every fucker down and whacked two bellends within one move and could conceivably have been sent off for two yellows and one foul.

Shaq: 7

Come on, couldn't get on the ball. Couldn't get on the ball. Started robbing freekicks off everyone else like it was literally his ball, and then sets up the winner. Scenes.

Big Div: 9

Scored the winner there, didn't he? If The Reds win the league this season we should be naming stands after him. Fucking statues.

NEIL ATKINSON'S REVIEW

THIRTY-SEVEN down. One to go.

Liverpool go and win at bottom half Newcastle. They show their class over the course of the 90 minutes and…

…As if you can talk about this being cut and dried. As if this is cool. As if this should become something which is never about how it feels. It feels like everything. All there is is feeling. All there is is being alive.

Tonight I saw all my friends strung out. I saw Emilia Bona rock back and forth while it was 2-2. I saw Ben Johnson with his back to me, on his knees at 2-2 shuddering. Stu Wright sitting on the floor blankly while Mo Salah was injured. Paul Cope in bits. Steve Graves cry for the first time since 2014.

When the final whistle went I sank to my knees, my sobs heavy. Liverpool still alive, Liverpool giving it one more go. I was and have been prepared to bleed, but maybe not quite that much.

It's no wonder Trent Alexander-Arnold kicks it out of play at times.

Someone made you fall in love with this mad game, these mad men in Red. Someone gave you bad advice, one thing lead to another and years later you are watching Liverpool playing Newcastle United at St. James' Park in the penultimate game in the closest Liverpool have come to the league title in a generation, and Newcastle equalise making it 2-2 and you and everyone you know is done.

Thirty-seven down. One to go.

The game starts brightly despite the weather. A Virgil van Dijk classic header in the 14th minute feels like a smash and grab. A set piece that will allow Liverpool to control the game. A head start that will allow the players some breathing space before the biggest week of their footballing lives. Breathing space for us was all that was wanted.

Liverpool are not blameless when it comes to the first equaliser. A scramble in the box allows Newcastle's Atsu in. Still, we've had shaky moments before. We've had plenty of dodgy 10 minutes before, and so it appears in the first half of this game as a cool Salah goal 15 minutes later restores the lead and calms heads.

At this point, Newcastle are supposed to give in. They are supposed to give in. But we all know, however much we love him, Rafa Benitez's Newcastle were never really going to give in. Not with the power and headwind provided by their fans, and frankly the skill and dignity of this Newcastle side.

Lascelles is a leader on the pitch and gets the ball in the correct places. Newcastle look fit and up for it, and Liverpool at times look tired. The Redmen are harried by the physical interventions of their opposition, and Fabinho and Wijnaldum can't really get control of the game.

Everything became unbelievably difficult. Salomon Rondon doesn't help, the unplayable bastard. He gives van Dijk a torrid time and leaves Lovren a mess. He is the essence of awkwardness, the definition of a difference maker. Thank Christ they didn't have Almiron tonight or Liverpool may have been torn asunder.

Liverpool's opener is a lovely goal; their second an excellent one. A backheel from Daniel Sturridge leads to Arnold's ball in, which leads to Mo Salah's delightful finish; Fowler-esque in its innovation.

Liverpool the better side throughout the first half should really find their way to a third and the same can be said for the first 15 of the second half. Chances are missed and defending is last ditch until Rondon scores a beautiful goal, so sweetly struck.

When he does so, what follows make you think that this side that was about to have scored its third will never score again. Hearts sink. Is this it? It that it? Done. And then, there is worse to come.

Mo Salah falls very badly after his head collides with Newcastle's goalkeeper Dubravka. He falls to the ground and reaches for his head. He barely moves. Our wonderful man, our clever, kind Mo is hurt badly, and it is more than anyone can take.

He is stretchered off and showing solidarity as ever, Rafa reaches out his hand to him as he is carried towards the tunnel, as if even now, Rafa understands how we all feel.

Liverpool are affected by that or the change of shape. Nothing is going to come until the very second it does; until the net bulges, until Divock Origi is there again. Divock is again fortunate, but he is again there to buy a ticket to win the lottery.

At this moment, and for the final 11 minutes as we struggle through eight justified but long minutes of stoppage time, we are watching stories flash before our eyes. We are thinking of all the other 3-3 draws we have ever known. Liverpool have been known to draw games at St. James' Park before.

We are thinking about the words 'bitter' and 'sweet' and how fucked up and wrong it is that a team as good as this Liverpool side doesn't just get all the medals now. We are wondering how long we have to go through this for. We are wondering why there is so much pain in what is supposed to be a fucking leisure activity.

Until the final whistle. Until that final blessed relief comes. And you want to run to that person who made you love The Reds and grab them by the shoulders and tell them perhaps it isn't all mad and painful after all. Perhaps it does mean something, perhaps there is some point to it all.

Perhaps this love is actually for something. Perhaps it is about the beauty, not just of the glorious gliding cross-field pass, or the power of a undefendable strike, but also of the beauty of these men, fighting for each other, wanting to be with each other, and to win this thing together. That love.

Thirty-seven down. Two to go.

Liverpool win and one more hurdle has been cleared, one more during this remarkable season. They now have 94 points, only beaten the once by the only side that can finish ahead of them. This is a remarkable performance which defines consistency but more than that it defines want.

Liverpool are where they are because they can be, but also because they want it more than anything imaginable. They crave it. Their manager has done an astonishing job of placing that need in them but without overwhelming them by the task.

Two to go. Two to go because there is Monday night, there is that moment when another side becomes something we can so directly get behind. Two to go for these Reds because there are two more things that need to happen and Leicester can make it happen.

Thirty-seven down. Three to go.

Three to go because we get to acclaim our magnificent men on Tuesday night. We get to adore them at Anfield when they face a great side. We get to roar at everyone. We get to live. You'll be glad of the summer. You'll be glad of the July 4 when everything works as it should, when your heart isn't pounding and your knees aren't buckling.

But it won't be living. Liverpool have shown you living. And there will be more of it on Tuesday. Let's roar our defiance; let's articulate the joy it is to be alive.

Thirty-seven down. Four to go?

It's unlikely but why not? Why can't this season have an encore? Why can't Tuesday night lead to Madrid still? Honestly, lord, the idea of only watching them twice more hurts as much as anything else. These are the best of us. The best of themselves.

CHAPTER SEVEN – THE HOME STRAIGHT

They are just a football team, trying to play the best season of their lives. Nothing purer. Nothing sweeter. They'll do for me.

Thirty-seven down. One to go. Let it break you. Let it leave little meaning and too much emotion. Let it all be about what it feels like. Our lives can be mundane, our football team is anything but.

This is what it is to be alive, my friends. This is what it is to be in love.

Thirty-seven down. One to go.

Liverpool v Barcelona

Tuesday May 7, 2019

ROB GUTMANN'S PREVIEW

THERE was always a possibility.

A possibility that Barcelona might dish out the kind of first leg beating to Liverpool that would render the second leg of this European Cup semi final all but redundant.

Liverpool had the capacity to have beaten the Catalans and beaten them well, but fate wasn't having it. I felt we'd either rock Barca in their own fortress and carry something like a 3-1 win back with us to Anfield or we'd be on the wrong side of a serious reverse.

No one imagined that Liverpool could both so comprehensively dominate Barcelona at the Nou Camp and yet take a proper hiding.

The bullish (deluded) among us think we can summon the spirit of 2005 and turn this tie around. But Barcelona are surely too good to be made mugs of, especially by a seriously weakened and distracted Liverpool.

The early news on the wires is that Mo Salah and Bobby Firmino are definitely out. I'm content with that if it increases the chances of them both starting against Wolves at the weekend. At the time of writing the odds are against us lifting the Premier League trophy next weekend but they're still better than our chances of yet being crowned European Champions this season.

Aside from Mo and Bobby, Jürgen Klopp will want to take as few risks with his main men as possible. I don't think that will extend to resting the likes of Virgil van Dijk or Sadio Mane but if anyone is nursing a minor niggle expect them to be benched at least.

Hey, I'm not giving up on us knocking Barca out entirely. I will be in my usual perch at Anfield on Tuesday night. By kick off I'll have talked myself into believing that if we can just get a first half one-goal lead that anything will become possible.

In the corner of the multiverse where Liverpool do stage a remarkable comeback and reach the Champions League final, Klopp will pick a front three which will feature Sadio Mane as its spearhead with Divock Origi and Xherdan Shaqiri providing the pace down the sides.

The latter two were cameo stars of the breathtaking and emotional victory over Newcastle on Saturday night. If ever you wanted to contrive a scenario where you were able to properly warm up stand-ins to come in from the cold then it was provided at St James' Park.

From being cast aside and left only as witnesses to the unfurling of an incredible Liverpool campaign suddenly, from nowhere, the likes of Origi, Shaqiri and Sturridge found themselves centre stage. None were exactly world class on the evening but all contributed and each would've felt themselves reinserted into the story of the club and the season. All three would've slept very sweetly on Saturday night and maybe for the first time in a good while.

Jürgen Klopp will know this and look to channel the positivity of freer minds for the team cause.

In the dream where The Reds win, this new front three, with Sadio running wild ahead of a pumped up supporting cast, Klopp has selected his bulldog midfield of James Milner, Jordan Henderson and Gini Wijnaldum. These lads certainly know the ropes.

They collectively rolled up sleeves and ran Liverpool to last year's final. They were all lungs and sinew and Europe couldn't deal with them. If each soldier finds his highest level then maybe even Barcelona will be blown away by their hurricane.

Of course, Barcelona will be the more rested side. Valverde put out the reserves in La Liga at the weekend. Liverpool won't care, though. Liverpool are brimming with adrenalin and ablaze with a burning sense of injustice that they will most likely end this campaign without silverware.

There may be a temptation to rest one flying full back but the clipping of attacking wings that the injuries to Salah and Firmino represent could lead Klopp to resisting. If he pulls Trent it will be for Joe Gomez. Andy Robbo would be replaced by Milner, with Fabinho then stepping into the midfield rather than being rested.

The other wildcard Klopp has to play is Alex Oxlade-Chamberlain. Out for a year but back in training and some first-team minutes under his belt against Huddersfield, it may be a case of 'If not now then when?' with Chamberlain. There's an argument for giving him 60 as the surprise element that Valverde will not have anticipated.

My hope is that this game is, at a minimum, an enjoyable, pride restoring (not that we have really lost any) exercise and *hors d'oeuvres* for a much more pressing engagement at the weekend.

Let's remind Barcelona that they are mortal and that we are coming for their crown. If not now, then most definitely soon.

Liverpool 4 Barcelona 0
BEN JOHNSON'S RATINGS

I WAS at a low ebb there before kick off.

This shit didn't seem fair. I needed something, someone to get me back on track, some kind of affirmation as to why footy is the greatest thing in the world.

Met the lads for four pints before kick off and that was almost enough. No one that arsed about the game, just having a laugh, buzzing off each other's company. Then the game kicked off and the first half unfolded and the sheer defiance all over the pitch.

In the crowd, with every whistle, with every 'fuck off Suarez, you fat cunt', with every song. Nothing but defiance. That is the Scousest characteristic of them all. Defiance.

We don't fucking care about you cunts not liking us, we don't fucking care about you cunts revelling in our perceived downfall. We are Liverpool and anyone who isn't can fuck the fucking hell right off.

This team, mate. This club. This is what they do to you. I was happy with 1-0. I was happy with us ruffling their feathers, with half a team, and getting had off a little bit. I was happy with us being alive at half time. And then that fucking happened.

Jesus Christ, no wonder every cunt hates us. Best there ever was, that.

Alisson: 10

He makes an unreal save at 1-0 just before half time. I thought it was offside and wasn't arsed, but he wasn't and in fairness he is the greatest keeper I have ever fucking seen. Like the greatest. Better than all the rest. Better than anyone. Anyone I've ever met. Makes it look easy.

Trent: 9

Is quite possibly the greatest full back I've ever seen apart from the lad on the other side of the pitch. Stunning performance. Didn't see the fourth goal cause I was talking to Melia about how we were going to get diddled 4-1, and when we looked up it was slapping the back of the net. Unbelievable awareness, unbelievable execution, won us the game.

Big Joel Matip: 9

Messi tries to diddle him, first 10 minutes, cuts inside, big Joelly gets a massive horrible toe to it. Like the biggest toe you have ever seen. Like a dinosaur toe. Might have burst the ball like a raptor. Incredible tonight.

Virgil: 8

Tremendous. Absolutely tremendous. It's amazing that he is that good and yet big Joel somehow managed to be better. Deserves to lift that cunt of a thing.

Andy Robbo: 8

Was a massive fan of him getting in Messi's head first half. Fuck off you fucking little beard midget with a magic foot. Carried on for ages with half a foot.

Fab: 8

Gets booked early doors and does incredibly well not to get another in the remaining 70. Front foot all day, twatting everyone, absolutely marvellous.

Henderson: 9

Might be the greatest ever centre mid to play the game. If not, he might have run more than anyone to ever play in centre mid.

Jimmy Milner: 8

Kicked a load of lumps out of all kind of bellends. Unbelievable workload, unbelievable. Then just went full back, to replace the best ever full back to play the game, and no fucker noticed the difference.

Div: 9

Was like a man possessed. Better than Shearer in his pomp. That finish for the fourth, lad. I wasn't even looking. Was having a lovely chat with Adam Melia about character and defiance, and this side maybe falling at the last but being everything you have ever wanted, and then turned round as it twatted into the top bin. Statues lad.

Shaqo: 7

Did a cracking demonstration of why he hasn't got a start in six months in the first half. Gave the fucker away every time he got it. Well better second half.

Sadio: 8

Was as lively as fuck. Everywhere first 10 minutes. Was our second best forward. Determined to be a nuisance.

SUBS...

Gini: 9

One of them, isn't it? Heard him coming on and was devoed that Robbo has gone off. Then he just bangs two. The second is some header, you know.

THE REST...

Suarez: 9

Not going to celebrate at Anfield. I know, lad. Cause you aren't even having a shot, you fat tramp.

JOSH SEXTON'S REVIEW

I'M gonna have to apologise.

Firstly, I apologise that Neil Atkinson can't bring you these words. That you don't get to read the absolute poetry he could conjure up in the aftermath of a whirlwind of football like that.

I apologise if these words don't do that for you. Don't have the Joni Mitchell and Lorde lyrics effect. I'm sorry.

I'm also sorry because when Jürgen Klopp joined Liverpool he spoke of turning doubters to believers. Until this week I had put myself firmly in the camp of the latter. I thought Klopp's lads could do anything. That they were capable of winning a deserved league and European Cup double.

And then this week happened.

We went to the Nou Camp bouncing, full of beans, confident that no matter what Lionel Messi could create this Liverpool team could deal with it and give it back tenfold.

You know the rest. You know that Lionel Messi happened. It was the influence of something otherworldly. A player whose talents may never be replicated – certainly not in my lifetime.

This Liverpool side have gone again and again for months. They've been pegged back every single time. Tonight though, we saw the influence of something otherworldly. Something that I have to apologise for because I was convinced it couldn't happen.

I doubted. I no longer believed Liverpool could finish this season with a trophy to hoist above their heads in May. They deserve it so much. More than anything in the world. It seemed so cruel. Fate had dealt The Reds a shit hand.

Well fate can absolutely get to fucking fuck.

Another apology goes to Anfield. That homogenous mass of 53,000 Reds that gather every other week, and so regularly on a midweek, to worship this football team.

I apologise because I didn't think worship was enough. I didn't think that even a higher power could save this Liverpool side tonight.

But Anfield created another magical setting tonight. It provided the platform which allowed these magnificent lads to go on and achieve their dreams, and our dreams.

I want to make sure I don't do down what those lads on the pitch achieved tonight. I don't want to have to make another apology.

I saw Fabinho run his actual legs off. He looked as though he could barely stand in front of the crowd.

I saw Trent Alexander-Arnold channel the spirit of every Scouser in our team who came before him. Who dragged a team to victory. If you still doubt Trent you can fuck off. He stood up on the big stage once again. He'll absolutely do for me.

I saw Virgil van Dijk marshall. Joel Matip tackle everything that came near him. James Milner experience the absolute shit out of the game. Jordan Henderson be a LIVERPOOL CAPTAIN. Sadio Mane do the work of his missing mates and more. Alisson do exactly what he was bought to do.

Andy Robbo gave so much for the cause that he had to be hooked on half time. Little did we know how much that sub would change our destiny. Gini Wijnaldum came on and absolutely boxed everything off. His goals, among others, have taken Liverpool to another Champions League final.

The others are Divock Origi, to whom my final apology goes to. I, and I'm sure I'm not alone, had completely written him off this season. I didn't believe he could do any of what he has done. Didn't believe he had the determination to score that goal against Everton. Didn't have the presence to score that goal against Newcastle. Didn't have the ability to run absolute rings around that Barca defence.

Liverpool Football Club went again tonight. Anfield rose again. The lads who we've loved all season stood up to the task. The lads who we (or I) wrote off did the same. Everybody at Liverpool Football Club should bask in the glory of tonight.

The abyss has been stared into today. Liverpool were staring at another trophyless season and it hurt. The doubt hurt.

I promise I'll never doubt this team again.

I hope you have the best night out of your lives. You deserve it and these lads deserve it.

See you in Madrid.

Liverpool v Wolves

Sunday May 12, 2019

ROB GUTMANN'S PREVIEW

THERE'S Gini Wijnaldum on Tuesday night, at the final whistle, on his knees, covering his eyes.

He's looked into the face of God. Can't take in what he's witnessed. He's seen pure bliss.

There's Trent Alexander-Arnold in the 79th minute prowling by the corner flag. He feigns to leave the kick to another but then in a blinking of an eye he's spun on a heel and into the ball. He whips it into the path of Divock Origi, who in turn sweeps it into Ter Stegen's goal.

Anfield erupts, manager Klopp later hails Alexander-Arnold's ruse as a moment of divine genius. But Trent's done that before. In the playground, in PE, in his back garden. The boy who just loved the game. The genius is that he's always the boy.

James Milner. He's got his arms around his comrades, tears streaking his features. He's openly weeping and all the world can see. James doesn't care. James is a real man.

Anfield, five minutes to kick off, Champions league semi final second leg, Liverpool v Barcelona. The ground collectively aches as every man, woman and child belt out You'll Never Walk Alone.

Liverpool's timeless anthem can be rendered in many different ways. Sometimes it is defiant, often joyous, other occasions angry but tonight it is a lament, a song of collective sadness and togetherness in the face of great disappointment. A Liverpool team, arguably the best the club has ever been represented by, looking increasingly like seeing out a magnificent campaign with little prospect of tangible reward.

Only at Anfield is everything possible. Only there could Tuesday night happen. The team that couldn't be broken lifted itself from a canvas it had never deserved to be prone upon, raised its guard and started to swing and jab.

The footwork was electrifying as Liverpool danced through and around the self-styled best football team on the planet. Barcelona were tenderised, dizzied and then floored, blows raining down, an onslaught they were powerless to resist.

Now Liverpool are ready. Finally, Jürgen Klopp's Liverpool are ready. Ready to step forward and accept the mantle of champions. Thus far they have been imperious, kings of all they've surveyed but kings without a crown.

The team that Klopp built deserve to be league title winners for the 2018-19 season and to step up and claim that prize by beating Wolves on Sunday. The record would show that the team that took 97 points from 114 on offer were the best team in the land.

Liverpool may not become league champions on Sunday because it is extremely likely that another incredible collection of footballers, Manchester City, defeat Brighton and finish top of the Premier League, ahead of Liverpool by the narrowest of margins.

At the beginning of the week, as a ridiculous Vincent Kompany goal took City back to the top of the pile, it seemed Liverpool's match with Wolves would be consigned to footnote territory. Heavy defeat in Barcelona a week ago looked likely to compound

Liverpool's misery and to provide a sad conclusion to what has for so long been a story worthy of having a glorious finale.

Then Tuesday night happened. Anfield happened.

Now everything has changed.

We'll be positively strutting down Walton Breck Road on Sunday. City really can't hurt us now. We have travelled two steps further than them in the competition they coveted the most. We are favourites to be crowned at last and crowned as kings of Europe.

Of course, it may not happen and we may not win the league either but the landscape has changed. We have more than a puncher's chance of real silverware. Sunday can now be treated as a potential incredible bonus. City can pip us to the title and we can shrug and wave them off as we pack our trunks for Madrid.

We haven't reached the summit yet, but it's very much in sight.

Regardless of what happens next, the view from up here is wonderful.

Liverpool 2 Wolves 0
NEIL ATKINSON'S REVIEW

THERE were maybe four to go when we last talked, you and I. Maybe four more love songs.

And now there is definitely just one. And how are we doing?

Proud but not that cool. Not really. Angry but at no one in particular. No blame, not because of a no-blame culture, but because no blame should attach itself. However, there is this: Liverpool have had an interest on one last day since last winning the bloody thing.

And for a moment the trapdoor is lifted and we get a sense of what it might feel like if Liverpool win the league, and the answer is this: absolutely crazy.

This team, these supporters have so much pent up desire to win the title, it bursts out as Brighton's goal goes in on the 28th minute. The noise shoots out of the corporate boxes in the middle of the main stand and swoops round the stadium in seconds.

People are up on their feet shouting about God knows what, as if someone had just discovered oil or diamonds under the Anfield Road end. As others scream 'What? What? What has happened? Please someone tell me. What. Is. Going. On?'

My head went. Which is nothing compared to what happened to The Reds for whom the first half had started incredibly well. The passing is fluid, and Origi looks more comfortable than he ever has, no doubt basking in recent heroics. Liverpool keep shape and ball, waiting for the opportunity to come.

The captain is all about the clever moves and the Liverpool shape is still evident as it has been for 99 per cent of this season. On the 17th he couples up with Trent, to allow Sadio Mane to slot one in deflected off Boly.

Then the goal on the South Coast and then just moments later as City equalise the craziness takes a turn for the worse. Panicked Liverpool fans desperately try to make phones work. 'Is someone making this up for a laugh? What. Is. Going. On?'

The game continues but for a period in the first half, it feels like we are all playing someone else, somewhere else, and that transmits to a team of lads in their 20s who look suddenly like lambs shot through with serotonin. Frisky isn't the half of it. Frisky isn't always good and is bad news against Wolves.

Against Wolves you need focus and certainty because they have it in the bucketload. A gang of massive lads who love and trust their shape. A million diagonals later and here I am trying to tell you Dendoncker is enormous. They are always dangerous without a load of actual danger. But they do hit the bar.

They are a better side than their Mancunian-obsessed support deserve on the day. They are bantz writ large while the side has no jokes and a ton of elbows. An old school 'who the fucking hell are you?' rings out from The Kop.

But that's not really the question here. Who the fucking hell are we? That is what matters. Are we brave? Are we strong? Do we believe in our lads?

We all bounced into the ground and now we realise. This is torture. It is horrendous. We are making it harder for our footballers and kettling our own heads. Not knowing whether there was still hope was actually physically painful for a few minutes.

This isn't what Jürgen meant when he discussed being prepared to suffer through games, but it is what I meant when I spoke to you about being prepared to bleed. We bled.

CHAPTER SEVEN – THE HOME STRAIGHT

There was a moment when I realised the rollercoaster was at the point where vomiting is an option.

By half time, though, everyone knows that it is 2-1 to City, and that the mighty Brighton & Hove Albion were not to be our knights in shining armour this year. But it is that gradual realisation that allows Liverpool's crowd to find itself having lost itself in the early excitement.

There was a moment we realised the rollercoaster was just that; not a runaway train where crashing and burning was a possibility, but something with a solid safety harness and that harness is called Madrid.

Wolves continue to impose themselves and perform well but Alisson is remarkable in his unfussiness. He is always exactly where he needs to be and personifies reliability. This isn't accidental. His brain is constantly whirring. It makes the saves look mundane when they are anything but.

The checking of phones doesn't stop. We couldn't really ask Brighton to give us that miracle. The expectation wasn't fair. Manchester City are a really great team. There will be discussion of how that gang of lads came together. But that shouldn't in anyway lessen the brilliance or achievement of that gang of lads nor the journey of their supporters. Far from it.

They have shown astonishing grit and spirit, Bernardo Silva and Raheem Sterling have impressed beyond belief and it should be possible to salute them and love Liverpool. When in doubt, be kind. In fact just be kind in general. We've spent the season together, you and I. I'd hope it is always within the essence of these words.

Mane's second goal on the 82nd from the boot of Trent, to Sadio's head to the back of the goal is glorious and takes him level with Mo Salah for the golden boot. Which leads to Mo Salah having a ton of shots which make me laugh, anyway.

Mane now has scored the most goals at home of any player this season, too. He takes his place among the greats in this team and the greats of our club. That he happens to play alongside other greats ought not to overshadow his achievements.

However, our brilliant lads were tired in the second half, and despite substitutions, looked like they could all use a breather. They had had midweek exertions. They didn't need a stellar performance, they just needed a win, in case of miracles. Today's match ends as a routine win but a good win.

So it's a strange one. You get a win that feels like coming second. Because it is coming second. That's what has happened and sugarcoating it is pointless. Let it taste sour. But you can't help feeling amazed by it all nonetheless. It's weird. And something of a hiatus now that we have Madrid to come.

We have that one to go. We are brilliant and beaten. Unimpeachable but bettered. Touched by greatness but unlucky.

But. But. But. Lucky. That's what I feel. Lucky. You get to a point in life when you think that there are no more love affairs. You think, there were players, teams, games before that made me giddy. But surely you get to a certain age, and all that's gone. You still support them, but not with childish excitement anymore.

People say it's the hope that kills you. And that is true to a certain extent, but it's also a total lie, because we haven't been killed by hope this season, we have been brought alive by it. Here is a team, that for 38 games has held us captivated. This is the real thing. The romance. It had had it all.

More than anything it had the ability to make us giddy, to make fools of us in the best way and we get one more go round the carousel with them, one more time to send our stomach west. One more awfully big adventure. Giddiness is reason to live, giddiness is reason to clamber out of bed, giddiness is your stomach and your heart in unison.

It is what Liverpool at their best do to their opponents, what making people turn around again and again is about. What they do at their best to us, make children of us, make lovers of us.

Liverpool have made us lucky, Liverpool have made us proud. Liverpool give us something to do, something in common and a reason to write love songs, a reason not to be cynical, a reason to be kind.

Thanks lads. Thanks Jürgen and the backroom chaps. Win in Madrid because you deserve to lift something up and hang something around your necks.

One to go. One more love song.

Liverpool v Tottenham Hotspur
Saturday June 1, 2019
ROB GUTMANN'S FINAL PREVIEW

'OVER and over and over and over,
'Like a monkey with a miniature cymbal…'
That song by Hot Chip. Can't get it out of my head. My head is cluttered, my swede is cabbaged. Buzzing, full of noise, full of songs.

I'll be in Madrid. Not sure where yet. You may find me in a bodega, down an alley not far off the Plaza Mayor. You may find me in O'Malley's near the Plaza de Santa Ana. You're unlikely to be greeting me on the terraces of the Wanda Metropolitano.

I'm a travelling ticketless Red, you see. Wherever I can find a spec in front of a TV in the centre of the Spanish capital, that's my home. Me and about 40,000 other hapless ticketless souls.

Reminds me of that Radiohead song: 'You do it to yourself you do, and that's what really hurts.'

We do it to ourselves. I'm spending a small fortune to travel to watch Liverpool play on a TV screen in a bar somewhere, and to kip over in a shitty bed in a crap hotel 1,500 miles away from home comfort. And if the same scenario transpired again next year, or in 10 years' time, I'd still rinse and repeat.

I'd almost gotten to the point of jibbing the entire enterprise. Writing off flights and rooms already paid for, to experience. Then you talk to people. You realise we're all in the same boat. Tens of thousands of us, all with no hope of tickets but hearts full of hope.

We're all migrating, trekking across Europe, not so much as a conquering horde more a defiant flotilla. This is our Dunkirk. We have to go, to leave, because to stay would feel like defeat. We have to get to Madrid, our sanctuary and we will get there by any means possible.

My two boys, Danny and Raffy, are going with me. They're still a bit confused as to why we'll travel without tickets. They just want to see Liverpool play in a European Cup final.

Lads, so do I. So do I.

I've followed Liverpool the length and breadth, and go home and away. I've been to all manner of semi finals and cup finals with the team. But I've never been to a European Cup final. I was 18 by the time we'd reached our fifth, and I'd not been able to afford to go to any of them.

When we started getting to these things again, from 2005 onwards, I was in a very different phase of life. I'd had kids and successfully indoctrinated them into being Liverpool diehards. We watch every game together.

In 2005, my Danny was seven and had been home and away with me all season long. The final was in midweek and I couldn't get him out of school. I could've gone on my own, but doing so felt like it would've been a betrayal. Like all that I'd preached to him, about him and me and The Reds. About us being bound together forever.

'Once upon a time when we were friends, I gave you my heart , the story ends...'
ABC's All Of My Heart in my head.

I couldn't leave him. Or I couldn't let him leave me. Either way, 2007, Athens, was broadly the same sketch.

Then Danny grew up, and didn't have school commitments to thwart us both, but by 2018, his second coming, my youngest, Rafa, was nine and as smitten with Liverpool as his big brother and dad. Kyiv was a journey too long and too far. Once again we settled ourselves to stay home and watch the game on the TV.

As we consoled each other in the aftermath of last season's losing final, we vowed, like the musketeers we are, that should our team reach the following year's final, in Madrid, that neither heaven nor earth would prevent us going. Of course no one believed that night that we would have to face this incredible prospect.

'If you wish upon a star...'

Running out by the back of The Kop onto Walton Breck road. Liverpool have beaten Barcelona 4-0 and it's the greatest night of our lives. We're literally dancing in the street. We're all the same age momentarily. Me at 52, Danny at 20, Raffy at 10. Dancing in the street singing 'we're going to Madrid'.

'Porto, Barcelona, who the fuck ya tryna kid...'

And we are going to Madrid. I've never been to see Liverpool play in a European Cup final and I may never do so, but I am going to Madrid. The lack of a ticket will not prevent that.

I feel we have to keep trying for tickets, mind. Like Liverpool keep trying. Like Mo Salah's T-shirt that said 'never give up' was trying to tell us. Loving our team means we must be like them because we made them.

'Never gonna give you up. Never gonna let you down.'

UEFA may continue to let us down with their crappy ticket allocations, the club's administrators maybe should do better with the way they regard loyalty, life can deal out all manner of poor decks of cards. But Liverpool will not let us down because Liverpool never give up.

Whatever is thrown at us and our team on Saturday in Madrid we will not yield. No team will be more readied to step forward and claim what is rightfully theirs than this Liverpool side.

It may well be the greatest Liverpool team of our lifetimes. It smells and looks like it might be, but only the anointing that winning the European Cup represents can confirm that. Our will to lift this trophy cannot be measured but it is mightier than theirs.

This sport notoriously thwarts the processes of natural justice and laughs in the faces of fairness. But now, surely now, Liverpool's moment has arrived.

I'm going to Madrid. I'm going with my boys, and with all the boys and girls, and mums and dads, and nans and granddads to represent a city that will not sleep on Saturday night, come what may.

I've been singing songs in my head all day every day since that night dancing outside Anfield, four weeks back. The pace is quickening now, rhythms getting faster, the melodies sweeter, the orchestra louder.

'And the piano it sounds like a carnival...'

Well, it will do if Liverpool do what Liverpool are born to do. To win and to sing.

Like a team that's going to win the European Cup.

Champions Of Europe 2
Tottenham 0
BEN JOHNSON'S RATINGS

MADRID Airport. Sunday, June 2.

I mean, I was up at 6.45am, not a mark on me. No hangover, no nothing. Mine was an unusual Champions League final day. Friday night, you see, got a smidgen out of hand. European Cup nerves and that, the ale flew, bevied twice in a day. Shapes were thrown.

Saturday morning breaks and I'm a mess. A fat baldy mess of a man, with no ticket, no plan and no hope of either.

Couple of hours before kick off I went to meet the lads in what can only really be described as a fucking butty shop with the ale in, a fucking subway, to watch the biggest game of our lives. A fucking butty shop. Think about that.

The telly went off. There was nearly a riot. The telly come back on. The Reds had a pen. What the fuck. The Reds were shite. The Reds were shite. The Reds were Shite. We score the second. Nothing else matters. Mayhem. The leccy goes in the gaff. Mayhem. We watch the last five minutes on a phone. Nothing else matters.

With love from the bottom of my heart.

Alisson: 10

We don't win that game if he isn't in goal. He was just so good. His footwork. His fucking saves. His positional sense. His fucking sense. His frame, his everything. Best I've ever seen and I seen Westerveld, mind you. The save from the freekick is unbelievable. The save from Son when he pure twatted it then the one right again from Lucas Moura. Unreal.

Holding the European Cup with one hand. Souness.

Trent: 9

What can you say about him that hasn't already been said? Twenty years of age and he's winning European Cups. Imagine that one goes in when he did his best Ste Gerard impression, there. Gave it away with some mad decisions first 20 but fuck me, it's the European Cup final. I'd be trying to score with every touch.

Was great defensively. But honestly we won, nothing else fucking matters.

Big Joel The Leccy Conqueror: 9

Mad the way he was fourth choice, everyone is binning him in the summer and a couple of lads get injured and he turns into a really, really, really good player, and ends up better than van Dijk for a bit.

Still does mad shit with his body now and again, like has involuntary twitches and that. Scousecharms has got a mate who got struck by lightning while he was stood under a tree. Two of his mates exploded. Literally exploded. He lost 40 per cent of his body weight, and can now turn the telly on and that without touching it, like a fucking X-Man.

Reckon it might be Joel, you know. Zapping his way to glory.

Virgil: 9

I have heard a rumour that he cried before we lifted the cup. I mean, Jesus Christ that would have broken me. I'm glad the telly went off. His recovery run when Son was in was incredible. He looked for the first time in his life like he weren't getting back and then he just lashed the burners on and boxed it. An unbelievable footballer.

Made up for him that his decision to sign for us has been vindicated. What a hero.

Andy Robbo: 9

Cope was obsessed about his body shape. It was pretty fucking good, to be fair. Some of them balls he put in were unreal. Great effort. Didn't stop running and that takes some doing in that heat. A fabulous footballer. One of the best.

Gini: 8

Struggled to have an impact really, but then in fairness he fucking got us here. The right sub to take him off, but so fucking what? Nothing else matters. Harder job than it looks that midfield shuffler. Shows how good Henderson is that he could keep going.

Jordan Henderson: 10

I'm not even rating his performance. I'm rating him as a man. I reckon I'm happier for him than I am for me. A wonderful, wonderful human being. The video with his auld fella was pretty cry-y, wasn't it?

Fabinho: 9

What a tremendous signing. Absolutely steel. As in as hard as steel and a bargain. Seriously impressive in them little holes, isn't he?

Sadio Mane: 10

Unbelievable, wasn't he? We had a really big discussion yesterday about what we would do if our birds get sick of us and fuck us off. It was decided that I was moving to Senegal. Heavy that, isn't it? I mean I would miss my wife and family and that because, you know, I love them, but Senegal would be pretty nice, I reckon.

Unbelievable ability to kill time/take fellas on, get The Reds up the pitch and nearly set up a goal in one move. Just pipped to man of the match by me and Alisson.

Mo Salah: 9

Redemption song. I mean, it was pretty nice, wasn't it? I hope Sergio Ramos was watching it in his gaff with a bit of a cob on. He twats that pen in fairness and it's a fucking good job cause it's only the speed that beats the keeper. Made some poor decisions really, and wasn't at his best, but he's sat in his gaff with a big gold medal round his neck.

Nothing. Else. Matters.

Bobby Firmino: 7

Was nowhere near fit, was he? Couldn't press, couldn't control it, couldn't really do much, in fairness. The right decision to sub him obvs, but so fucking what? We won. Nothing else matters.

SUBS...

Milner: 8

Made up for him, you know. Absolutely come on and got The Reds through. What a fella.

Div: 10

Was absolutely shite for 20 minutes there, wasn't he? Shite. But then, that little shift onto his left, bang, the only place it could go in. Want to watch that again for all eternity. Wish I was in that end for it but never mind.

I got to watch Adam Melia, sat down, watching his timer on his phone instead of the match, unable to see the telly, look up with little hopeful eyes, as all hell broke loose around him, look straight into my eyes for confirmation, with a little smile on his face, start laughing and crying and celebrating all at the same time. I will never forget that.

It's 11am in Paris as I write this and he still hasn't seen the goal.

Jürgen: 10

I don't think I have ever been happier for anyone in my life. He is a remarkable man. A true leader of men. Unbelievable what he has pretty much done single handed for this club. He wouldn't have a word of it being just him, though. That's the marker of him.

I hope to meet him some day and I can tell him how much he means to me and maybe say thanks.

NEIL ATKINSON'S REVIEW

COME and adore them.

They're the kings of Europe.

To adore, to love. To love is an action, it is active. It isn't a passive thing. In the book *The Reasons For Love* by Harry Frankfurt he explores why we love, what love actually is. He determines in short that love is about care, its essence is there. What we care about deeply is what we love.

So we may say we love ice cream but unless we are Ben, unless we are Jerry, unless we are Haagen or Daas do we truly care about ice cream?

Do we feel ice cream's concerns? Do we live its highs and lows? Ice cream we can like but we cannot truly love it.

We love Liverpool. Love.

I can't stop crying. I can't stop crying because I can't stop thinking of those lads, those footballers who have given us everything, who have themselves shown such care and love. Since August this has been a love song. And you know who you are.

These words, this reaction has been very much about what it is and who it is we love. It's been a discussion of how it feels, for the collective, for the individual, for them the players, for us the supporters. Discussion of the shape and the goals and the mistakes matters but what matters more, what matters the most is how it feels.

So often for the love you show a football team you get nothing in return. That's fine. It's the way it works. You don't get the highs if you can't hack the lows.

And I can't stop crying. It's unedifying. I am a soppy, sloppy mess. Because it just feels. Because we have cared so much for these lads and we see it reflected back to us.

Virgil van Dijk collapses when Divock Origi scores. He just hits the deck. It was bedlam, it was pandemonium and when it finished all I saw were people in tears and I now know that Virgil would have been in tears too but he has to be the grown up, he has to see it out.

The final whistle sounds and Jordan Henderson falls to his knees, head in his hands and while his face is hidden he is just shuddering, shaking. The release and the relief breaks through in sobs. I can't stop thinking about it, what he has been through and what he has achieved and what failure would have done to him this time.

I see Dan Morgan who got a grip of me last year after Kyiv and I collapse onto his shoulder. Everywhere there are faces moist with sheer delirium, sodden with delight.

What's astonishing about all this is that I expected to win. Expected Liverpool to be better than Tottenham. But the game was an absolute dog, defined by the early penalty and then the tension of it was everywhere. It was in every pass. Liverpool had suddenly so much to lose. They had been favourites, they had the early goal, they are the better side.

The second half killed but for the first half of it Tottenham couldn't land a glove. There was a flurry of half chances for both sides after Milner put an effort wide, and just when Tottenham were maybe turning the screw Divock Origi turned the ball home and there was carnage and we were out of purgatory and into euphoria.

Sadio Mane had been the best outfield player. Strong and precise and makes other forwards look strangely average. Divock had been frankly rubbish. Gave it away cheaply. But there he was again. Yet again. He has a claim to have had a better season than many true Liverpool legends. And now he is one, a legendary figure in this journey which needed the denouement it got.

Pound for pound, time on the pitch no one has a better massive goals to minutes ratio for The Reds I can think of. Build him a statue now. For providing Liverpudlians around the globe with massive relief and boundless joy.

But without a single doubt man of the match has to be the goalkeeper. Alisson stretches and shines where previous Liverpool goalkeepers in this game have given the whole thing up. He makes it look effortless and shot after shot in the second half of the second half. He ensures the half chances are left exactly as that – half chances. His positioning and focus is tremendous.

These two – Divock and Alisson – embody what is so good about the job Jürgen Klopp has done. Origi should theoretically be an outcast, someone just to improve upon. Instead he shows what some belief and fantastic coaching in the right environment can do.

Alisson shows what investing big can do as well. But investing in personality along with talent. We have so much emotion, so much cascading love and care that sometimes we just need someone to be very sensible indeed. He is just the very finest and he helped enormously on the night without being truly brilliant.

Expecting to win is something but living that win was something else entirely. Their concerns are our concerns, their dreams our dreams, their needs and wants our needs and wants. What they deserved we deserve. We are as one with them because of the love, because of the care but that second half hurt so much. Craig Hannan had to ask me to stop saying the time, every minute counted.

Winning was everything today. It's nice to be nice and it's good to play well but winning was absolutely everything. Coming second is not who we are, who we have been and who this team has become. And yes that hurt this season.

Liverpool got the points and played the football of champions but weren't able to lift the main thing up domestically. They needed to be the winners, the fuck-off winners of a major trophy. Not winning the league hurt but tonight nothing hurts and everything is wonderful and Paul Senior turns up and now I am shuddering, shaking, head buried into his shoulder.

I told you. I can't stop crying.

In a good season you get to fall in love with them, go on the journey and live with them. This has been a great season. And this is sort of the last time we watch them.

There's Daniel Sturridge doing the arms – the magnificent bastard; Dejan Lovren going bananas; Divock being Divock. Adam Lallana the first to go to Henderson, to pick him up, to see his cheeks drenched. They all play their part, play a part in the chapter we have just seen which adds to the tapestry which is this football club.

To all the boys I have loved before. To the boys I will always love. For the journeys we have shared with one another, I have an endless loop of people I need to hold and to sob on the shoulder of. This is a love song. And you know who you are.

Saw Fuad coming out. Saw Phil Blundell in a boozer. Can't wait to see Steve Graves, can't wait to be in Glastonbury Tuesday with Ben Johnson. Can't wait to watch Sadio Mane and Mo Salah play football for us again. Can't wait for what happens next. The journey doesn't stop.

Elsewhere you will get the calm analysis. Jonathan Wilson and Michael Cox will speak some sense. Barney Ronay will be wry. Rory will be different class. Me? I just want to snog the face off you and off the Liverpool players.

Thank you for coming here and reading these words. In a sense this is sort of the end of a bit of storytelling but the journey doesn't stop. All of this has happened before and all of this will happen again. You are here because you care, because you love. This is a love song. And you know who you are.

Jordan Henderson on his knees, Sadio Mane with the trophy. Loving life, loving Liverpool. The kings of Europe. Adore them.

I can't stop crying.

How Klopp And Co Brought The Fun Back
DAN MORGAN

ARE you not having fun?

How can you not be?

This isn't the current state of mind. I'm on a train from Madrid to Barcelona the morning after watching Liverpool win their sixth European cup.

The trophy is intoxicating in its sheer presence. It engulfs you, it is a beautiful, unapologetic elephant in the room whenever it is in your presence.

Whenever it is in your presence.

An oxymoronic turn of phrase. There are those who have never got through the door to share a room with it.

Those whose only reference is of European elite being dwarfed through the prism of a screen in a far away dystopia.

We have six of them. Six.

I don't often engage in the things that surround my day to day which I consider slightly bourgeois.

But mark my words, I will make a concerted effort to get into Anfield's trophy room this summer and feel the sheer overwhelming sensation of being in the company of half a dozen giant pots.

You can be grounded by triumph at times. In this sense it can remind you of what you've endured to get that sweet sensation of winning.

But in this case, you become grounded by modesty. By realising that your Liverpool bubble, framed by your own insularism, is the European hub of performing arts, of football royalty.

Are you not having fun?

The reason I ask is because I'm not actually thinking of now. I'm thinking of the question in its source.

Jürgen Klopp asked the question to Maurizio Sarri in the melee of being a goal down at Stamford Bridge in October's league encounter in which the game finished 1-1.

In many ways, it is my moment of the season. It is Klopp to his core. His infectious humanism has been a mirrorball which has bounced around all of us.

He reminds me and you on a regular basis that you should be having a good time doing this.

That he will politely disagree with one of the most notorious Shanklyisms that football is more important than life and death.

His mantra remains that football is about people and experiences. It is about opening your eyes to the world and its beauty in front of you.

It is about seeing people grow. To know that at some point there will be an end, but you will look each other in the eye and by God you will know you have savoured every second with each other.

That is why what should be a culmination of a post-2012 famine in Madrid only feels like the warmup act.

It's because we are grounded by the honesty we see in front of us by the 11 in red.

Liverpool's sixth was ours. I told as many people I could hug and love in that stadium.

Ours is not defined by age or generation, however. Ours is purely all of us old, young, man, woman, local or global who've invested into this manager and this team.

They deserved their turn. We very much deserve ours.

Are you not having fun?

If not, that is completely your own prerogative, and you will have your own valid reasons away from football as for why not.

But in all of our hardships, there are chinks of light. Reminders that things are possible if you see a way, if you remain honest and hard working, if you believe and erase doubt.

In the end, we all get a turn in some way. In our sheer divinity we have had more than most, which is enough to tell you that we may well never stop – in our lifetime, at least.

Fun? We're not just having fun, we're having the time of our lives.

How Liverpool Brought People Together
GARETH ROBERTS

WE'VE all got our own tale to tell about life – and every moment means something different to each of us.

Our own story is continually being written, and written in only a way that we really know about. We have our own context behind our eyes.

As much as life offers up its rules – written down, enforced or just the softer cultural pressures to cede to a norm, there are no real rules. Not really. All the rules are what you make of them.

And so, when we first come into this world, our life is a blank canvas. We love nothing and hate nothing. Purpose and perspective comes later. We're a brand new sponge, unopened, yet to soak up a drop, dry as a bone, still in the wrapper.

Then comes life and its many influences. A steady flow of family, friends, school, work, sport, media, the arts. We travel, we experience, we change. And different things will mean different things to different people – every one shaped by life, experience, luck, love and everything else that comes with our time.

Some pour their heart and soul into work – it means everything to them. All their hours, all their time, all their thinking space – it's about work, or business, or money. They live to work. They change who they are to be better at it. They follow rules written by the successful. They interpret life through the prism of business speak and that gives them a glow inside.

For others, it's family first – a child's smile, a mother's hug, quality time with dad. Some have that, some don't. Some crave it, some lose it.

And then, among it all, is football. Your club. Your team. It can easily be waved away as what my dad once described as '22 fellas kicking a ball'. For him, football never bit hard. It wasn't for him. It's not a big part of his life story.

But it is a big part of mine. From the magnificence of unboxing that first red Umbro kit under the Christmas tree as a kid in 1984, wanting and yearning to go to Anfield ever after, finally doing so and then the decades of obsessing that have followed, Liverpool FC and everything to do with it has been a daily infatuation.

It's left me with moments I'll remember all my life.

The first time I glimpsed the green of the Anfield turf. The first time I saw a Liverpool captain lift a trophy. The thrill of watching a lad from the same streets I had trodden worshipped as a hero. Cardiff, Dortmund, Istanbul, Wembley. Steven Gerrard's goal against West Ham. Michael Owen's against Arsenal. Jerzy Dudek's save. The list goes on and on.

And yet. That story. My story. Whether it's age, mental state, life, love, money, work, a general sense of 'what am I doing?' or all of the above, over the last 12 months or so I've questioned everything. Repeatedly. Obsessively.

Like countless others the world over, no doubt, my story hasn't been a great one in recent times for lots of reasons. I wasn't quite sure what story my life was writing. I'm still not.

As part of that, football inevitably came into the equation. Perhaps more than ever before, I was overthinking it. The money involved. The time it takes. The mental space it occupies, particularly when it's your work as well as your pleasure.

There's the fact, too, that we're never far away from something that suggests the game is eating itself, that it's changing and not necessarily for the better.

So off that inner voice goes. What would it be like if you didn't go so much? Would it be better to spend more time with family and friends, not just the people you know via football? Saved some money? Did something else?

Because, after all, isn't it all an unfair fight with the financially-doped clubs anyway? And how much is brilliant and how much not so? How many dark days are endured for the bright and sunshiny ones?

Being honest, a season when Liverpool clocked up a record 97 points in the Premier League and still didn't win the thing was hardly going to help with matters. For me, for us, for them. How could all that effort, that will, that skill, those performances go unrewarded?

But then, to quote Michael Corleone in *The Godfather: Part III*: 'Just when I thought I was out, they pull me back in.'

This is not to say I was throwing everything up in the air and walking away from it all – far from it. But I perhaps needed a reboot, some romance, something brilliant – and the club did, too. The players did. The manager did.

Now we have it. And then some. By the bucketload. For the sixth time.

I didn't go to Madrid. Ticket availability and finances were top among the reasons for staying home. But even that has ended up being part of the story.

When Divock Origi continued to write his own legend by putting the ball in the corner of Hugo Lloris's net in the 87th minute I was overcome. Frozen for a second. Tears flowed, my head swirled and all I had left was just enough to accept the gleeful embraces of my closest friends as all around the packed bar exploded with emotion.

And that's why we do it, really. That's what football is about. The shared experience. The unbridled joy. Enjoying that moment together and knowing that in those precise seconds your life stories are the same – there is mutual meaning, the extreme enjoyment is intertwined and there and then nothing else matters.

Had I travelled ticketless to Spain, minus those mates, would it have all been the same? I mean, I'm sure I would have enjoyed seeing a sixth European Cup being lifted regardless, and we've all hugged a stranger at the footie (right?!), but I'm glad we wrote it this way. I'm glad I shared it with them.

There were more tears on the whistle, more tears when I saw Jordan Henderson and his dad, and yet more when the children I've failed to convert to football passed on the experience of a European Cup parade. And then, the parade itself.

I've seen lots of these – from being a child clutching my nan's hand by a bus stop through to adulthood and alcohol-fuelled dancing in the street. They're always special. Not just because you get to see the smiling faces of the people who won it for you, but because you get to see the smiling faces of the people they won it for.

All ages. From all places. Matchgoers, telly watchers, occasional attendees and the most dedicated of all. All together. All as one.

In that moment, none of it matters – the stresses, the strains, the worries, the pressures. Life becomes simple. What you look like, what you wear, who you are, where you're from. All the stuff so readily stressed over.

The life obsession with comparing and contrasting. All of it forgotten, gone, wiped away to just enjoy it, to drink it in and celebrate – and feel the same from all around you.

Liverpool loves its football. We've shown the world that once more. But does it mean more? I don't care. Is it bigger and better or different than somewhere else? Does it matter?

Instead, what does matter is that we know, that we feel it, and that we enjoy it. And everyone did.

CHAPTER SEVEN – THE HOME STRAIGHT

On Saturday night and Sunday afternoon, millions of people shared the same chapter of their life stories before they veered off once more to write their individual tales.

And that's why it's special. That's why we love it. In those times, we're part of something – we're together and the emotions on the face of Jordan Henderson, Trent Alexander-Arnold, Jürgen Klopp and the rest of the heroes who made it happen in Madrid are our emotions too. They cried, we cried. They partied, we partied. They're proud and so are we.

We're made up for them, for ourselves, for our mates, for the club, for the city. And we should be. Because what a story this is. Our story. The story of the six-time European Champions.

They beat the odds versus Barcelona, saw it out versus Spurs and were cheered home by 750,000 people on the streets of our city.

Liverpool, Life, Love And
The Tales We Can Tell

PAUL COPE

AS my Nan might have said, thank Christ for that.

It's funny building up to these things these days. It's strange being a part of other people's stories. It's fascinating meeting you in person and hearing how this impacts your life when we're all just normal fans doing what we can to add to the occasion.

The drama. The anticipation. The hope.

But more than anything else, for me and for many of you, the relief.

The overwhelming relief that Jordan Henderson is now a European Cup-winning captain. I'll never debate him again. Say what you want about him. He's done something only four other Liverpool captains in history have done. If you don't rate him you can, quite frankly, fuck right off.

If you love to spend your time moaning and complaining and being negative about any of this, you can fuck right off.

That's how I feel. I didn't celebrate the goals like I usually would. I looked Rob Gutmann in the eyes and grabbed his shoulder. I watched Adam Melia watching his clock on his phone and told everyone around me to calm down. Just fucking win. I'll celebrate properly when it's over.

The overwhelming feeling of relief pouring out of every part of my body. The release. I could see it everywhere I looked and hear it from everyone I spoke to.

You can even see it in the slow motion video of the trophy lift that I can't stop watching. Our captain's entire body visibly shaking with the release of energy while his teammates go wild in a way I can't remember another group of players doing when lifting the greatest of trophies.

Thank Christ for that.

I've never been happier to hear Liverpool players, coaches and pundits saying we played badly. And won. We just fucking won. And that's what we needed to do. Because now we're winners again.

Don't get me wrong. I believe everything I've ever said to you here. I believe in never giving up. I believe in always trying one more time. But I also believe in winners and losers. I believe in stories and drama and adventure and excitement. I believe in fate. I believe in love and hope and dreams.

But you have to win. Sooner or later you have to win or it's all a waste of time. Rocky movies don't carry on after a heavy loss unless he comes back to win.

I'm not sure what we would have done if we'd lost. I had a song in my head for an article if I had to write something in that scenario. My mate played his playlist in our room in Ibiza on our way to Madrid and we sang our boy-band songs like the 1980s boys we are.

How do you get up from an all-time low?

A part of my brain started thinking about that piece. About what I'd say. About how I could lift myself and try to lift you.

What if we lost? After everything. What if we still didn't win?

CHAPTER SEVEN – THE HOME STRAIGHT

The unbearable pain. The agony. The despair.

Then I thought of the alternative. The article if we won. This piece. The imagery. The trophy lift. The stories and the parade.

I believe that we should always prepare for the worst but believe in the best. Focus on the positives. On the sunshine not the rain. Visualise your life the way you want it to be and sooner or later you'll get there. Believe it or call it bullshit, but whether you believe you can or believe you can't you're right. You'll always be right.

I believe we can. I believe you can. I believe in us and I believe in joy and hope and happiness.

I believe in love. I believe in serenity. I believe in fate taking us to where we want to be.

If you've been with me before you'll know it will always come back to the same things eventually. It's why I have to leave. Why a break is needed. Why it can't go on forever. There are only so many messages. Only so many poems and articles and inspirational things to say.

Once you've learned them the only thing left is to follow them. You'd be amazed how rare it is. How rarely anyone just does the basics they need to do to change their lives.

Trent Alexander-Arnold is praised by his coaches for listening and learning and working hard. It has always amazed me that it's enough to make him stand out from his peers. But I've seen it. I've witnessed first-hand how just smiling at people and being polite is enough to separate you from the masses.

Just being nice to people changes your life. Just being positive. Just believing that things can be better and reminding other people of the fact.

Believe things can be better. Watch these lads and feel this joy and believe it can all be better.

Wherever you are, whatever you do, it's never the end. It's always just a story you're telling yourself, so choose a good story. If it's bad right now, tell yourself you're in the middle of your own Rocky movie. Remind yourself you're in Kyiv, or Basel or Athens. Remember the day is darkest before the dawn.

Remember the clichés. They exist for a reason. They stand the test of time because they're largely true.

If things have been hard in parts of your life away from this incredible football team over the past few months or years, let it inspire you to keep going. To get up. Stand up. Smile. Find someone less fortunate than you and help them. Give them a hug. Embrace the world and embrace the pain.

From your darkest tunnels comes the greatest light. We don't get Madrid without Kyiv. We don't get redemption without deprivation. We don't get light without dark. We don't get to stand back up without first falling down.

These are the greatest moments in the greatest times, but we only have them because we have felt the pain. We have walked through the storms and felt the rain soak our souls. And we know there is always a golden sky. Sooner or later. If you dare to believe. If you are prepared to risk it all. If you can be prepared to feel heartbreak rolling the dice for love.

Whatever it is, believe in it. Believe you can be whoever you want to be and believe you can do whatever you want to do. Look at these lads. Read their stories. Look where they've come from. Every one of them a story to inspire us all.

To work hard, to carry on when others might stop. Believe that you can change things over time. Don't overestimate what you can do in a week and underestimate what you can do in a year, or five years, or 10.

Be a European Cup winner in every aspect of your life.

I last won a European Cup 14 years ago at my first final. I watched the victory parade in Liverpool via still images being shown on a tiny hotel screen in Istanbul. Now I stream them live from a magical box I carry around in my pocket while wandering through the streets of Paris on my way home from my fourth European Cup final. My fourth.

I had an argument with my girlfriend before Athens. She didn't want me to go because I'd been to one two years earlier. I said I might never see one again in my lifetime, yet now I've seen four of them in 14 years.

Fourteen years.

Where will I be in another 14? Where will you be? What will have changed? What will we have done?

Births, deaths, marriages, divorces. Whole lives. Yet we can decide. We can choose what happens. Where we want to be the next time. What we want to have done. To be.

Be you. Be the very best of you. Watch Jordan Henderson and let him inspire you to never give up. To prove time and time again that all things are possible for those who believe.

I say I won a European Cup in 2005 and I mean it. I won. You won. They won. My generation won. And now a new one has won. Another victory for all of us. To filter into whatever story we want to tell.

Make no mistake that's all this is. Our lives are just a series of stories we tell ourselves. The beauty is we can decide what stories to tell. A person who shared my life for so long used to joke that we could both experience the same thing and I'd walk away telling a positive story and she would do the opposite.

The facts never changed, only the stories we told ourselves.

So, tell yourself a good story. Tell yourself when times are dark that it's just a moment in time. The darkness needed so that you can feel the light. Don't allow the world to convince you that it has to be this way, that you have to stay on the floor because that's just the way it is. It isn't. Believe in that.

And, just as importantly, when times are good remember to savour them. To soak them up and be grateful.

It's where most of us go wrong. Be grateful for your wife doing the things she always does, or your husband doing the same. Be thankful for your kid giving you a hug or your parents fussing over you. Let the small moments be as joyous as the big. Hold the people you love. Whistle and sing and dance. Stare deeply into the eyes of your dearest friends and tell them you love them.

Savour it all, because you never know when it will be your last. Your last kiss, your last smile, the last time your kid holds your hand.

Soak it up. We live in the greatest of times and we allow people to convince us they're the worst. People are generally good. Focus on the goodness. Look for what you want to see in life and you will find it. Believe in things getting better and they will.

We talked a year ago about it just being the start and we were right. Let that remind you every day of your life. A philosophy of one man who believes in everyone taking care of each other. Of community and friendship. Of joy and happiness.

Enjoy yourself. Whatever happens, find the silver lining. Find the best way to be the best of you. Don't worry about the news telling you that the world is a bad place. The world will look after itself if we all just make sure we're the best we can be, one at a time, and help others to be the best that they can be. Viral growth of peace and love and happiness. Imagine.

I love this journey. This adventure. We've reached the end of a truly great book and the sequel promises so much. A drama like no other. A love affair without compare.

Hold it all close. Cuddle the person next to you and let them feel your love. Be prepared to risk it all and be prepared to fall. And always be ready to stand up again. No matter what. Always remember Kyiv. And Athens. And Basel.

And always remember Istanbul and Madrid.

The joy can never be the same without the sadness. So, enjoy the sadness for what it gives you. For what it represents. Opportunity. A chance to create the comeback story that everyone loves so much. The greatest stories of our times.

This is the end of this part of the story, but there's always another part. I will leave again and begin another chapter with new places and new people. With fun and laughter and memories. With tears and pain. With life. Savouring what I already have and anticipating the unknown. Energy rippling through me as I dream my dreams and let the images of what has already been wash through my mind.

What will you do next? Where will you be in 12 months' time? When I write to you on the way to Istanbul. On the way to number seven. What will have changed? How will your life have improved? Allow these boys to inspire you. To be your fire. Your catalyst. To convince you that it is all possible if you believe that it is.

So believe.

Don't allow this to just be a game of football, because it's so much more than that. What we have is special. Watch those images of Liverpool during the victory parade and tell me this isn't something mystical. Scenes from an epic movie, played out in real life.

Crushing lows followed by exhilarating highs. Fire and colours and magic. Make no mistake we live inside the greatest of all fairytales and we owe it to ourselves and to whoever or whatever put us here to make sure it means something more. To inspire others. To change our lives. To dream our biggest dreams and make them a reality.

We have witnessed miracles, so we know they exist. Others aren't so fortunate. Many don't get to see with their own eyes what is possible if you truly believe. But we do. We get to see it so often I almost feel bad for the others. So for me it must mean something.

I go now to revel in being a European Cup winner again. Somewhere in the world. To be proud. To smile. To know. Even when others don't. To appreciate what it means. To tell more stories that have been added to the collection.

To sit in a bar somewhere on the planet and Rotterdam by The Beautiful South to filter faintly through the speakers. For Saturday Night by Wigfield to play in a cheesy nightclub. For Sit Down by James to play in a cafe. For a gentle smile to spread across my face as the lyrics we have for those songs reverberate around my mind, and for someone sitting with me to ask what I'm grinning about.

It's a long story, I'll say. The greatest of stories. Maybe the greatest ever told. I'll tell you all about it if you really want to know, but it will take some time to tell it properly and you might not believe it's true.

I feel it now as I picture the scenes and tears come to my eyes. Again. My heart swells with pride and emotion. The images I find it impossible to describe. The photographs I'll show to other people and they'll ask where it was and what had happened. It doesn't look real, but it is. It's our magical reality and that's all that matters. A life beyond compare.

I leave you again and I leave with an article that's not really about football. I know you know they never really are. They're about you and your life, and me and my life. That's why they do what they do. We don't cry at movies because of the people on the screen, we cry because we put ourselves in the story.

So I leave this time wanting to say that you should dream your biggest dream. Don't be afraid. Don't let them tell you it's not possible. It is. It's all possible, whatever it is.

You can be whoever you really want to be and do whatever you truly want to do. Let this maddest of things be your inspiration. Let this craziness drive you forward.

Someone dear to me who knew nothing of all of this before a few months ago has told me more than once how the look in my eyes is different when I talk about this. How it's funny to watch.

I'm now a grown man and this magical thing still moves me like nothing else. I can feel it when I talk about it, when I write. The exhilaration in my voice, my quickening heartbeat. The joy rippling through my veins and my tingling skin.

I love this more than I ever really appreciated before. It stirs something in me that nothing else does. So I will be happy and, for once, completely unashamed of that happiness. It might be daft to many, many people, but it's not to me. This is mine and this is yours and we can have our stories, together. This is our tribe and these are our people. So enjoy it for everything it is.

European Cup winners for the sixth time. Our boys. These Reds. This era. Maybe even the best one.

Of all of the thousands of images and videos I've watched over the past few days, one has resonated with me more than any other because it said it all. Virgil van Dijk interviewing Gini Wijnaldum and Joe Gomez on top of the bus during the parade. He ends by saying three words to them both as half a question, half a statement.

'What a club.'

They both stare at the incredible crowds with a look in their eyes you don't usually see from footballers. A gaze usually only seen in religious imagery. In spiritual moments. And both, at once, repeat it back, as if in a trance.

'What. A. Club.'

We love you Liverpool, we do. Thank you for everything you give to us.

See you in Istanbul.

CHAPTER SEVEN – THE HOME STRAIGHT

ACKNOWLEDGEMENTS

EVERY performative enterprise needs an audience.

The Anfield Wrap's oxygen is its listeners, viewers and readers. We can't thank them enough. Can't thank you enough. The response and support is consistently terrific. Our concerns are their concerns. We are in this together.

Every performative enterprise needs collaborators. It needs co-conspirators.

The Anfield Wrap's lifeblood is its contributors. This book is dedicated to them first and foremost. They have been friends or become them, they have been kind and generous with themselves, their thoughts, their ideas and their jokes. Whether it is one AFQ or phone call right through to those who are there three or four times a week, it all matters, it all helps.

Every performative enterprise needs support.

The Anfield Wrap team, some of whom are seen or heard from rarely if at all, are a constant source of energy, have backed our essence to the hilt and given themselves to this strange venture that still barely makes sense. We have all been part of telling the story of supporting Liverpool from the heart of the city.

What a story it has been. We hope we have done it, that manager, those players, and our collective hopes and dreams justice. That manager and those players deserve our acclaim and our thanks. They deserve the moon on a stick. They deserve the European Cup. They got it.

Come and adore them. Come to town, handsome. Come to town, gorgeous. They're the Kings Of Europe.

Neil Atkinson

ACKNOWLEDGEMENTS